China-Pakistan Economic Corridor and India's Strategic Interests

China-Pakistan Economic Corridor and India's Strategic Interests

Ashutosh Kumar

PRASHANT PUBLISHING HOUSE
DELHI-110094

Published by :
Prashant Publishing House
C-34, 28 Foota Road, Gali-3,
West Karwal Nagar, Delhi-110094
Phone : 011-22963970, Mob. : 9810396373
e-mail.: prashantpublishinghouse@gmail.com

China-Pakistan Economic Corridor and India's Strategic Interests

First Published 2017

ISBN 978-93-80565-16-3

PRINTED IN INDIA
Published by Mr. R.K. Jha M/s Prashant Publishing House and Published at H.S. Offset House Press, Delhi.

Contents

Preface

China-Pakistan Economic Corridor (CPEC), a mega development project signed between China and Pakistan is considered to be a "game changer" on economic and geo-strategic grounds. On one side, the project would help China in achieving its foreign policy goals to expand from the South China Sea to the Indian Ocean and Arabian Sea, it would ensure economic growth in Pakistan and subcontinent as a whole.

While China is pursuing multilateral partnerships with other South Asian states, Pakistan is central to China in many respects to achieve its geo-strategic goals in the region. CPEC is one such flagship project which both countries are determined to implement and see the envisioned benefits. This fact has been rarely acknowledged in academic circles that Sino-Pak relationship as a legacy of relationship based on mutual trust and credibility, began with recognition of China by Pakistan and instrumental role in secret diplomacy by Pakistan that helped in bridging gap between the U.S. and China.

It is in this environment of multi-faceted conflict that the China-Pakistan Economic Corridor programme (CPEC) is anchored. The programme amounts to over 45 billion US dollars and was agreed between the two countries in April 2015. The corridor has its starting point in the Chinese-built port of Gwadar, on Pakistani Balochistan's southern coast at the Arabian Sea, and is linked to Chinese-funded, infrastructural mega-projects that are regional in nature,

The programme has been flaunted as a turning point for the fragile Pakistani economy and an upcoming backbone of regional connectivity, which is supposed to create jobs and prosperity for everyone, the Baloch included. The government's reasoning seems to be that, once the recalcitrant Baloch nationalists discover the benefits of improved infrastructure, they will return to the fold of the Pakistani motherland. However, until this spirit of cooperation takes root, the Chinese workers involved in the project will be protected by an additional security division comprising army battalions, as well as civil armed forces.

Of all China's neighboring countries, China-Pakistan relations are the closest and friendliest. With the kick-off of Xin Jinping's proposal, the "China-Pakistan Economic Corridor", the relations of both countries have upgraded to a new level from high-level political and military relations, extending to the full range of contacts and comprehensive relations.

However, China does have some concerns regarding Pakistan, particularly the problems associated with containing Islamic terrorism as well as the rising Islamic identity within Xinjiang's Uyghur minority. Nonetheless, both the United States and China have a common interest in allowing China to play a bigger in the reconstruction of Afghanistan and constrain opportunistic moves from Pakistan; and this political change is welcomed mostly by other regional players including Russia, Iran, Saudi Arabia, and other Gulf countries.

This book will definitely prove to be a boon to teachers, students and research scholars.

—*Editor*

1

Introduction

The Chinese designed One Belt- One Road (OBOR) project will surely be a mega changer for the economic and political future of the entire Eurasian region. OBOR aims to connect the Chinese mainland with Europe and Asia through a network of roads, rail and sea routes. An important part of the OBOR is the South Asia bound land route connecting Kazhgar in Xinjiang (Chinese autonomous region) with the Pakistan's Persian Gulf port of Gwadar. The Kazhgar- Gwadar connectivity is bilaterally implemented as a part of the China Pakistan Economic Corridor Project (CEPC).

The 3000 km long route comprising of rail and road networks and development of the Gwadar port by the Chinese has a project cost of $46 bn. Of the US $46bn, between $35bn to $38bn were allocated for the energy sector, the rest for constructing rail and road networks. Despite the secrecy and confusion surrounding the project hope about the project is sky high in Pakistan. Following are the implications of the project for the two participants – China and Pakistan and the neighboring India.

WHAT CHINA GETS FROM THE PROJECT?

On the economic front, China is the biggest beneficiary as the project gives it a shortcut to Indian Ocean, bypassing the Strait of Malacca. It can access the Western part of the Indian Ocean in the most politically easiest way because of its friendly and strategic relationship with Pakistan.

At present, China transports 80% of its oil through the strait of Malacca. This can be deviated through the Pak route. On the political front, a decisive advantage for China is that Pakistan historically shows willingness to play the role of satellite state to major powers including the US.

Because of the India factor, Pakistan will remain an ally of China even by surrendering several rights to Chinese economic and strategic interests. This means that among all the OROB associate country, Pakistan offers more strategic value to China. There is a future option for Beijing to retain a significant army in Pakistan in the pretext of providing security to the CPEC.

What the project means for Pakistan?

The project is described as a 'game changer' for Pakistan's economic future, which otherwise has only meagre prospects to develop its economy. Pakistan's economy can get a rejuvenation due to Chinese investment. If Pakistan is able to overcome its security problems, the CPEC can be a game changer. At the same time, the benefit it can get from being a transit country for Chinese goods depends upon its ability to change itself by achieve industrial progress.

The word game changer is to be carefully read along with the past *great game* played between US, Pakistan and Saudi Arabia on the one side and Russia, Iran and India on the other side to establish a land route to Central Asia. Pakistan's effort to be the entry point into Central Asia foiled because the opposite side tried hard to retain their control over Afghanistan. Now, with Chinese help, Pakistan can get a chance to become at least one of the transit points.

Pakistan can get an opportunity to develop its infrastructure – especially energy. Bulk of the CPEC is aimed to develop Pakistan's energy sector including the construction of the largest solar energy plant in the world. China will help Pakistan to develop its resource based industries so that they can be exported to China. Another advantage of the project is that with the potential economic decline of the Gulf States, Pakistan as a natural resource exporter can sell its commodities to the lucrative Chinese markets through the CPEC transit route.

What the project means for India?

India is the third party on which the CPEC impacts a lot of intangible and indirect effects. Given the political synergy between China and Pakistan, the CPEC will be a disguised political disturbance for India. Its strategic content is high and capable of restricting New Delhi's maneuverability in the region. In an extreme scenario, Pakistan may act as a 'rented house' for Chinese Military.

The project goes through the disputed Pak occupied Kashmir (Gilgit- Baltistan) is a nuisance for India. Already, CPEC is getting lot of attention because of the direct involvement of the Pakistani military at the insistence of the Chinese leadership.

So far, the quick progress in Gwadar Kazhgar project has compelled an otherwise slow New Delhi to get an agreement with Iran to construct a port at Chabahar. In future also, the India-Iran alliance for a geographic connectivity with Central Asia partnering Afghanistan will continue; but without hurting both Beijing and Islamabad.

INDIA ABOUT THE CHINA-PAKISTAN ECONOMIC CORRIDOR

The CPEC may be a bilateral endeavour, but New Delhi cannot ignore its spillover effects on regional governance and regime creation in South Asia. Beyond sketching out the broad considerations, India's foreign policy planners are yet to study the impact of the China-Pakistan Economic Corridor (CPEC) on South Asia's politics.

Views in New Delhi to the CPEC could be divided into two groups: the first believes the CPEC serves China's singular agenda of extending its strategic footprint to Gwadar and beyond, and freeing the country of the Malacca Strait chokehold that currently serves as the lifeline for Beijing's global commerce. Another section believes, with good reason, that many CPEC projects are simply not viable enough to sustain the interest of Chinese investors in the long run. Either outcome may materialise, but the CPEC is an important enough project whose economic and strategic consequences require methodical assessment. Three aspects of the CPEC in particular stand out as relevant questions for India to consider:

- Will economic cooperation through the CPEC lead to regional military architectures in South Asia?
- How will the US respond to the CPEC – will the Trump administration offer counter-benefits to Pakistan or other regional actors to blunt China's overtures?
- Will Beijing see the CPEC as a case study for regime creation in Asia? That is, use it as a template to create and influence investment and trade standards in the region?

The CPEC may be a bilateral endeavour, but New Delhi cannot ignore its spillover effects on regional governance. The inequities in the China-Pakistan relationship and the nature of proposed Chinese investment in the CPEC merit a comparison with the Marshall Plan, the most successful foreign assistance project of the 20th century.

Analysts in India and Pakistan have expressed bewilderment at Pakistan borrowing from Chinese banks to pay for Chinese projects in the corridor, but Beijing is simply taking a leaf out of the US playbook. The Marshall Plan – known formally as the European Recovery Plan — involved the US extending lines of credit and assistance for Western European economies ravaged by the Second World War. Credited with restoring stability in Europe, one needs to look no further than the then US under secretary of state Dean Acheson's words to gauge the real goals of the Marshall Plan. In May 1947, Acheson laid out the objectives of the recovery project in a speech at Cleveland:

"Our [US] exports of goods and services to the world during the current year, 1947, are estimated to total 16 billion dollars [...] In return for the commodities and services which we expect to furnish the world this year, we estimate we will receive commodities and services from abroad to the value of 8 billion dollars. [...] The differences between the value of the goods and services which foreign countries must buy from the United States this year and the value of goods and services they are able to supply to us this year will therefore amount to the huge sum of about 8 billion dollars.

How are foreigners going to get the US dollars necessary to cover this huge difference? [This is one] of the most important questions in international relations today."

In 1947, the US needed to finance and create captive markets that would continue buying American goods while offering their own services (cheap labour, highly skilled professionals) to the US in return. China today is looking to move its assembly lines outside the country, create cheaper supply chains and limit its economic externalities (such as environmental pollution) at home. Then, as is the case today with the 2008 recession, the global economy had slowed down after two devastating wars. The US, like China, was facing an export glut.

In many Marshall Plan projects, moreover, the strategic interests of the US government were at odds with that of its private sector. The case of oil is illustrative. Soon after the Second World War, oil prices shot through the roof.

With Russian influence over Eastern Europe limiting their access to energy resources, Western European countries turned to the US for help. The US government, which saw the Marshall Plan as critical to staving off communism in the continent, sought to ensure Europe's access to oil at low prices. US oil companies, which controlled the lion's share of global oil supply, strongly resisted this move but eventually gave in to many of their government's demands.

In that case, the situation worked itself out since recipients of Marshall Plan aid used US dollars to buy US oil-refining equipment, with an eye on cheaper crude oil. But the episode highlights the important lesson that financial viability – often used to dismiss the China Pakistan Economic Corridor – is not necessarily the sole determinant of the CPEC's future. Beijing's strategic relationship with Islamabad, and its continuing quest to underwrite strategic parity between India and Pakistan in South Asia, will certainly contribute to the CPEC's longevity.

Spillover effects of CPEC

But what of the unintended or spillover consequences of the CPEC on security in South Asia? Here too, the Marshall Plan is instructive. Two years after the Economic Recovery Plan was formally announced by secretary of state George Marshall during his 1947 commencement address at Harvard, the North Atlantic Treaty Organisation (NATO) came into effect. The trans-Atlantic military alliance had been in the making for a while and the Marshall Plan by itself did not contribute to NATO's creation. But the plan freed up European coffers for rearmament and militarisation, acting as an "indirect economic subsidy". In fact, US President Harry Truman then expressly linked military support to Europe and the Marshall Plan, adopting a no-questions-asked policy to recipient NATO countries, who could then channel national budgets for defence spending.

The lines blurred between the Marshall Plan and the strategic environment in which it operated. If the CPEC's future will be determined by China-Pakistan ties, Indian policy planners should also be wary of the corridor's impact on the bilateral relationship. If China begins to guarantee the security of major projects along the corridor, would that free up Pakistan's budget and resources to target defence spending elsewhere? Support from Iran and Afghanistan would be indispensable to the CPEC's stability – will Beijing create an informal, four-way grouping aimed at securing CPEC currently, but aimed at adopting a bigger role in the years to come? New Delhi has just not visualised the regional impact of the CPEC, wishing it away as a bilateral enterprise. In cash-starved South and West Asia, the economic corridor will be closely tailed by smaller countries to see if similar projects can be replicated elsewhere.

China, US and Pakistan

Will the CPEC grow into a large enough project to invite the US's attention? If so, what will be the consequences for

South Asia? Historians generally agree that the Marshall Plan and NATO directly contributed to the Cold War, triggering a series of alliances and counter-alliances across the globe led by the US and Russia. During this process, smaller countries often played off the major powers against each other, using their insecurities to buy weapons and aid. No doubt, the US is keeping a close watch on the China-Pakistan Economic Corridor. But before Washington D.C. gets involved in the CPEC debate, New Delhi should modulate its entry. India and the US should begin serious conversations on the CPEC and its role as a force multiplier for China's strategic footprint in South Asia. Pakistan is unlikely to play the US off against China – its relations with both countries have evolved somewhat independently after US President Richard Nixon's 1972 visit to Beijing – but the Trump administration may yet be convinced of stronger ties with Islamabad to ward off pervasive Chinese influence.

And finally, India should observe the potential impact that the CPEC may have on regime creation in Asia. If China is unencumbered by financial viability – at least in the short and medium term – many countries will perceive Beijing to be more interested in strategic ties than purely economic arrangements. To attract 'quick and dirty' investment, therefore, autocratic regimes in Asia will invite strategic linkages with China. Indeed, the newly announced Shanghai Cooperation Organisation Bank is a sign that China itself seems to be convinced of the interdependence between military and economic regimes. This churning in economic and strategic architectures in Asia is a natural consequence of China's rise and the US's withdrawal from the region, but CPEC will be a litmus test to see whether Beijing can balance both.

India, therefore, cannot sustain its single-minded strategy of isolating Pakistan when it has clearly not had the desired effect on China and other regional players. For now, the CPEC seems to be on course for completing some of its milestones, and India would be ill-advised to rely on the false comfort that profits alone will drive China's business with Pakistan. Understanding the CPEC's regional impact and mitigating its negative effects will require a comprehensive strategy from New Delhi that goes beyond the India-Pakistan narrative.

THE ECONOMIC RELATIONSHIP: SURPRISINGLY LIMITED

Pakistan's portrayal of its relationship with China features exaggeration of the economic dimension of the relationship. Pakistani media routinely report huge numbers for investment and financing with the People's Republic of China (PRC), numbers that cannot be verified by any independent source, including by the Chinese government or the Chinese companies supposedly involved. While Pakistani officials talk of a total of $25 billion in Chinese investment in Pakistan so far, the PRC's official figure of direct investment through 2010 is $1.83 billion.

The Heritage Foundation's China Global Tracker documents investments as well as engineering and construction contracts of $100 million or more since the beginning of 2005, as reported by the companies. The China Tracker shows only $1.2 billion in such investment and contracts combined through 2010. These are dominated by telecommunications, with China Mobile acquiring Paktel and investing in improvements in Pakistan's telecommunications system, such as paying the Chinese engineering company Great Wall to launch a satellite.

The Heritage Foundation figure precludes transactions initiated before 2005 and is therefore too low for a country like Pakistan, where Chinese involvement is long-standing. But it also does not include road and port projects that have not begun and are unlikely to look anything like the gigantic endeavors advertised by Pakistan. While Pakistan touts the expansion of Gwadar and other ports as multibillion dollar projects, the leading enterprise China Communications Construction notes only a modest project to expand facilities in Karachi. In sum, Chinese investment activity in Pakistan is quite modest. It is a negligible fraction of total Chinese outward investment of more than $250 billion since 2005 and dwarfed by Chinese activity in Indonesia, for example. This should not be a surprise. Chinese outward investment is motivated more by domestic economic needs than by foreign policy goals. What the PRC deems to be strategic sectors — iron, copper, oil, coal, and gas — are materials needed to keep domestic industry humming and hundreds of millions of people employed. Farmland is similar, though it has proven more difficult to acquire. Pakistan has comparatively little in the way of any of these resources.

Chinese private investors, which are far smaller than their state-controlled counterparts, seek either an asset that will considerably strengthen their position in the home market, or a new market they can sell to because they are hampered at home. Textiles might be attractive now that Chinese costs are rising, but most of the textile investment moving out of the PRC to this point is foreign-funded. Pakistan again has fairly little to offer commercially and the political connection has proven inadequate to spur exchange.

While China is not spending much money itself in Pakistan, it might be financing Pakistani spending. Here the evidence is not clear because the principal vehicle for Chinese financing, the China Development Bank (CDB), does not provide information of the same quality or quantity as many Chinese enterprises investing overseas. The CDB's foreign loan portfolio has been stated as more than $140 billion, but the many claims made around the world about its loans add up to far more than that. One important reason for the gap is that countries boast about lines of credit, not actual loans made.

In this somewhat unclear environment, it does not appear that realized Chinese lending to Pakistan is large or even moderate. Scattered claims of large loans are again unverified by independent sources and tied to projects or shipments that have not yet been made. The PRC typically lends large amounts in barter — such as loans for oil — or to fund sizable engineering projects, and neither is frequent among Chinese-Pakistani economic transactions.

Indirect evidence comes from the Pakistan-China Investment Company (PCIC). The PCIC is an alliance between the China Development Bank and the Pakistani government.

Elsewhere, the China Development Bank uses such entities extensively.

The China-Africa Development Fund, for instance, was set up about the same time as PCIC but is 25 times larger in terms of capital, and far more active. According to the public record, PCIC does not seem to be doing much of anything.

Chinese humanitarian aid to Pakistan also has been modest, especially when compared to that provided by the U.S. After massive flooding in Pakistan in the summer of 2010, for instance, the U.S. provided nearly $700 million in flood relief and in-kind assistance. China eventually committed to providing $250 million, after a meagre initial contribution of $18 million.

While U.S. humanitarian aid outstripped that from China, Beijing has provided much-needed reconstruction aid for the worst-hit flood areas. U.S. media reports claimed in September 2010 that 7,000 to 10,000 People's Liberation Army (PLA) troops were deployed to Gilgit-Baltistan in northern Pakistan to help rebuild areas devastated by the 2010 floods.

Indian analysts also noted the presence of PLA logistics and engineering corps in the region to provide flood relief and to build infrastructure projects, such as roads, railways, and dams. In early October, Indian army chief General V. K. Singh noted that about 3,000 to 4,000 Chinese troops were stationed in northern Pakistan focusing on construction projects.

The final, and perhaps most important, indication of the limits of the China-Pakistan financial relationship is the PRC's not-so-gentle shunting of Pakistani aid requests to the International Monetary Fund (IMF).

The IMF denied large-scale aid requests made by Pakistan immediately after the September 2008 financial shock, forcing Islamabad to accept a multi-billion-dollar IMF program with stringent economic conditions. In the end, China did agree to provide around $500 million in concessionary lending to Pakistan, but its refusal to provide large-scale loans indicates clear limits on China's willingness to take primary responsibility for Pakistan's financial woes.

CHINA'S ECONOMIC INTERESTS WITH AFGHANISTAN AND PAKISTAN

China's economic interests in both countries are also substantial. In Afghanistan, the China Metallurgical Construction Group's $3.2 billion Aynak copper mine investment, in the eastern province of Logar, is the country's largest, with the mine holding as much as the equivalent of a third of China's total copper reserves. Chinese companies have interests in mineral deposits elsewhere in the country and are also active in the irrigation, infrastructure, telecommunications, and power sectors.

China has an even wider-ranging set of investments in Pakistan. In addition to large-scale projects in telecommunications and hydropower, the Chinese-built port at Gwadar in Baluchistan potentially provides both an energy transshipment route_once connected to the expanded Karakoram Highway (KKH)_and a future naval facility. Not only does rising extremism in the region threaten these projects, it also puts Chinese nationals at risk, and calls into question the very viability of China's most important ally in the region, Pakistan.

The theoretical result, therefore, should be a China willing to find ways to support international efforts to combat militancy and bring stability to both states. But the reality is different, even if Sino-U.S. cooperation on Afghanistan and Pakistan is not itself new. In fact, few regions have played as prominent a role in the Sino-U.S. relationship in recent decades. Islamabad was the conduit for the normalization of relations between the United States and China in the 1970s.

It was the Soviet invasion of Afghanistan that provided the final catalyst for establishing joint Sino-U.S. signal intelligence bases in Xinjiang to monitor Soviet military activities. China, in close conjunction with the Central Intelligence Agency and Pakistan's Inter-Services Intelligence (ISI), became the leading weapons supplier to the mujahideen in the first years of the Afghan campaign, while Chinese arms, mules, and military training were an integral part of the mujahideen's war throughout its duration.

Recent examples of Sino-U.S. coordination during crises in the region have underscored the necessity of bilateral cooperation. Officials from both sides have described close bilateral liaisons over issues ranging from the Kargil conflict of 1999 to the financial turbulence in Pakistan in 2008 as well as the Mumbai attacks of the same year. China played a supportive role in the immediate aftermath of the September 11, 2001 attacks, backing Pakistan's decision to withdraw its support for the Taliban, and developing a limited program of cooperation on counterterrorism issues with the United States, which included the establishment of a Federal Bureau of Investigation office in Beijing.

Formal bilateral consultation mechanisms were expanded under George W. Bush's administration, which launched a South Asia dialogue at the assistant secretary of state level as part of a package of new exchanges on regional issues established under the U.S.-China Senior Dialogue. Without necessarily translating into immediate outcomes, these dialogues set down broad markers for both sides, established a basic tradition of coordination, and brought into regular contact parts of the U.S. and Chinese bureaucracies that would otherwise have had little interaction. The prospects for upgraded cooperation with China under the Obama administration seemed good. Aside from Beijing's own concerns about the worsening situation in the region, China has traditionally felt under pressure to appear cooperative on the top tier of U.S. security priorities and Afghanistan and Pakistan were set to occupy a higher status for President Barack Obama than for Bush. Officials in the Obama administration were less ambivalent than those in the previous administration about the virtues of greater Chinese involvement in Afghanistan, particularly on the security side where limited offers from Beijing had been rebuffed in the past. The greater prominence given to Pakistan in U.S. strategy exemplified by the "AfPak" coinage also placed China toward the top of any possible list of countries whose cooperation could have a major impact. And the promise of a broader regional engagement strategy meant that a more extensive and systematic U.S. diplomatic effort to solicit that involvement was anticipated.

This was reinforced by Special Representative for Afghanistan and Pakistan Richard Holbrooke's early initiatives, which included visiting Beijing in March 2009 and attending the U.S.-China Strategic and Economic Dialogue (SED) in Washington in July 2009, which featured discussions on Afghanistan and Pakistan under the strategic track. capacity, investment, trainers for police, peacekeepers, and allowing its territory to be used as a part of the Northern Distribution Network for the NATO-led International Security Assistance Force.

Even more importantly, some think that China could use its leverage over the Pakistani military to press it to rein in the Afghan-focused groups operating out of Pakistan, such as the Haqqani network and the Afghan Taliban itself, as well as refocusing its "India-centric" doctrine toward a more effective set of counterinsurgency capabilities. It is hoped that some of these steps can be coaxed out by a more sustained U.S. effort to engage China on regional policy and to draw Beijing into an active role in the various multilateral groupings that deal with Afghanistan and Pakistan.

SUPPORTING BALOCHISTAN IN INDIA'S INTEREST: BALOCH LEADER

A Baloch woman leader and rights activist has accused Pakistan of "genocide" in Balochistan and says India must support the "freedom movement" in the restive province for its own "strategic interests" as an "antidote for the Pakistan-China anti-India coalition".

Naela Quadri, 50, said she was here to make a "conscience awakening call" to the government and people of India who helped liberate East Pakistan from Islamabad in 1971 to help it become an independent Bangladesh.

"It is not only for us. An independent Balochistan is the only antidote for Pakistan-China anti-India coalition," Quadri, a Harvard graduate and a champion of Baloch rights, told IANS in an interview.

The Balochistan Independence Movement leader made a passionate plea to Prime MinisterNarendra Modi to get involved in the "freedom movement" of the sprawling western region which borders Iran and Afghanistan.

"India has to take a stand, not only against gross human rights violations in the neighbourhood but also because its strategic interests are involved," said Quadri, who also heads the World Baloch Women's Forum and campaigns for Baloch people's rights worldwide. She was once jailed in Pakistan.

Pakistan has been accusing India of stoking trouble in Balochistan, which is the size of France and is rich in gas, gold and copper reserves. It is also home to massive untapped sources of oil and uranium. Angry over Pakistan's exploitation of the resources and alleged repressive rule, Balochis have so far launched five armed insurgencies since the territory, a princely state under the British, was annexed by Islamabad in 1948.

She accused Pakistan of resorting to "genocide" in Balochistan in response to the "political, democratic and secular" freedom struggle.

"They have killed some 200,000 Balochis in the last decade. The Pakistan Army has participated in enforced disappearance of 25,000 people including men and women," she said.

"They are using all the eight UN indicators of genocide including dehumanization, polarization, extermination and denial."

Recalling the May 28, 1998 Pakistan nuclear tests, Quadri said the army "illegally" used Balochistan for testing its atomic weapons that it got from China. "They have hid the weapons in Balochistan.

"The Balochs are facing all this in isolation and loneliness. No country has come to our help. Not India, so far.

"India is not what it was in 1971 (when Bangladesh was liberated). You had a strong headed and brave leader in Indira Gandhi. She was determined and had a tough foreign policy to deal with Pakistan.

"Unfortunately, the case is different now."

She hoped that Prime Minister Modi would come off "as strong as Gandhi" to help Balochistan win its freedom.

"Modi has a popular mandate and I am sure Indian people would support the Balochistan initiative," said Quadri, an activist since her childhood.

NAELA QUADRI DENIES INDIA'S ROLE IN 'BALOCH STRUGGLE'

India, despite its strategic interests, has not been forthcoming in support to the Balochistan freedom movement, says a prominent author-activist from the restive western Pakistani province, rebutting Islamabad's allegations that New Delhi was instigating separatist trouble there.

Naela Quadri Baloch, 50, also refuted Pakistan's fresh claims that it had arrested from Balochistan an alleged Indian spy, Kulbushan Jadhav.

"These are all lies. Had India helped us, we could have made a breakthrough and gained our independence. Where are the Indians? We don't see them. They don't come to us," Quadri told IANS in an interview on the margins of a talk on Balochistan hosted by Indian think tank Observer Research Foundation (ORF) here.

Jadhav, a former Indian Navy officer, was arrested last month. Pakistani envoy in India Abdul Basit claimed that Jadhav's alleged confession recorded in a video "irrefutably corroborates what Pakistan has been saying all along" that India was stirring unrest and destablising his country.

Quadri categorically denied India's involvement. She said Balochis, in fact, want India to get involved and support their fight against the "brutal and barbaric" Pakistani rule in Balochistan.

"India has to take a stand, not only against gross human rights violations in the neighbourhood but also because its strategic interests are involved," said Quadri, the leader of the Balochistan Independence Movement.

Balochistan is a vast territory, the size of France, rich in gas, gold and copper reserves. It is also home to massive untapped sources of oil and uranium. Angry over Pakistan's exploitation of the resources and alleged repressive rule, Balochis have so far launched five armed insurgencies since the territory was annexed by Islamabad in 1948.

There are about seven armed groups currently fighting the Pakistan Army in the region that gets little attention in the country's mainstream media.

Quadri said Pakistan was only interested in Balochistan's resources, and added that Islamabad has involved China and gifted it a share of the resources only to contain India.

She said China's development of the Gwadar port, in the Arabian Sea bordering Balochistan, should be a cause of worry for India. China has also signed an agreement with Pakistan that grants rights to more than 2,000 acres of land in Balochistan for a Chinese company.

"China wants to control the Indian Ocean. Tell me how do you think India will be safe, and trade peacefully in the face of Chinese naval presence on the sea route," Quadri said, adding, "Isn't this enough for India to help us drag the army out of Balochistan?"

Asked what precisely she wanted from India, the activist said she was looking for "every possible support".

"Be it diplomatic, financial or armed. We need it badly. Every kind of support," said the Harvard graduate, who was once allegedly injured on the head during a clash with the Army. The injury claimed the vision of her right eye.

She said if India could do it in Bangladesh "why not Balochistan".

"India is not what it was in 1971 (when Bangladesh was liberated). You had a strong headed and brave leader in Indira

Gandhi. She was determined and had a tough foreign policy to deal with Pakistan. Unfortunately, the case is different now." She hoped that Prime Minister Narendra Modi would come off "as strong as Gandhi" to help Balochistan win its "freedom".

"Modi has a popular mandate and I am sure Indian people would support the Balochistan initiative," said Quadri, an activist since her early childhood.

She accused Pakistan of genocide in Balochistan — a region crisscrossed by the borders of Iran, Afghanistan and Pakistan. "They have killed some 2,00,000 Balochis in the last decade.

"They are using all the eight UN indicators of genocide including dehumanization, polarization, extermination and denial," Quadri asserted.

2

China-Pakistan Economic Corridor Challenge to India

Conventional wisdom has it that India is worried about CPECBSE -4.45 % at its two ends: Gwadar, where the Chinese are building a maritime presence, and Pakistan-occupied segments of the former kingdom of Jammu & Kashmir, where Pakistani and Chinese territorial and military frontiers are merging. However, there is a deeper issue, one that has hitherto underpinned India's long-term Pakistan strategy. The very fundamentals of that strategy are now under question. Indeed, CPEC is rewriting the economic geography and regional integrity of the subcontinent in a manner that will require more than a tactical, episodic response.

Historically and across the world, trade routes have tended to flow from north to south. There have been exceptions, such as when Britain northern Europe became an economic power and a significant consumer of commodities, and trade routes moved south to north. Yet, for the most part that trajectory has been maintained.

This is no coincidence. Most of the world's people live in the northern hemisphere and trade has tended to seek a route to the sea (to the south) to explore new markets. So it has been in the Indian subcontinent too, for centuries and millennia. Trade routes came down from Central Asia to modern Pakistan, into contemporary northern India, before finding their way to peninsular India.

Partition interrupted this perennial free trade zone (before we knew what the expression meant). Economically this hurt India, especially north India, and cut it off from markets such as Afghanistan.It hurt Pakistan even more and left it trapped and locked out of its natural trading hinterland. More than the political act of Partition - a fact of history nobody seriously wants to change - it was the trade walls that came up on the Radcliffe Line that negatively affected the destiny of the subcontinent. As India opened up its economy in 1991, this absence of sufficient economic osmosis with its neighbours emerged as a paradox. Every prime minister since then, irrespective of party and whatever his individual instincts and political beliefs, came to accept that as India's economy grew, Pakistan would be compelled by business and commercial logic to engage with India.

This could be a product of enlightenment or self-interest, internal pressure or global currents: but it would happen.It would make Pakistan, depending on where it was placed, India's Canada or India's Mexico. The persuasiveness of the north-south trade route could not be rejected forever. CPEC alters that supposition. It replaces Pakistan's dependence on a north-south trade corridor with its bet on an east-west corridor, from Kashgar (Xinjiang province) to Gwadar. This trade route is fairly unprecedented and is an expression of a new economic and strategic geography that China wants to define.

Admittedly CPEC is not quite the "corridor of opportunities" that its advocates contend. Many of its projects are financially unviable. The power plants it is building will require tariffs that are unsustainable for most Pakistanis. CPEC follows a familiar pattern of Chinese investments in South Asian countries - including for instance Hambantota port, the white elephant Sri Lanka has been saddled with.

In this model much of Chinese "investment" is actually a loan that the host nation has to repay. The bulk of Chinese money goes not to locals but is transferred from a state-owned Chinese bank or credit institution to a state-run or state-associated Chinese infrastructure company that executes the project using Chinese workers. Project costs are gold plated to account for both bribes for local elites (generals in Rawalpindi or politicians in Punjab and Balochistan) as well as to ensure windfall gains for the Chinese.

By all accounts, CPEC is going down this path as well. Having said that, its strategic importance for China is greater than usual. This is because of the access it allows western China to the Indian Ocean, as an alternative to the Straits of Malacca.It also gives China a presence and for all purposes a colony that will allow it room for immediate military and political influence in India's neighbourhood and in West Asia.

Whether CPEC's power plants eventually light up homes in rural Punjab or not, the fact is Pakistan's political and military elite has willingly signed on to this Chinese strategic blueprint. As in the case of another superpower in the past, it has happily sacrificed its country's realisable, long-term interests for personal benefit and in the service of an external benefactor.

By embracing the east-west corridor (CPEC) Pakistan is not just abandoning its obvious north-south trade alignment but in effect turning its back on the subcontinent and on South Asia. It sees itself as culturally in West Asia and strategically as located within the Chinese politico-economic zone.

This means that irrespective of how quickly or impressively India's economy may expand in the coming decades, Pakistan is not interested in a linkage let alone integration. New Delhi's assumption that this was a longterm inevitability no longer holds. How does India respond? It can wage a political and diplomatic battle to make CPEC un-implementable. This is possible but not probable.

A harder school in the Indian establishment believes that if the subcontinent is no more the unit of reckoning for Pakistan, then India's interest in recognising and preserving shared tangible legacies, including natural and water resources, should correspondingly decline. Expect more on that in the coming days.

THE CHINA-PAKISTAN ECONOMIC CORRIDOR

The Chinese plan to invest $46 billion dollars in Pakistan to strengthen the China-Pakistan Economic Corridor (CPEC), announced by President Xi Jinping during his April visit to Islamabad, is remarkable for its size and scope. The plan has the goal of providing a direct link between the Pakistani port at Gwadar and the city of Kashgar in China's Xinjiang Uyghur Autonomous Region, and has sparked a flurry of commentary. The size of the plan far exceeds total U.S. aid to Pakistan since 2002 and dwarfs Pakistan's generally paltry FDI figures. The decision by China to make such a high-profile investment in its long-time partner is indicative not only of the enduring regional dynamics that have compelled the two countries' alliance but also of China's increasingly global ambitions. While the details of the CPEC have been discussed and debated at length, the geopolitical factors underpinning China's decision to invest so heavily in its troubled neighbor merit further examination.

The "All-Weather Friendship"

Close relations between China and Pakistan are certainly nothing new and are generally framed in terms of the two countries' mutual rivalry with India. Indeed, this strategic triangle has been the greatest impetus for Beijing and Islamabad's "all-weather friendship," which extends to the diplomatic, economic, and military realms. China has proved to be a reliable alternative for Pakistan to the United States in providing military assistance, including support for its nuclear program. The two states have collaborated on major infrastructure projects in Pakistan in the past, including Gwadar Port and the Karakoram Highway—both of which will play essential roles in the proposed economic corridor.

The Pakistan-China relationship, for all its rhetoric, is also increasingly uneven. For instance, while China is the number one source of imports to and number two destination of exports from Pakistan, trade with Pakistan accounts for a negligible portion of the Chinese economy. The gap between the two countries extends to popular perceptions: while an overwhelming majority of Pakistanis view China favorably (in part, at least, the result of relentless government campaigns extolling the strength of the two countries' friendship), Chinese tend to view Pakistan with far greater ambivalence. Finally, while Pakistan remains stubbornly fixated on India and mired in internal strife, China is a growing world power with correspondingly global ambitions. This last dynamic is particularly important in understanding the motivations and goals of the CPEC project.

Project Goals

The motivations behind China's promised investment in Pakistan are primarily threefold, in order of global relevance: providing economic support to a long-time ally and strategic hedge, facilitating trade, and building linkages to the west by which China can expand its influence.

China's most parochial motivation for the CPEC is to provide economic support to a flagging ally struggling with internal instability. Pakistan and China, as mentioned, have historically viewed each other as balances vis-à-vis their shared rival, India. Now, with the United States explicitly turning its attention toward India to counter Chinese regional influence, and with India's economy primed to grow, it is logical that Beijing would seek to apply a formidable counterweight. Pakistan's previously announced purchase of eight submarines from China is a more overt manifestation of this dynamic. The plan's emphasis on energy projects, to which $37 billion is said to be devoted, is particularly pertinent for Pakistan, which has been struggling with an acute energy crisis for much of the past decade. Moreover, China has real cause to be concerned about Pakistan's susceptibility to terrorism and insurgency. Elements of China's own Muslim Uyghur insurgency in its westernmost Xinjiang Uyghur Autonomous Region are reportedly tied to extremist networks in Pakistan and use the country's lawless western regions as a base of operations. Beijing hopes that a massive economic infusion will promote economic growth and stability both at home and abroad, while strengthening its struggling ally.

China's second interest in the CPEC is its potential to diversify energy trade routes to and from the Middle East. In recent years, China has worked hard to develop linkages to the energy-rich Central Asian states as a way to reduce its dependence on imports through the Indian Ocean and South China Sea, regions where a strong U.S. naval presence could allow for blockades at choke points, such as the Strait of Malacca, in the event of a confrontation between the two powers.

The CPEC intends to make full use of the Chinese-constructed and operated Gwadar Port, situated along the Strait of Hormuz in Pakistan's western Baluchistan Province, as the access point by which energy shipments could arrive and be sent through Pakistan via proposed pipelines, thus bypassing easily disrupted shipping lanes.

The famed Karakoram Highway, linking Pakistan and China via the Karakoram mountain range, is also scheduled to be upgraded. In addition, China has agreed to pay for the Pakistani portion of the oft-delayed Iran-Pakistan natural gas pipeline. Indeed, the promise of a Chinese-built economic corridor likely played a central role in Islamabad's decision to avoid antagonizing its energy-rich western neighbor by remaining out of the Saudi-led coalition in Yemen, despite a history of close military ties to Riyadh.

These reasons alone, however, do not justify such a massive investment in a single country facing as many challenges as Pakistan. China's geopolitical goals are increasingly global, expanding beyond its immediate neighborhood, and the decision to announce its massive investment in the CPEC is a clear indication that Beijing views Pakistan as an important partner in meeting its ambitious economic and political goals. China views its investment in Pakistan, particularly its goal of a rail corridor between the two countries, as the "flagship project" of its "One Belt, One Road" initiative. This initiative seeks to link China's economic partners in Southeast Asia to Europe by means of overland and maritime trade routes, including key Middle East energy resources and emerging African markets. Pakistan, by virtue of its status as a long-term ally and its geographic position linking western China to sea routes through the Middle East, Africa, and, perhaps most importantly, Europe, could serve as a central crossroads for Beijing's expanding global ambitions. The potential for Gwadar to be used in support of future Chinese naval operations is also very real, although the nature of this usage is the source of ongoing debate. Regardless, when viewed in the context of China's broader strategic aims, it is clear that the ambitions behind the CPEC go far beyond strengthening bilateral ties.

Implications and Recommendations

The Chinese plan to invest an enormous $46 billion into the planned CPEC clearly has implications for U.S. policymakers, particularly when viewed in light of Beijing's apparent long-term strategic objectives. That being said, it is important that decision-makers understand that a plan of this scale inevitably faces equally significant obstacles, not least of which are Pakistan's own deteriorating security environment and complex domestic political dynamics. Furthermore, the evolving regional landscape presents U.S. strategists with opportunities, as well as challenges, to ensure that our interests remain protected.

For all of their fanfare, the announced investment projects face significant hurdles, including a fractured Pakistani political environment, in which an apparent change in the CPEC route has already sparked protests from local and provincial leaders in Pakistan's underdeveloped western provinces of Baluchistan and Khyber Pakhtunkhwa. Given both countries' penchants for opacity, corruption appears to be an inevitable challenge. Additionally, the fact that Chinese companies, employing primarily Chinese workers, will carry out many of the projects may only serve to increase political resistance. While navigating political turmoil is not particularly unusual in a development context, the ongoing insurgency in Baluchistan, where separatists have targeted Chinese workers in the past, and Pakistan's continuing struggle with Islamic extremist networks present an enormously challenging security environment. Pakistan's early commitment to establish a 12,000-man security force to protect Chinese workers is an indication of the seriousness of the challenge. An attack on Chinese civilians by militants with links to Pakistan could throw a wrench in diplomatic relations, as it has in the past.

That being said, even if many of the proposed projects are not completed (which is probable), the impact on Pakistan is likely to be significant—$46 billion is an enormous figure. More importantly for U.S. policymakers, however, is the message that the proposal sends regarding the sincerity of China's intentions to utilize Pakistan as a means by which to expand its global influence. This obviously presents challenges for the United States—challenges that are best met by continuing to engage with regional partners (including India) and allies, while reaffirming commitments to bolster the U.S. presence in the Asia-Pacific.

Improving U.S. relations with Iran, particularly now that a nuclear accord has been reached, could be an important element in promoting regional stability, while building linkages across the South Asian subcontinent. As mentioned, China has already announced an agreement to build a natural gas pipeline from Iran to Pakistan, and Washington would be wise to engage with Tehran to work toward expanding energy trade between Iran, Pakistan, and India. Promoting energy linkages between South and Central Asia, in addition to the stalled Trans-Afghanistan pipeline, can be an important step toward reducing Central Asian reliance on Russian and Chinese markets by providing alternative markets for the region's energy exports. Opening diplomatic channels in the region will also be vital to ensuring long-term stability in Afghanistan—an interest Beijing shares. China's potential to play a role in facilitating dialogue between the Afghan Government and the Taliban was on display in recent reported meetings between representatives of the two parties in Urumqi.

Finally, although U.S. policymakers should not simply accept platitudes regarding shared U.S.-China interests at face value (as has been demonstrated, Chinese interests go far beyond Pakistan's stability and economic growth), this does not mean that diplomats and defense officials should not explore areas of trilateral cooperation, including in the field of counterterrorism. The United States, however, must not be seen as complicit in the unjust and counterproductive marginalization and oppression of China's and Pakistan's respective Uyghur and Baluch minorities.

China's planned investment in Pakistan is motivated by an array of factors, including strengthening a useful regional ally and building advantageous trade routes that bypass potentially hostile waters. Most importantly, however, is Pakistan's utility in furthering China's growing power ambitions. For U.S. policymakers, this will require further rebalancing to the Asia-Pacific, solidifying old alliances and building new partnerships, while finding creative methods to build regional linkages that support U.S. interests.

THE CHINA-PAKISTAN ALLIANCE AND SCRUTINY

Over the course of 2011 the relationship between China and Pakistan came under greater scrutiny, primarily owing to Pakistan's faltering relations with the United States. The US-Pakistani relationship went from being troubling right to the brink with a spate of incidents beginning with the arrest of a CIA contractor followed by the killing of Osama bin Laden on Pakistani soil, a NATO strike that killed two dozen Pakistani soldiers and the Memogate scandal, which exposed the persistent internal tensions between the civilian government and military in Pakistan. Concurrently, China and Pakistan celebrated 'Friendship Year' and marked 60 years of diplomatic ties with high- profile state visits, multi-billion-dollar economic deals, the announcement of joint infrastructure projects and joint military exercises.

As Pakistan and China strengthen their relations, questions have arisen around the changing nature of this alliance, the rhetoric that sustains it and the implications of greater Chinese influence in Pakistan for the region. On the one hand, more hardline elements in Washington and New Delhi argue that souring US relations have pushed Pakistan closer to China, giving the latter influence and access in a pivotal region where both US and Indian interests are at stake. Recent reports that Pakistan is likely to hand over the operations of Gwadar Port to China have only aroused further suspicions. Meanwhile, the official Chinese and Pakistani rhetoric promotes the relationship as an 'all-weather' alliance that will endure the test of time.

This chapter examines the image that China and Pakistan have tried to create through a combined approach of multi-dimensional cooperation bolstered by an effective media strategy for their alliance. It argues for a measured interpretation that recognizes the obvious strengths of the Sino- Pakistani relationship but also the less understood parameters of the alliance. How this 'all-weather' narrative has been built to illustrate why China's engagement with its neighbour is contingent upon the drivers of its own national security, regional ambitions and view of the changing world order, and not on unequivocal support of Pakistan. It analyses the challenges and contradictions of the relationship because the official rhetoric highlights similarities but often glosses over the challenges of the relationship. The role of the media is considered here as it seems set to become increasingly important in how the alliance is perceived both by the two countries' domestic audiences and externally, particularly by India and the United States. The chapter concludes with an examination of the regional implications of Pakistan's relationship with China.

The flurry of commentary on Sino-Pakistani relations, particularly after the killing of Osama bin Laden, has only underscored why China has been, and is likely to remain, a different type of partner to Pakistan than the United States. Using economic and defence cooperation as indicators to juxtapose the Chinese–Pakistani and US–Pakistani partnerships is instructive. It illustrates how the United States and China are managing their relations with Pakistan as they both try to secure their national interests while facing similar challenges in the region. However, there are salient differences between the goals and strategies of US and Chinese military, economic and civilian cooperation with Pakistan. Despite the flowery and saccharine words used to describe the depth and strength of their relationship, the level of people-to-people contact and cultural links between China and Pakistan is woefully low.

Looking beyond the rhetoric, there is a mismatch between the importance placed on the alliance by the public in Pakistan and China. What is often less appreciated in the discussion of Sino-Pakistani relations is how heavily dependent they are on the ties between government and military officials. Playing down the effects of Chinese assistance on existing domestic tensions and how they are perceived on the ground by ethno-nationalist and militant non-state actors in Pakistan could lead to a further increase in violence directed at Chinese interests in the country. Pakistan knows it has more to gain from the relationship via Chinese investments and political support, and reacts swiftly to any attacks on Chinese interests.

But its chronic instability has prompted China to reassess its 'all-weather' ties with Pakistan behind the scenes, while it publicly remains a staunch ally.

BUILDING THE ALL-WEATHER NARRATIVE

The rhetoric between the two countries is based on emphasizing their historical ties, Pakistan's loyalty to China and China's memory of that loyalty, 'mutual trust' and 'mutual areas of cooperation'. In reality, examining the rhetoric over the past decade shows that much of it consists of neutral statements that are often aimed at keeping US and Indian regional ambitions in check. These include 'all-weather friend', 'ties that are deeper than the Arabian Sea', 'mutual respect' and 'multi-dimensional cooperation'.

The historical memory of loyalty that is stressed is often subject to the shifting economic and political environment of the day, illustrated by China's changing stance on Indian–Pakistani conflicts and its own relations with the United States and India. The economic and trade links, investments and aid are significant but, given China's capacity and compared with what Pakistan receives from other countries, are still fairly limited. The foundation of the alliance is built on defence cooperation which is constantly deepened by bilateral visits from high-level military personnel.

The areas of cooperation in which this 'sweeter than honey' rhetoric continues to strengthen the veneer of a deep friendship. In addition to public official statements, the print and broadcast media in both countries are playing a more prominent role in shaping and influencing the image of the relationship.

PAKISTANI LOYALTY AND CHINESE HISTORICAL MEMORY

Understanding why the rhetoric between China and Pakistan is so strong lies in the historical origins of the relationship and the value the Chinese place on Pakistan's loyalty, which is a cornerstone of the alliance. However, the relationship has, like most alliances, had its ups and downs and been influenced by each country's bilateral relationship with India and the United States. After diplomatic ties were established in 1951, the early years until the 1960s were characterized by inconsistent policies between China and Pakistan. After the Sino-Indian war in 1962 over Aksai- Chin and Arunachal Pradesh, the dynamics of the relationship altered as this marked the first instance when China took advantage of souring relations between Pakistan and the United States, as Islamabad saw US support for India in the war as a sign of betrayal. For example, although Pakistan had voted against the People's Republic of China's admission to the United Nations in

1960, its sympathies shifted as it became clear that the Kennedy administration would be prepared to intervene on the side of India if China became aggressive, as well as doubling military aid to India. China and Pakistan signed two landmark agreements on trade and territory, and agreed to jointly construct the Karakoram Highway linking northern Pakistan to western China.

The 1965 Indo-Pakistani war gave depth and meaning to this new alliance. The United States placed the blame for the skirmishes in Kashmir largely on Pakistan – thereby reneging on the 1959 Agreement of Cooperation, which stipulated that the United States would come to the military aid of Pakistan at its request – and issued a statement of neutrality. China, along with Iran and Indonesia, provided significant support to Pakistan. While the United States cut off arms sales to India and Pakistan, China gave Pakistan the political support it desired, backing its position and threatening to intervene if necessary. After the 1965 US embargo on weapons to Pakistan, China also became a strategic supplier of conventional weaponry. China's role in building Pakistan's defence industry grew as the United States imposed severe nuclear-related sanctions in the 1970s. The Chinese offer of military assistance and economic aid to Pakistan as the United States suspended economic assistance only served to reinforce 'a new friendship that came into being on account of American neglect and a powerful shared antagonism with India'.

As President Richard Nixon sought an opening with the Chinese against the Soviet Union, and then as China began its programme of economic reforms in the 1970s, Pakistan became one conduit by which US–Chinese relations began to normalize. The 1971 India–Pakistan war over Bangladesh marked another significant juncture in Sino-Pakistani relations. Again China supported Pakistan, albeit in a more restrained manner than in 1965, and vetoed Bangladesh's application for recognition as an independent country at the UN General Assembly as it considered it to be a province of Pakistan. China used its first veto as a permanent member of the UN Security Council over Bangladesh.

Meanwhile, China also sought a rapprochement of its own with India. With economic development becoming a top post-Mao priority in the 1970s, Beijing saw the potential of India, and Chinese policy prioritized development in a peaceful neighbourhood. The impact of this rapprochement with India was limited as Sino-Pakistani relations again took centre stage with the Soviet invasion of Afghanistan in 1979. As the Sino-Soviet split intensified, China and Pakistan again found common interests against a mutual enemy as Islamabad feared the Soviet Union would want to move into Pakistan next to gain access to a warm-water port. Concurrently, Pakistan became a closer ally of the United States to fight the Soviet Union as both countries trained and aided the mujahedeen. The significant moment in Sino-Indian relations came when Prime Minister Rajiv Gandhi visited Beijing in 1988. With the re-escalation of conflict in Kashmir a year later, China diluted its previously pro-Pakistani rhetoric and subsequently withdrew its support for a plebiscite on the Kashmir dispute.

China's strategic relationship with Pakistan and its approach to Indo-Pakistani disputes in the first decade after the Cold War reflected its desire for better relations with India to advance its economic agenda, to counter the US–Indian alliance and to respond effectively to the changes in a fluid geopolitical environment. Whereas Sino-Pakistani relations had a strong foundation in anti-Indian sentiment, they were gradually recalibrated to reflect India's changing role as a global actor and as a market for Chinese goods. Pakistan no longer benefited from the kind of support, at least in tangible terms, that it had once received in disputes against India in the early years, notably on the issue of Kashmir. China's changing policy towards the two countries was in evidence in 1998 when India and Pakistan tested nuclear weapons, during the Kargil war in 1999 and after the terrorist attack on the Indian parliament in 2001; in all three cases China held its position of neutrality.

After the terrorist attacks of 9/11 and the invasion of Afghanistan, the Sino-Pakistani relationship entered a new phase in which Pakistan once again became strategically vital to the United States, now as an ally in the 'War on Terror'. Pakistan's relations with the United States have always been marred by mutual suspicion and mistrust, yet the countries remain inextricably tied to each other. In February 2009, a cable from the United States embassy in Pakistan stated: 'The relationship is one of co-dependency we grudgingly admit – Pakistan knows the US cannot afford to walk away; the US knows Pakistan cannot survive without our support.' American actions in the aftermath of the Soviet war in Afghanistan and 9/11 have left enduring legacies in Pakistan, not least the scourge of Islamic militancy that continues to afflict the country today.

Multidimensional Cooperation

In January 2012, the Chinese Ambassador to Pakistan underscored the country's strategic importance by declaring it 'the fulcrum of Asia'. 6 In the last decade the areas of cooperation between China and Pakistan have evolved and been re-prioritized. Significantly, China only began taking more of an interest in Pakistan's internal security after 9/11 and has since deepened security cooperation.

Its specific concerns about China's Xinjiang autonomous region, where the government confronts what it has described as an Uighur separatist movement, has become a critical arena of cooperation since 2001. China also continues to sell Pakistan nuclear reactors for its civilian nuclear energy projects, military aircraft and inexpensive conventional hardware. In return, Pakistan does not directly oppose or challenge any of China's 'core' interests, including Xinjiang, Taiwan, Tibet and the South China Sea, and it is routinely thanked by the Chinese leadership for this loyalty.

In a speech delivered during his visit to Pakistan in 2006 President Hu Jintao outlined five main drivers of China's 'multi-dimensional' relationship with Pakistan:

- deepening strategic cooperation and consolidating traditional friendship,
- expanding 'win-win' business ties,
- expanding cultural and social exchanges and strengthening the basis of friendship,
- strengthening cooperation in international affairs and upholding common interests, and

- promoting exchanges among civilizations to enhance world harmony.

The 2005 'Pakistan–China Treaty for Friendship and Cooperation and Good Neighbourly Relations' is promoted as a fundamental instrument to strengthen strategic, economic and cultural relations. Of these, strategic cooperation, especially around counter-terrorism, and enhancing economic cooperation are the core drivers of the Sino-Pakistani alliance.

Counter-terrorism in Xinjiang

'Pakistan is at the important forefront in the international counter-terrorism campaign and has made outstanding contributions in combating terrorism. China and Pakistan are friendly neighbours and have conducted sound cooperation in the field of counter- terrorism.'

Xinjiang is the largest political subdivision of China, accounting for more than one-sixth of its territory and a quarter of its boundary length. It is also China's largest gas-producing and second largest oil-producing region, with one of the largest networks of pipelines in the country.

The region is home to nine million Uighurs, a Muslim population of Turkic origin, among which separatist sentiment has historically run high. In the western part of Xinjiang, which borders northern Pakistan, ethnic tensions have grown between the Uighur population and the Han, China's ethnic majority, as increasing numbers of them move into the region in response to the promotion of economic development by the government.

During the Soviet war in Afghanistan in the 1980s, hundreds of Uighur militants were trained in Pakistani madrassas and returned to Xinjiang to join violent ultra-nationalist groups. Many madrassas continue to be hubs of radical ideology.

Uighurs travelling via Pakistan on their way to Saudi Arabia for religious pilgrimages are given accommodation at madrassas where they are often exposed to radical Islam. Although there is no evidence for Islamabad supporting these groups, Beijing has in the past reacted to militant attacks by closing the Karakoram Highway and suspending land-based trade agreements.

China has aimed at maintaining a positive image in the Muslim world to avoid attacks on its soil and its interests abroad, and it has sought more support from Pakistan on its policies towards Xinjiang after 9/11.

In 2002, Pakistani forces captured 22 Uighurs crossing the border, suspecting them of preparing to carry out a terrorist attack in China. This was followed by the assassination by Pakistani forces of Hasan Mahsum, head of the East Turkestan Islamic Movement, which China has classified as a terrorist organization for its activities in Xinjiang and is based in Waziristan.

In the regional capital of Xinjiang, Urumqi, almost 200 people were killed in ethnic riots in 2009, according to official numbers. This was followed in 2011 by further violence which led the Chinese government to step up security measures. Statements from security officials in Xinjiang's Kashgar directly linked the 2011 attacks to militants based or trained in Pakistan, the first time China has publicly pointed the finger at Pakistan. This signalled the Chinese government's increasing frustration over Pakistan's ability to check cross-border militancy, a linchpin of Chinese support.

Military-to-military cooperation

The role of military-to-military ties and cooperation is often used as a highly symbolic tool to signal the strength of the relationship: China expedited the delivery of 50 additional JF-17 fighter jets to Pakistan after the death of Osama bin Laden, assisted Pakistan in building its first indigenously built frigate a month later and in August 2011 launched a communications satellite for Pakistan.

This was followed by Pakistan's keen expression of interest in sending an astronaut on a Chinese spacecraft. Finally, reports that the Pakistani military had given China access to the US helicopter that crashed and had to be abandoned during the raid on bin Laden's compound in Abbottabad caused alarm in Washington, although China and Pakistan both vehemently denied the accusations. All these events made headlines during 2011 and only served to further fuel the suspicion that shrouds the relationship.

For China the purpose of enhancing military-to-military cooperation is to ensure Pakistan facilitates, not hinders, domestic stability within China's borders. Cooperation pivots around supply of weapons, intelligence-sharing, counter-terrorism and joint exercises.

Pakistan and China carry out military exercises every two years and have tested their capacity to conduct operations from a joint- command centre, including simulation of large-scale intelligence gathering by Chinese and Pakistani troops, and search-and-destroy missions.

In November 2011 the two armies held their joint exercises, Youyi-IV (translating into 'friendship'), which was aimed at building capacity and intelligence-sharing for counter-terrorism. According to one analyst, 'joint-military exercises send a message of support for Pakistan's approach to counterterrorism and exemplify the generally satisfactory state of the military-to-military relationship, as illustrated by the attention paid to the closing ceremonies.'

Stronger military-to-military ties also help China maintain continuity and withstand the instability that ensues when Pakistan lurches between democratic governments. Pakistan may not be able to provide China with equipment or technology but the capacity for joint production, like with the Sino- Pakistani JF-17/FC1 fighter means China can skirt the European Union embargo on weapon sales to China imposed after the 1989 protests in Tiananmen Square. The scope for joint production has also created unease in India's security establishment as it is a cost-effective means of enhancing Pakistan's military capacity and capabilities.

China assisted in building Pakistan's nuclear weapon capability and civilian energy programme. China signed a civil-nuclear agreement with Pakistan in 1986 and has subsequently supplied it with two nuclear power plants. China claims to have ended support for Pakistan's nuclear weapons programme after signing the Non-Proliferation Treaty in 1992, although assistance is widely believed to have continued.

While it appears cooperation heavily favours Chinese interests, official statements by China supporting Pakistan's fight against terrorism gives the latter the kind of political support it desires and that is largely lacking from the international community. This was most clearly illustrated by Chinese support for Pakistan after the US raid in May 2011 that killed bin Laden. Foreign Ministry spokeswoman Jiang Yu stated: 'China will continue staunchly supporting Pakistan developing and implementing its own anti-terror strategy based on its own national conditions.'

3

The Geopolitics of South Central Asia and the China-Pakistan Economic Corridor

The US has aligned India to itself in pursuit of its "pivot" to the Asia Pacific and its compulsive drive to manage the rise of China. Its ingress into India is direct, emphatic and in line with its stated policy objectives in the region. This portends deep economic, political and strategic connotations for the region. India has readily mustered to the US call and has ventured into the South China Sea imbroglio too, ostensibly to prove its credentials as a "strategic partner" of the US. The US "pivot" to the Asia Pacific and India's role in it is however now subject to President-elect Trump's review of it. The possible fate of the Trans Pacific Partnership may be an indicator of things to come! China and Pakistan's multidimensional interests continue to converge and the CPEC now epitomizes the continuously growing strength of their alliance. The Russians have started engaging Pakistan at the economic, political and strategic levels. Its historical interest in the perennial warm waters of the Arabian Sea is getting revived by the success of the CPEC. The CARs, Iran, Saudi Arabia, Turkey and even the EU amongst others have shown interest in getting involved with the CPEC.

The geo political, geostrategic and geo-economic dimensions of the Mekran Coast and the CPEC are thus acquiring truly gigantic and ominous proportions. The interplay of conflicting and competing interests of many countries around the CPEC makes for a fascinating new Great Game. The emergence of a multi polar regime with all its dynamics and consequences is all but certain.

There appear to be two time-based groupings that may emerge as a consequence of US policies in the region. Eventually, one might morph into the other to form an even larger, more potent entity to challenge it. First, a possible alliance of China, Russia, Iran and Pakistan (CRIP) could evolve as a competing pole to the US-India combine in the region. The CRIP would make for a very potent regional grouping with a massive strategic, economic and political clout and an evolving sphere of influence.

Foraying forth from the Mekran Coast it would potentially dominate the oil and gas rich Greater Middle East Region (and the CARs by default) and also have an oversight on all Sea Lines of Communications (SLOCs) to and from the Hormuz Straits/Persian Gulf. It's strategic reach and oversight will cover the global East-West trade that transcends the Indian Ocean, Red Sea, Suez Canal and Mediterranean Sea and beyond. With the CPEC crystallizing China has literally outmaneuvered the US in the Asia Pacific. It also outflanks the menacing Malacca Straits with all its devastating implications. In one stroke it has literally become a two-ocean nation. Coupled with a potential draw down on the "pivot" to Asia Pacific by the Trump Administration it may even force groupings like ASEAN and its members to rethink their priorities at the regional and extra regional levels.

The other option is for the SCO (logo right) to emerge from its self induced slumber, become proactive and present itself as an alternative to the US at the global level. Till date it has had a political dimension only. It is now time for it to acquire an economic and military one too. It incorporates the CARs and the weight of the geo political grouping in itself will force Afghanistan to fall in line. The US presence in Afghanistan may yet turn out to be the spoiler in the game with India playing the side kick. Regardless, the SCO must move positively to bring the areas including the Indian Ocean, Arabian Sea and the Greater Middle East Region into its sphere of influence.

The CRIP could ensure the trouble free grounding of the CPEC, stabilize the region and then become the core around which an expanded, reinvigorated and multi dimensional SCO could evolve and grow. It has the potential of becoming the major competing pole to the US and its allies and creating some balance of power at the global level. India's role however will have to be carefully examined. Will it be willing to get off the US band wagon? Or will it want to milk both cows simultaneously, as has been its wont? How will its relations with Russia and the US effect the formation of CRIP and its *evolution into a stronger SCO?* Or are we in for a *battle royale* in the SCAR or even Eurasia, with the major powers and their surrogates involved in a geopolitical game of gigantic proportions and ramifications? Russia and China could actually use the CPEC and the emerging groupings to wean India away from the US. This could become a reality if President-elect Trump follows an isolationist policy, withdraws west of the Atlantic and decides to concentrate on "Making America Great Again" – starting with continental US!

The CPEC is bound to become the massive centre of gravity around which the regional and even extra regional economies will thrive in the near future. It's very pronounced economic dimensions will have a direct bearing on the political and strategic relationships within and outside the region. Interstate relations will be cast anew. Inter and intra regional connectivity will evolve to ensure effective utilization of the many East-West and North-South trade corridors that will crisscross Pakistan. New alignments, new realities and new partnerships will emerge. Old ones will be recalibrated. Old festering issues will need to be resolved post haste. Increasing economic stakes in the CPEC will force belligerents to seek and maintain regional peace. Outstanding issues will have to be resolved justly and according to international covenants. It applies directly to India-Pakistan and Pakistan-Afghanistan issues. India is likely to be left out of this economic bonanza if it does not rethink its approach towards Pakistan and towards conflict resolution with it.

PAKISTAN'S STRATEGIES AND GEO-POLITICAL

After the emergence of the CARs, Pakistan moved actively into Central Asia, but policy makers were clearly divided as to what Pakistan would gain out of Central Asia. While some wanted an Islamic revolution in Central Asia, others wanted open trade links through Afghanistan. The dichotomy of views revealed the limits of Pakistan's Central Asia Policy. Moreover, during this period, the Central Asian leaders were extremely wary of Pakistan because of its involvement in the Afghan war and its support to the mujahideen. During the Pakistan-backed Taliban era in Afghanistan, bilateral relations between Pakistan and the Central Asian states touched rock bottom.

After Pakistan joined the global war against terrorism as a frontline state, bilateral relations began to be revisited. During the past few years, frequent visits by Central Asian and Pakistani officials to each other's states reflect the changing nature of their bilateral relations. A number of agreements have been signed covering such areas as trade and tourism, cultural and economic cooperation during these visits. Pakistan has developed institutionalised arrangements for this purpose. Joint Economic Commissions (JECs) have been established with all the Central Asian states. Under a Special Technical Assistance Programme (STAP) initiated in 1992-93, Pakistan provides training facilities, which are fully funded by Islamabad. The programme includes courses ranging from English language, banking and accountancy to diplomacy.

In this context President General Pervez Musharraf's visit to Uzbekistan and Kyrgyzstan in March 2005 was significant. Earlier, the two-day official visit of President Nursultan Nazarbayev of Kazakhstan in December 2003 to Islamabad was a step towards strengthening bilateral ties between the two countries. During this visit, both the leaders decided to hold annual foreign ministerial consultations. While speaking at the Pakistan-Kazakhstan Business Forum, President Nazarbayev identified three zones of technological parks of information and biotechnology where Pakistani companies could invest significantly.

It is important to note that during the Tajik Foreign Minister's visit to Islamabad in January 2004, he assured President Musharraf that Tajikistan would not allow Indian military bases on its soil. This was followed by the visit of Tajik President Emomali Rahmanov to Islamabad in May 2004. During this visit, eight agreements were inked covering abolition of visas for holders of diplomatic passports, avoidance of double taxation, cooperation between the education ministers and justice ministers, combating drug trafficking, and cooperation between official news agencies and promotion and protection of investment. Pakistan-Uzbekistan relations have also been improving over the past few years given the changed security paradigm. During Uzbek President Karimov's recent visit to Islamabad in May 2006, both sides agreed to expand trade and economic ties and coordinate anti-terrorism activities. It was also planned to extend road and rail links that would enable the CARs, particularly Uzbekistan, to make use of Pakistan's seaports to develop commerce with other regions. A joint fight against extremism and terrorism has, of late, been on top of the list for both the countries. During his March 2005 visit President Musharraf assured the Uzbek leader of his determination to wipe out terrorists, including a substantial number of Uzbek nationals, from the tribal areas. How far these promises will be fulfilled is yet to be seen.

In an attempt to build strong ties with Central Asia, Pakistan has sought to use its cultural links with this region. It is perceived that Pakistan is the cultural extension of the Central Asian region that in turn is seen to be in fusion with the South Asian social milieu. In this context, a Pakistani scholar opined, "Pakistan's political existence and emergence on the world map would not have materialised but for the primordial relationship that glues us together. The roots of our faith, undoubtedly, lie in the Arabian soil but our cultural linkages are with Central

Asian civilisation, which in itself is an amalgam of diverse influence and cross-cultural fertilisation"

Cooperation in the fields of education and culture is an important aspect of Pakistan-Central Asia relations. There are number of Central Asian students studying in Pakistan and similarly Pakistani students in the CARs. The lack of information makes it difficult to provide the total number of Pakistani students studying in all CARs. However, the example of Kyrgyzstan can be cited. Kyrgyz students have been pursuing studies in Pakistani educational institutions in various fields such as engineering, business administration, information technology and the English language. Kyrgyz civil servants also attend training programmes in Pakistan. Conversely, over 350 Pakistani students are currently pursuing studies, mainly in medical colleges, in Kyrgyzstan.

Quest for "Strategic Depth"

The emergence of Central Asia was viewed as an opportunity for Pakistan to spread its sphere of influence beyond Afghanistan thus providing "strategic depth" against India. As mentioned earlier, Pakistan's desire to expand its influence in Afghanistan has been very central to Islamabad's strategic thinking. In the view of Gen. Mirza Aslam Beg, "...Afghanistan will be a great source of strength to Pakistan to face any crisis and danger that it may encounter. In fact, the security of Pakistan, Iran and Afghanistan is interlinked and is indivisible..."

While examining Pakistan's Afghan policy, it has been argued that its defence planning has been handicapped by the lack of territorial depth to absorb an attack by India and then to retaliate. This elusive quest for strategic depth has guided Pakistan in its ambitious involvement in Afghanistan in spite of the multiple implications for its social fabric and political culture. Thus, Pakistan's Afghan policy was constructed with an objective to create a subservient government in Afghanistan that would be friendly to Pakistan, militarily too weak to question the Durand line and unstable to raise the Pushtunistan issue. In addition to this, the military strategists argued that a friendly Afghanistan would give Kashmiri militants a base from where they could be trained, funded and armed. The Central Asian region was seen as an extension of Pakistan's strategic space.

The end of the Taliban regime in Afghanistan has not brought any fundamental change in Pakistan's Afghan policy. Afghanistan is still very central to Pakistan's strategic thinking, and is akin to being Pakistan's backwaters. Wary about how the current situation would unfold in Afghanistan, Islamabad is trying to cement its ties with the current regime in Kabul while supporting Taliban elements and has not given up its grand strategy of establishing a friendly government in Kabul.

It is believed that Pakistan's new proxy war in Afghanistan is slowly unravelling itself. There is the resurgence of Taliban in Afghanistan. The Taliban are supported by the Pakistani establishment itself – from low-level military officers and some ministers to religious parties and their jihadi infrastructure. The ISI too has been proactively working to bring the Taliban back to its life.

There has been constant accusation by Afghanistan of Pakistan's interference and its support to the Taliban and Al Qaida elements to create trouble for Kabul. Afghan President Hamid Karzai during his visit in February 2006 provided evidence to President Musharraf implicating Pakistan in the recruitment, training and equipping of Islamic radical suicide bombers.

The senior Afghan official who accompanied President Karzai said, "In places like Karachi, Pakistani extremist groups working on behalf of the Taliban for a fee, carry out the recruitment and then bring them to safe houses in Balochistan for training and equipping with vests." In a recent visit to Islamabad, Gen. Johan Abizaid, the head of the US Central Command reportedly showed the Pakistanis, intelligence photographs of Taliban training camps at an undisclosed location and asked for them to be shut down.

Three years ago, Dr. Timothy D. Hoyt, Associate Professor of Strategy and policy at the US Naval War College, in a hearing before the House Committee on International relations in October 2003 accused Pakistan of providing sanctuary to terrorist groups, that enjoy strong support among active and retired Army officers and intelligence officials. He said: "So long as Pakistan relies on terrorism to achieve its political objectives, it will be impossible to eliminate terrorism and the Al Qaeda presence in the region."

Regional Organisations

Apart from using its Islamic card to tie the CARs in its strategic fold against India, Islamabad also sought to use multilateral bodies in the region. Its desire to balance India through regional organisations got manifested in their wooing neighbouring Iran, Turkey, Afghanistan, and the CARs into the Economic Co-operation Organisation (ECO). Under this forum, states are expected to develop closer economic interaction.

In November 1992, Pakistan, Iran, Turkey, Afghanistan and the five former Soviet republics of Kazakhstan, Azerbaijan, Kyrgyzstan, Turkmenistan, and Uzbekistan created an extended Muslim economic bloc linking Asia and Europe.

Former Prime Minister Nawaz Sharif noted in a speech marking the occasion that the ECO "now corresponds to the boundaries of the ancient area, which brought prosperity and civilisation through fruitful exchanges along the historic silk route. The people of these lands have a shared history and common spiritual and cultural values."

Nawaz Sharif added his belief that extensive investment in infrastructure and encouragement of the private sector were the most important immediate objectives. He noted that Pakistan was building a major highway network to link Central Asia to the Arabian Sea and that its railroads were "poised to link not only member-states but also ECO with Europe, Russia, and South Asia." He added: "peace in Afghanistan is essential for political harmony and fruitful cooperation in our entire region."

Speaking about the achievements of ECO, Pakistani foreign minister Khursheed Mahmood Kasuri stated that it had made considerable progress in the trade, transport and energy sectors. The second ECO Commerce Ministers' Meeting held in Islamabad in July 2003 approved the ECO Trade Agreement (ECOTA).

The agreement envisages reduction of tariffs up to 15 per cent over a period of eight years (15 years in case of Afghanistan) on at least 80 per cent of goods on tariff lines. Para-tariff and non-tariff barriers would be eliminated within a period of two years. He further stated that the implementation of ECOTA would pave the way for economic integration of the region. New strategies and plans are expected to be adopted to make the organisation more effective.

Despite claims made by Pakistan's ministers about ECO's progress, it has so far been a non-starter. The establishment of a free trade zone is difficult when basic infrastructure necessary in this regard is lacking. Moreover, the competing interests of Iran, Pakistan and Turkey limit the role ECO can play in the region. Instability in Afghanistan remains a major obstruction for expanding the area of cooperation.

Islamabad also sponsored the membership of the newly independent Central Asian countries in the Organisation of Islamic Countries (OIC). This was yet another drive to bring the CARs into the Ummah. Pakistan has also been keen to join the SCO. In early 2001, Pakistan applied for observer status but the Central Asian members of the organisation blocked its entry. A major stumbling block was Pakistan's support for the Taliban government in Afghanistan.

Though China supported Pakistan's membership, Russia wanted India to simultaneously join SCO. It was only in June 2005 that the applications of Pakistan, Iran and India were simultaneously considered and approved with consensus for granting observer status in the SCO at the Council of Heads of States Meeting in Astana on July 5, 2005. Pakistan is also a member of Conference on Interaction and Confidence-Building Measures in Asia (CICA). Much to the chagrin of Pakistan, India is included in both these organisations.

CHINA-PAKISTAN ECONOMIC CORRIDOR: A ROAD TO PEACE?

Three weeks ago, trucks carrying goods from China began offloading containers to ships at the Pakistani port of Gwadar, marking the operational opening of the Chinese built-and-financed China-Pakistan Economic Corridor (CPEC). The scale of the $51 billion infrastructure scheme will change Pakistan in ways that offer hope for easing its internal conflicts and its destabilizing fear of international isolation, experts said in a discussion at the U.S. Institute of Peace.

CPEC, which includes upgraded highways and rail lines, new power plants and the deepwater port at Gwadar to ease the path for exports from western China, is creating new, positive confidence in Pakistan's security and foreign policy establishment, said Hussain Nadim, a Pakistan expert at USIP and a former special assistant to the country's minister of planning, development and reforms. While political battles continue over local opportunities created by CPEC projects, its overall impact has been to reduce tensions among the country's fractious regions and political parties, while the strengthening ties with China are fostering a broader internationalist outlook, Nadim said in the Dec. 1 event. "Even ethnic nationalist parties that may have had separatist tendencies in the past are very keen on partnering with China and benefiting from the influx of Chinese capital that can increase jobs, electricity and improve livelihoods," said Arif Rafiq, a fellow at the Center for Global Policy and president of Vizier Consulting. Neither he nor his firm is involved with the project. "There's also an electoral advantage," he said.

"Even ethnic nationalist parties [in Pakistan] that may have had separatist tendencies in the past are very keen on partnering with China." — Arif Rafiq, Vizier Consulting

Investing in Pakistan meets multiple objectives for China, according to Zhao Hai, a research fellow with the National Strategy Institute at China's Tsinghua University. Most immediate is the need to deploy excess capacity built up within

China by stimulus spending during the financial crisis of 2008, he said. Most of CPEC construction is financed at very low rates by Chinese state banks lending to Chinese companies. The foreign enterprises—often state-owned—do the work using some Pakistani subcontractors and locally buying steel, concrete and other construction materials.

Still, the more familiar China becomes with Pakistan, the more it worries about domestic politics including relations between the government and the military, and regional and religious tensions, Zhao said. Gwadar and the roads and rail lines leading to it, for instance, are in Balochistan, a province that has experienced an insurgency fighting for autonomy. China tries to keep its distance from these disputes, he said. China also hopes CPEC can help address its own concerns related to the Uighur population in Xinjiang province, where the corridor begins, Zhao said. Xinjiang has been the site of frequent flare-ups between Chinese authorities and the Uighurs. The central government hopes CPEC will revitalize the region's economy, and therefore reduce tensions with the Uighurs and attract a more diverse population, Zhao said.

INDIA AND CHINA: OPPOSITE DIRECTIONS

But CPEC for now offers little prospect of reducing China's and Pakistan's immediate tensions with India, panel members said. India is proposing its own transportation corridors that run in the opposite direction from those of China's "One Belt, One Road Initiative," an overall project intended to link China with Central Asia, Europe and East Asia. Theoretically the Indian and Chinese projects could be linked, Zhao said. But mutual distrust precludes potential cooperation, he said.

"India remains vigilant and cautious, but they do somehow want to participate," he said. How to bring in India is the biggest question facing the CPEC project, Nadim said. When Prime Minister Nawaz Sharif took office in 2013, his primary focus was improving relations with India, not China, Nadim said, adding that he's confident India remains a priority. Sharif and his party recognize that the benefits of CPEC for Pakistan could be enhanced further with a significant easing of tensions with India, but that is likely further in the future, Nadim said "Realistically, the government of Pakistan isn't thinking beyond Balochistan," he said.

In the most hopeful scenario, CPEC could serve as the gateway for connecting Pakistan to India, Afghanistan, the Central Asian republics and even Iran, Rafiq said. "But the economic promise of regional integration is really held hostage by strategic challenges," he said.

India's long-running suspicions about the project were heightened by recent reports the Chinese navy intends to patrol Gwadar and that it provided an escort for the first ships leaving the port with Chinese cargo, said Sarah Watson an associate fellow and India specialist at the Center for Strategic and International Studies. More broadly, China's deepening involvement with Pakistan makes it more likely to move beyond traditional verbal support for its ally to military backing in case of a conflict with India, she said.

While there is cause for optimism that CPEC could contribute to a more peaceful future for South Asia, the massive construction underway in Pakistan is no panacea, said Jennifer Staats, the director of USIP's China program, who moderated the discussion. It's hard to know the ultimate effect on regional dynamics because the story is just getting started, she said. The first freight train on an upgraded line left China for another Pakistani port, Karachi, just last week.

GEOPOLITICS OF CHINA'S EMERGENCE AND ITS TRANSATLANTIC IMPLICATIONS

China's economic emergence is laden with geo-strategic implications, many of which cannot but recast crucial elements of the transatlantic relationship. It is not yet a truly global power, certainly not in the way the United States is. China is, however, a major power in East Asia and its reach is extending. It is, of course, a nuclear state possessing inter-continental missiles; it has a very large military establishment in possession of ever more sophisticated weaponry, it is a permanent member of the UN Security Council; and its global economic weight is increasing by leaps and bounds. One would therefore be utterly remiss to look at China simply in static terms. It is an ascendant if somewhat contradictory world power, and its growing presence on the global stage is altering the strategic and economic map.

At the same time though, China has dramatically abandoned the revolutionary ideology which once inspired its foreign policy. It is increasingly understood as a status quo power, with a deepening interest in sustaining a global and regional economically liberal order that its leaders now embrace as the key to national prosperity, internal stability and continued party hegemony. It has also altered its foreign policy at least tactically. Where China once considered the developing world as its greatest foreign policy priority, now its relations with the United States, Japan and Europe receive pride of place, followed by its regional neighbours, and then by the developing world. (European Policy Centre Conference, Remarks by Xinning Song) China's recent accession to the WTO and its clearly expressed goals within that body reinforce the view that it has become more of a status quo power dedicated to the preservation of an open trading order. This approach has eased China's relations with developed countries, most of which enjoy improved and fruitful economic relations with China. Yet tensions persist over issues like human rights, China's military ambition, Taiwan, Burma and arms sales. Although Taiwan is certainly the region's most likely strategic flash point, there are other dangerous regional security challenges including North Korea's attempts to manufacture nuclear weapons and China's alarmingly poor relations with Japan. Accommodating an ever more powerful and wealthy China was invariably going to pose challenges to the world's other great powers. (Schwarz)

Since 2003, China has hosted four rounds of the six-party talks among Japan, North Korea, Russia, South Korea, and the United States. It considers itself to be a mediator between North Korea and the United States in negotiations over the burgeoning North Korean nuclear programme. China crafted the framework for the negotiations.

The United States has commended China for its broad efforts to facilitate the six-party talks, but has criticized China for not using all its influence to convince North Korea to commit to Complete, Verifiable, Irreversible, Dismantlement (CVID). China provides North Korea with approximately 40% of its food and 90% of its oil and is North Korea's sole formal military ally. Prior to the recent agreement, some US officials and experts had speculated that China prefers to keep this nuclear issue unresolved because it counterbalances US policy in the Taiwan straits. China has a strong interest in preserving stability in North Korea, which it views as a buffer state, and it resisted threatened use of sanctions or force to resolve the North Korean problem. The United States has now applauded China's role as mediator in the six-party talks, which appear to have resulted in an arrangement that will end North Korea's nuclear programme.

The level of hostility between Japan and China has risen in recent months, in part because Japanese Prime Minister Junichiro Koizumi has paid several visits to the Yasukuni shrine where war criminals, who were responsible for terrible atrocities in China during the Second World War, are buried. Japanese owned businesses in Shanghai were attacked earlier this year after the introduction of a history textbook in some Japanese schools that glossed over Japanese atrocities during World War II. Mr Koizumi, however, recently apologized for the wartime invasion and declined to visit the shrine this year. (People's Daily Online, August 15, 2005) The creation of a bilateral panel of historians to review the legacy of the occupation could also help ease tensions. But difficulties in the relationship persist. Japanese recent endorsement of the American view that China's Taiwan policy represents the greatest threat to regional stability at a recent "two plus two" bilateral security meeting raised alarm bells in Beijing. (Briefing by Lanxin Xiang) Tension is also arising out of the fact that Chinese economic power is threatening to eclipse that of Japan. Managing this shifting relationship is proving difficult. Finding ways to accommodate the new China while delineating what cannot be given up in the process poses a genuine intellectual and political challenge for the entire western community. (Brzezinski)

Perhaps the most apparent manifestation of how China's evolution might alter US-European relations has been the recent transatlantic tension over a European push to lift its long-standing arms embargo imposed after the military crackdown on demonstrators in Tiananmen Square. In December 2004 EU leaders announced their intention to replace that embargo with an export code of conduct. This would include provisions on arms brokering and technology transfers and supposedly would trigger no increase in quantity or quality of weapons sold to China. But it would also be non-binding, and as such might not constrain members eager to sell more sophisticated systems to the Chinese. (Financial Times, January 22, 2005.) Over the past year, American officials communicated to their European counterparts that lifting the embargo would seriously complicate transatlantic defence trade and cooperation. American leaders strongly oppose any move by Europe that might help tip the delicate balance in the Taiwan Straits. European advocates of lifting the embargo maintain that they have no intention of doing so; but this has hardly quelled US concerns.

American officials and many in Europe strongly oppose lifting the embargo for a range of strategic and political reasons including the fragile military balance in East Asia, the possibility that Western weapons might be used by China in a possible confrontation with China, and the fact that China's political system remains fundamentally undemocratic and unaccountable. Washington is committed to helping Taiwan defend itself in the event of a Chinese invasion; but it is engaged in a delicate balancing game. The Americans have helped arm Taiwan to the point where its self-defence capability is credible, but not sufficiently to tempt it to declare full independence. US officials welcome dialogue and negotiation as the best means of preventing a military conflict. The Americans do not generally share the view of those in Taipei who would abandon the single

China ideal, although they are committed to deterring a Chinese military intervention.

American policy should be understood in terms of a classic balance of power politics. Historically great powers have never welcomed the rise of new powers and often work to impede that rise. (Mearsheimer) Several Chinese analysts, including Lanxing Xiang, have suggested, however, that there are risks involved in pursuing this course as well. Xiang uses an historical analogy to point out that Britain's tough policies toward an authoritarian Wilhelmine Germany helped make conflict between the two powers a preordained conclusion. Xiang worries that a policy of aggressive containment toward China might have the same effect, contributing to a climate of suspicion and tension and adding to the risk of miscalculation. (Lanxin Xiang, "Survival", Autumn 2001.)

American officials are somewhat divided on all of this. Those focused on commercial matters have a different view than those responsible for managing strategic-military issues. The US navy, for example, foresees a future Chinese "blue water" naval challenge (Kaplan) although the Chinese currently express an ambition to develop naval assets that would only advance their navy from a posture of coastal defence to a posture that would allow its fleet to exercise some suasion power in the China Sea.

At this point, the building of a genuine "blue water" navy is beyond the means of the Chinese, who recognize that they are prepared neither to match American naval power nor to challenge America's overall geopolitical superiority. (Jisi) The US navy will therefore exercise ultimate control of the sea-lanes that are vital to Chinese commercial and energy needs for some time to come. (Mallet, Financial Times) China's growing energy concerns certainly inform its evolving strategic orientation, but so too does its focus on the Taiwan question.

The recent Chinese-Russian military exercises included an amphibious assault of the kind that could one day be used in Taiwan. That exercise was coupled with a joint Russian-Chinese demand that the United States abandon bases in Central Asia

- something that certainly raised the level of concern in Washington.

China's National People's Congress recently adopted a law that explicitly states that a Taiwanese declaration of independence could be met with a Chinese military response. Chinese officials who met members of this Committee in Beijing insisted that this law has been misinterpreted in the West and that Americans and Europeans do not seem to understand how central Taiwan is to Chinese identity. The Taiwanese government's flirtation with independence has raised a red flag in China. According to the Vice-Chairman of the Foreign Affairs Committee of the National People's Congress, Wang Yingfan, and a number of Chinese foreign policy experts, no Chinese leader could ever concede to the establishment of a separate Taiwanese nation; to do so would be seen by the Chinese people as an act of treason. Ambassador Yingfan asserted to this Committee that China "would pay any price" to preserve what it sees as its territorial integrity and admitted that the law does imply the existence of a military option. (Meeting with Wang Yingfan, July 2005) Ambassador Yingfan suggested that the new law expresses China's desire to resolve the Taiwan question in a peaceful manner, while calling for the tightening of already substantial links between the island and the mainland. The law has certainly not been seen in such a benign light either in the United States or in Europe.

Indeed, the newly promulgated law on Taiwan certainly provoked second thoughts in Europe about revoking the arms embargo. For example, four parliamentary Committees in the British House of Commons - Defence, Foreign Affairs, International Development, and Trade and Industry - expressed strong reservations last spring about lifting the embargo without first clarifying how the European Council will ensure that this does not result in any qualitative or quantitative increase in arms sales to China. The Committees were alarmed by the ongoing human rights problem in China and felt that to lift the embargo would send the wrong political signals to Beijing. They also expressed concern that lifting the embargo could poison armaments cooperation and broader diplomatic relations with the United States. (House of Commons Report.)

Indeed, if not properly managed, trans-Atlantic fall-outs on China policy, like the recent spat over arms sales to China, could collectively weaken the recent efforts of some European and American leaders to deepen trans-Atlantic defence industrial cooperation. It is worth noting that the mood in the US Congress in recent years has not been particularly receptive to open trans-Atlantic defence markets. Secretary of Defence Donald Rumsfeld and other officials have actually fought some of the more restrictive bills coming from Capitol Hill. There is a sense now that were the European Union to end the embargo without stringent controls, the Department of Defence could no longer defend the very notion of a transatlantic defence market in the halls of Congress. While the United States has long enjoyed a privileged relationship with the Chinese both because of its extensive economic links to that country and because it too is a key power in the Pacific, Europe's relationship with China has expanded rather dramatically.

In 2004, Europe passed the United States as China's largest trade partner. (Kynge) Some in Europe now suggest that Europe and China share common views on a range of questions like the central role of the UN Security Council in dealing with international crises and in the desirability of a multi-polar as opposed to a unilateral global order. The Chinese themselves have picked up on this and have recognized the potential economic and strategic value of developing stronger ties to Europe. There is indeed a certain symmetry in Chinese and EU global ambitions. They are both powerful regional actors playing important, if not hegemonic, global roles. They see each other as potential partners with a common need to bolster their respective global influence and prosperity. This symmetry is certainly one of the sub-texts in the battle over the arms embargo, and it likely presages the rise of other transatlantic tensions that will involve China. The European Union defines its relationship with China as a "strategic partnership", a status it accords to its most important partners including the United

States, Canada, Russia and India. (European Policy Centre Conference, Remarks by Dirk Sterckx) At the recent EU-China summit, both sides reaffirmed their commitment to building an effective multilateral order.

Not surprisingly, some European and North American Atlanticists see this thinking as a direct challenge to the primacy of the NATO alliance. This is one reason why it may be an opportune moment to develop a nascent NATO-China dialogue. There have already been informal diplomatic contacts in Brussels; the Chinese have participated in several NATO seminars and were invited to observe a NATO exercise. Several NATO officials have also visited Beijing in recent months. Given China's participation in a number of peacekeeping activities, there is clearly ample room for dialogue. Zhang Yesui, China's Vice Foreign Minister recently told a NATO PA delegation that his government is closely following NATO's transformation and that his country warmly welcomes NATO's role in peacekeeping. He also indicated that NATO's presence in Afghanistan has contributed to regional stability. Yet China and Russia have also called for the closing of American bases in Central Asia, so its position is nuanced if not somewhat contradictory. The public's view of NATO is equally ambiguous; the bombing of the Chinese Embassy by US planes operating in a NATO mission over Belgrade provoked a strong nationalist outcry in China and this event, according to Mr. Yesui, is not entirely forgotten

Notwithstanding the improving European-Chinese relationship, there are also tensions between the two. These include China's policy toward Burma, its relationship with Taiwan and human rights issues in general. Europe's central bankers had expressed displeasure with China's foreign exchange policy of tying the Renminbi to the falling dollar and so welcomed the recent decision to allow the Renminbi to appreciate. At the same time, a range of groups worry that Europe's less traditional manufacturing competitive sectors could be overwhelmed by Chinese imports. In recent months, trade tensions with China have risen with Brussels and

Washington alike seeking to limit Chinese imports and investments in sensitive sectors like textiles.

The Chinese see the EU model of regional integration as a way to build a more stable and prosperous East Asia. (Perlez) China is currently not a member of The Association of South Eastern Asian Nations (ASEAN), but it has struck up an important dialogue with that regional body through what has become known as the "ASEAN plus Three" process in which both Japan and South Korea are also engaged. Recently China and ASEAN agreed to negotiate an ambitious trade liberalization agreement, and China has negotiated bilateral deals with a number of ASEAN countries. Intra-Asian trade is growing explosively, placing six regional players into the ranks of the world's ten fastest growing economies. (Baucus) China's new tactic of extending its influence through trade policy and cooperative multilateralism, rather than by simply brandishing its military muscle, points to its growing international maturity and sophistication. It has learned to extend its influence through win-win and not just confrontational approaches, and this is opening new doors. (Xiang "Survival" Summer 2004) Yet China has hardly forgotten the importance of military power; and it is embarked on a major military modernization effort. Moreover, it is not reluctant to brandish this power when it feels key national security interests are at stake.

THE CHINA-PAKISTAN CORRIDOR: A FATE-CHANGER?

Over the decades during which I have worked in and written about Pakistan, there have been so many supposed national "turning points" at which the country failed to turn that I have almost ceased to notice them.

But when earlier this year the Pakistani Government described China's planned energy and transport corridor through Pakistan to the Arabian Sea as a "fate changer", it may - perhaps - have been telling the truth.

At more than $46bn, the planned Chinese investment in this project is some four and a half times the total US economic aid to Pakistan since 9/11 (though admittedly largely in the form of low-interest loans).

Apart from energy pipelines and road-and-rail links between western China and the Pakistani port of Gwadar, the plans include massive investments in Pakistan's own energy, transport and telecommunications infrastructure, including what would be the world's largest solar power generating complex at Bahawalpur.

Pakistani dream

These projects, if realised - and this is a very big if - have the potential to bring in tens or even hundreds of billions of dollars in additional investments. They could restore Pakistan's economic growth of the early 1960s, which led economists at the time to predict that the country would be one of the future leading economic powers of Asia.

This dream was lost when Pakistan recklessly attacked India over the Kashmir dispute in 1965, and Zulfiqar Ali Bhutto subsequently abandoned free market policies in favour of a horribly corrupt and badly managed populism.

China's commitment to the core energy and transport aspects of the plans does not seem in much doubt. This corridor will be a key part of Beijing's "One Belt, One Road" strategy, intended to link China by land with Europe, Southeast Asia and the Middle East.

This strategy is driven both by economic interests and security concerns. China depends on imports for 60 percent of its oil, and the great majority of this is carried by tanker across the Indian Ocean and through the Strait of Malacca. Beijing sees this as rendering China dangerously vulnerable to pressure from India and the US, as well as to attacks from fighters.

Improving security

Security obstacles in Pakistan have greatly diminished in recent years thanks to the successful offensives of the Pakistani army against the Pakistani Taliban rebels. These offensives were supported - at last - by a united Pakistani public opinion.

The separatist rebellion in Balochistan - where the port of Gwadar is situated - remains a threat, but so far its military capacity has been very limited. It would only increase radically if India decided to increase its support for the rebels via Afghanistan with the deliberate aim of blocking the Chinese corridor.

Apart from being extremely dangerous and irresponsible in itself, such an Indian strategy would lead to a breakdown in both diplomatic relations and trade with China. That would be a very unwelcome development as both the Indian National Congress and current Bharatiya Janata Party governments in recent years have tried to improve these relations.

Fears have been expressed in India about the ways in which this new Chinese corridor would both strengthen Pakistan and increase China's geopolitical and economic influence in the region.

It is important to note, however, that while Beijing certainly regards Pakistan as a potential strategic ally against India, it has also brought strong influence to bear on Pakistan not to back attacks on India, and to seek a reduction of tension with Delhi.

China certainly does not favour either international terrorism or a new security crisis in South Asia. Ideally, therefore, future Indian leaders might come to see an Indian interest in seeking reconciliation with Pakistan so as to link up with the Chinese corridor and open land routes for India to the Middle East and Europe.

This would require, among other things, serious work on a consensus between Delhi, Islamabad, Beijing and Washington on how to seek a peace settlement in Afghanistan.

Rampant problems

The biggest obstacles to China's plans lie not in strategic threats but in the corruption, dysfunction and incompetence of Pakistan's governing structures, and the culture of patronage which dominates Pakistani politics.

Thus in the area of transport, Pakistan railways are a shambles compared with those of India, though the two countries inherited the same systems at independence.

Pakistan International Airlines has been in crisis for years, above all because - as with state-owned banks and industries - politicians (and generals when in power) have used it as a source of patronage and stuffed it with their relatives and supporters. This has led to the grotesque figure of 776 PIA employees per aircraft, one of the highest rates in the world.

Pakistan needs a huge outside investment in infrastructure in part because of its own chronic inability to raise taxes. At barely 10 percent of GDP, Pakistan's tax-collection rates are among the lowest in Asia. Pakistan suffers chronic electricity shortages in part because it cannot get the population to pay its electricity bills.

It does not have to be this way. Under President Ayub Khan in the late 1950s and early 1960s, a combination of a relatively honest, dynamic and far-sighted administration with plentiful US aid (above all for infrastructure, as with China's plans) and sound international advice led to Pakistan achieving some of the highest rates of economic growth in the world.

If Chinese money and Chinese influence can return Pakistan to those rates of growth, then this will not only help to stabilise Pakistan and create a barrier to violence there. It will also mark China's arrival as a truly great - and positive - force on the world stage.

GEOPOLITICS IN THE INDIAN OCEAN REGION

The Indian Ocean has figured unmistakably in India's geostrategic computations since Independence and clearly thus, as topographically Indian landmass projects into the Indian Ocean. Because of this peninsular development India's coastline has Arabian Sea and the Bay of Bengal on its western and eastern flanks. Profoundly pulled in to Mahanian thoughts, Sardar K.M. Pannikar, the most powerful backer of India's matchless quality in the Ocean contended for a 'ring of steel' to control the indispensable maritime space and attest its supremacy. In any case, in the years to take after, such vital thoughts for the Ocean stayed on paper as guard spending plans stayed low when all is said in done, and all the more particularly Indian Navy, inside the three arms of military was given a crude arrangement by progressive governments.

The budget for the Indian Navy remained as low as 2 to 3% of the total annual defence budget till the late 1990s. The end of the Cold War, and more so the disintegration of the Soviet Union as a single state, led to a major restructuring of the world order at the global level, which had an impact on the Indian Ocean region as well (Singh 1997).

The period after the end of the Cold War also heralded a dramatic change in the Indian perception of its stakes in the Indian Ocean Region. The result was a major drive to modernize the Indian navy. From the mid-1990s, Indian has embarked on a major programme to develop a 'Blue Water' navy involving significant increases in naval expenditure (Brewster 2010).

Analysts like Scott peg the date of modernization of the Indian Navy with the election of the Bharatiya Janata Party in 1998. The BJP, with its string defence policies, reversed the neglect of the Indian Navy. Naval spending increased within a expanding defence budget (Scott 2006). Scott further cites that during the 1990s in general, there were vociferous demands of modernization of the Indian Navy from the naval establishment amid concerns that China was raising its presence and profile in the IOR. Naval figures argued that the Mahanian vision of command of the sea and seapower was being neglected (Scott 2006).

The calls for the emphasis on naval expansion were answered with the arrival of the BJP to power at the Centre. In any case the year 1998 marked a significant change in the nuclear policy and the Nuclear Tests were conducted for the second time by India in May of that year. Since then, India has made efforts to overcome the deficient deployment of naval forces in the IOR which, reflects its geopolitical concerns vis-à-vis other powers in the region.

The broader canvass of geopolitics in the Indian Ocean Region has an imprint of the presence of the United States of America with its bases in the Arabian Sea and Gulf Region and in the Indian Ocean. On the other hand, China's presence in the region has been increasing due to its efforts to build ports and harbours at crucial locations namely, Myanmar (Sittwe), Hambantota (Sri Lanka) and Gwadar in Pakistan. China has provided technological know how as well as aid for these ports.

China, in return has benefitted by anchoring its warships on these ports during times of crisis such as evacuation of its citizens from the Gulf region during the Arab uprisings and the recent Syria crisis. China claims that its movements in the IOR are reflective of the efforts to protect the energy flows for its mainland demands, which occur between the Gulf region and China through the region.

The proposed Maritime Silk Road by China is another major strategy by China to create a strong foothold in the region. With its bases spread across the its littoral seas to further west in the Indian Ocean, the proposed Maritime Silk Road creates the environment in the region wherein China is viewed as an extra-regional power interfering in the region.

These Chinese ventures and the Maritime Silk Road concept/ idea are countered by the other super-power in the region i.e. the United States of America through various existing (Japan, Australia and Philippines) and new strategic partnerships (India). With these partner countries, of which, Australia and India are important actors in the region, the United States conducts naval exercises periodically as show of strength and solidarity. The other important actors in the region are Singapore, South Africa and Indonesia. United States has a base at Diego Garcia in the Chagos Archipelago in the Indian Ocean, which forms part of its Pacific Command (USPACOM). United States is also present in the region through its various interventions and resultant bases in the Gulf region and Afghanistan. It, therefore, is not an exaggeration to say that United States is a power to be reckon with in the region.

Incidentally, the United States is revising its geopolitical imagination of the region with the promotion of the term 'Indo-Pacific'. The term has been aggressively used by Australia, Japan and India to describe the space extending from the African littoral of the Indian Ocean to the Asian landmass littoral to the Western Pacific.

Interestingly enough in the geopolitical re-production of the Indo-Pacific, China does not find any mention. With geopolitical insight in combination with the geographical location of the three states (Australia, Japan and India), one can argue that the term is directed against the Chinese influence in the region, namely Southeast Asia and to geo-strategically contain China.

However, the validity of the term remains questionable due to its roots in bio-geography and its links with the reviled German World War II geographer Karl Haushofer who argued for a Germandom in the region, if Germany emerged victorious from the War.

Furthermore, the term can be questioned from a climatology perspective if the climatic classification propounded by Wladimir Koeppen was employed as the region is not a uniform climatic zone and displays categories of climate under the scheme.

Geographically too, such a term is unviable as the expanse covered by it is too enormous to be conceived of as a region. However, the region has validity as geopolitical construct/ imagination as it serves the strategic purposes of the promoters.

India, in the Indian Ocean Region as well as the newly revised term the 'Indo-Pacific' holds an important place due to its geographical location. Also, India on its own military strength may not be able to counter the Chinese ventures in the IOR and the Indo-Pacific.

Therefore, a strategy, wherein strong partnerships and alliances are forged whether they are in the form of economic ties, military exercises or political groupings are an essential part of India's geopolitical vision for the near future. To carry out such a vision and to counter the Chinese influence/ presence in the region India will certainly have to shore up its naval strength in terms of the naval equipment as the geographical expanse of the Indian Ocean is too vast to be covered by the already available inventory with the Indian Navy.

BACK BALOCH, RECLAIM POK: MODI MOVES TO FIX INDIA'S BIGGEST GEOPOLITICAL FAILURE

The elephant isn't easily provoked. But if it is boxed into a corner and incited with a thousand cuts, the aggressor runs the risk of being trampled in the wake of its eventual rage.

For decades since Independence, India has historically and inexplicably let Pakistan run away with the Kashmir narrative. Pakistan has forced three battles on us over the Valley and lost each of those.

But Islamabad still managed a permanent seat on the high horse of morality. It got to set the terms despite being the vanquished. And as victors, all that successive Indian governments could do was to adopt a defensive posture. While we have always tended to ignore, even play down our legal claim over the part of Kashmir (the so-called Northern Areas now known as Gilgit Baltistan) occupied by Pakistan, our neighbours have never failed to claim its writ on the area on our side of Line of Control through diplomatic, overt and even covert means.

A combination of Pakistan's sustained campaign and India's lazy response meant that the world now assumes "Kashmir problem" to be pertaining only to the area under our possession. International spotlight has consequently remained permanently focused on India and the way it manages to handle an unquiet land, allowing Pakistan to carry on with large-scale muffling of voices and untold atrocities on PoK. Recent Chinese interest has served to complicate matters even more.

Forced to deny alleged human rights violations in the Valley, forever on the defensive and repeatedly goaded by international agencies to "fix" and "solve" the "Kashmir dispute", India has remained mired in its biggest geopolitical failure.

In the last few days, however, there have been visible signs of a remarkable shift in India's foreign policy. It remains to be seen how the script pans out but Pakistan's cynical attempt to turn the killing of a terrorist into an inflection point for Kashmir insurgency seems to have finally broken the elephant's patience. The green shoots of a new muscular, counter-offensive strategy is visible. The line of a new tactic, first articulated through external affairs ministry spokesperson Vikas Swarup and then hammered out by Prime Minister Narendra Modi at an all-party meeting on Kashmir on Friday is clear.

India will categorically reclaim its writ over Pakistan-occupied-Kashmir, no longer tolerate interference in matters internal and intrinsic to India's sovereignty, rebuff Pakistan's efforts of whitewashing cross-border terrorism and most significantly, expose globally its gross human rights violations, brutalities and untold atrocities in Balochistan and PoK. Turning the tables on Pakistan which has always sought to include Kashmir within the ambit of bilateral talks, Modi said: "When we talk about Jammu and Kashmir, we should talk about four parts of Jammu and Kashmir —Jammu, Kashmir Valley, Ladakh and PoK," thus totally redrawing the contours.

His categorical statement that "PoK is ours", is as big a strategic shift as any. This denies Pakistan the right to peddle a one-sided narrative on Kashmir and simultaneously stonewalls China's long-term ambitions in altering the ground situation in South Asia. This is of huge significance.

Defence analyst Alok Bansal who has earlier widely commented on the radicalisation of Kashmiri youth and the dangers posed by influence of the Islamic State in Kashmir, told ANI that Modi's statement on PoK is an important step.

THE GEOPOLITICS OF GWADAR AND CHINA-PAKISTAN ECONOMIC CORRIDOR

History indeed keeps repeating itself. The 19th century's Great Game – associated with the historic Silk Road – has since been reincarnated in a new great game linked to China's Silk

Road Economic Belt and the 21st century Maritime Silk Road. With the development of Gwadar deep- seaport and China-Pakistan Economic Corridor (CPEC), connecting Gwadar to Kashgar, Pakistan's Balochistan province not only became restless but also attained strategic significance. With the launch of Gwadar port project (2002–2006), its operational control first handed over to the Port of Singapore Authority (2007–2012) and later to the China Overseas Port Holding Company in February 2013, Balochistan erupted into a separatist movement – quite different from previous four insurgencies in the past 68 years.

Pakistan merits much of the blame, owing to its perpetual disregard of Baloch rights through political neglect, economic deprivation, and military heavy- handedness. Yet the sudden international interest in this region is mysterious.

Selig S. Harrison had noted in his book, In the Shadow of Afghanistan: Baloch Nationalism and Soviet Temptations, "If it were not for the strategic location of Balochistan and the rich potential of oil, uranium, and other resources it would be difficult to imagine anyone fighting over this bleak, desolate, and forbidding land."

Except for Pakistan's nuclear explosions of May 1998 and the Metallurgical Corporation of China's Saindak Copper- Gold mine project since 1995, Balochistan remained unknown to the world.

However, the province generated a lot of controversy when Pakistan's Supreme Courtannulled Tethyan Copper Company's Reko- Dik gold and copper mining agreement – aUS$3.3 billion joint venture of Canada's Barrick Gold and Chile's Antofagasta Minerals, resulting in a loss of US$220 million in 2013.

It is equally interesting that Baloch separatist leaders found asylum not only in Afghanistan and India but also in Britain and Switzerland.

India's External Affairs Ministry admitted the presence of Baloch leader Hyrbyair Marri in New Delhi in October 2015, further confirming their policy of extending support for separatist movement in Pakistan. BBC also revealed that India supplied weapons, funds, and training to Pakistan's ethnic Muttahida Qaumi Movement in past decades. Proposing a "defensive- offense" strategy (i.e., use of proxies) in February 2014, India's national security advisor, Ajit Doval had dared Pakistan to "do one Mumbai and lose Balochistan."

In a rare departure from diplomatic norms Pakistan's military leadership not onlywarned India about causing terrorism in Balochistan, but the government also handed over three dossiers to the UN and the US carrying details of subversive activities in Pakistan by Indian intelligence (Research and Analysis Wing).

Furthermore, US Congressman Dana Rohrabacher headed a Congressional hearing on human rights violations in Balochistan on 8 February 2012, tabling a resolution (which was rejected) for Balochistan's right for self- determination. Meanwhile, UN Working Group on Enforced or Involuntary Disappearances also visited Balochistan in September 2012 to investigate the issue of 'missing persons' – miscreants allegedly picked- up by the intelligence agencies never to be produced in any court of law.

Gwadar's development and its linkage to Xinjiang province through CPEC – a 2,395 km long corridor with economic and industrial zones en route, arising from a US$46 billion Chinese investment – has started an undeclared war for naval dominance in the Indian Ocean. CPECnot only shortens China's crude oil route, which presently passes through the Straits of Malacca, but also grants it closer access to the resource rich Middle Eastern and African countries. China's control of Gwadar can be seen as another "string of [naval] pearls" in the Indo- Pacific Corridor.

A view into India's western coast of Gujarat and Maharashtra as well as monitoring the hub of Strait of Hormuz has made India construct a sprawling naval base atKarwar. Iran has also begun establishing a naval base at Pasabander, while India and Iran have sped- up the development of Iranian Chahbahar port near Gwadar.

Geopolitics, a game of competing power interests, has turned lethal after been eclipsed by geo- economics. Therefore, as we would never see a stable Afghanistan (or Kashmir or India'sRed Corridor for that matter), there is little likelihood of having a peaceful Balochistan. Despite Pakistan bending over backwards for the realization of Gwadar and CPEC, several factors hinder what Pakistan calls a game- changer in the region. First, Pakistan has a capacity problem, amplified by mega- corruption and incompetence.

The government is running on foreign and domestic loans mortgaging the future of the nation. Despite bypassing Pakistan Procurement Regulatory Authority's rules of international bidding, granting all CPEC projects to Chinese companies, the sovereign guarantees for minimum 18percent internal rate of return would be backbreaking.

Even as the world abandons coal- run power plants, Pakistan plans to build a number of them in several economic/ industrial zones, which are yet to be earmarked and financial allocations made for land acquisition. Bureaucratic hurdles and slow pace of work would further frustrate China's strategic patience.

The water and power and petroleum ministers are already mud- slinging the minister for planning and development. Notably, China is not entirely relying onCPEC; developing the alternate Bangladesh- China- India- Myanmar (BCIM) Economic Corridor simultaneously.

Furthermore, the provinces and government disagree on CPEC's route: Prime Minister Nawaz Sharif prefers the route over his Punjab province, while the Khyber Pakhtoonkhwa government insists on its western alignment, which is not risk-free due to the ongoing insurgency in the tribal areas.

Despite establishing four- layered security by the Pakistan army's 12,000-strong special force, boosted by the Chinese military, safe passage over a 2,000 km long route cannot be ensured.

More than 200 security- related incidents have already taken place on the870 km Baluchistan stretch since the work began. While CPEC's economic benefits may mitigate threats in the long run, the route will remain prone to regional and geopolitical mischief.

Secondly, under Pakistan's sham democracy, it is unlikely that the current semi- feudal and tribal system (*Sardari Nizam*) – in which 'Chieftains' pocket development funds and rule through their own militias – will be reformed. Pakistan's continued neglect towards water- scarcityissue has further made the experts warn of Balochistan becoming a wasteland. Moreover, no one knows the fate of the country amid its ongoing civil- military frictions and power merry- go- round, especially if one projects over the 15 to 20 year completion period of the CPEC project.

Third, with the 'missing persons' issue and revelations of a 'kill and dump' game in Balochistan, Pakistan's army and intelligence agencies have been further discredited. Pakistan is likely to come under increasing international pressure for its poor human rights record, especially after recently losing a seat at United Nations Human Rights Council.

Finally, Balochistan is likely to remain unstable, due to Pakistan's encirclement by a hostile Afghanistan (owing to its support of the Taliban), an antagonized Shiite Iran (arising from Pakistan's sectarian conflict, Saudi kowtowing, and anti-Iran Jundallah's presence in borderlands), and a belligerent India. India's backing by the US, evident by recent nuclear anddefence pacts, has further encouraged New Delhi to call CPEC "unacceptable." Moreover,CPEC's conspicuous omission in US public statements during Mr. Sharif's and army chief, General Raheel Sharif's visits in October and November 2015 underline its disapproval.

Pakistan is, however, relying on its time- tested friend, China. While prematurely announcingthe end of Baloch insurgency, Lieutenant- General Amir Riaz (commander, southern command) highlighted Pakistan's expectations: "Chinese influence in the region will lead to rebalance of power in the world and Pakistan will be a great beneficiary." The general, however, was silent on the key issue of security of

Chinese workers and their regular killings in Pakistan. Religious extremists and jihadi groups use the so- called persecution of the Muslim Uighurpopulation in Xinjiang by (atheist) China as justification for their terrorist attacks.

In his book *The Future of Pakistan*, Stephen Cohen had predicted the country to "muddle through" (from crisis to crisis). Pakistan urgently needs to extend its (reformed) democratic and constitutional reach not only in the lawless tribal areas but also to Balochistan. Until and unless economic dividends and prosperity reaches every deprived Baloch, Balochistan will remain a pawn on international chessboard.

4

China Pakistan Economic Corridor Needs a Counter Strategy of India

Snubbing Pakistan for sponsoring terrorism and calling upon Pakistan to vacate the portion of Kashmir that remains under its illegal occupation is not new to the Indian policy approach. What is new is the assertion by the Narendra Modi Government on the need to reverse the game by shifting the discourse on Kashmir. New Delhi's new move is accompanied by the sudden sprouting of videos showing Pakistani atrocities in Gilgit and Baltistan (GB).

While Pakistan has effectively sustained its Kashmir agenda for seven decades, India has been defensive and sporadic in its claim over Pakistan-occupied Kashmir (PoK). Hopefully, the rhetoric this time is not a propaganda stunt and the policy shift will gain traction. As a step to wreck Pakistan's agenda, India has correctly proscribed the Hurriyat factor from the NSA-level talk – denying Pakistan any leeway on both terror and political dialogue.

While changing the Kashmir narrative is important, India needs to pay serious attention to the changing nature of power play that has brought PoK to the forefront of China's geopolitical calculations. The region came under spotlight after Xi Jinping announced plans for developing the China-Pakistan Economic Corridor (CPEC) and pledged USD 46 billion for building transport and energy connectivity to link Pakistan with China's ambitious flagship project 'One Belt, One Road' (OBOR). The August 2015 "Karamay Declaration" detailed Pakistan's role in China's global scheme. Lately, even Russia has indicated its interest in joining the bandwagon to prop up Pakistan's strategic significance for Eurasian integration.

While the Sino-Pak axis in PoK is nothing new, the sheer magnitude of the CPEC plan makes it clear that it is not confined to the single limited objective of boosting Pakistan's prosperity. On the face of it, CPEC signifies the laying of a crucial bridge for China to access the Indian Ocean and conversely for Pakistan to access Eurasia. While the need to capitalise on their political and geographical proximities explain this logic, this is not the entire truth. There is far more to China contemplating heavy investments in a country as perilously poised as Pakistan is.

Significance and Implications of CPEC

India needs to grasp the motivation, significance and implications of this new China-Pakistan nexus. First, CPEC implies a further deepening of the Sino-Pak alignment which began to intensify after the Osama Bin Laden episode. Moving from "all-weather friendship" to "iron brother" status, China began to liken its ties with Pakistan to the US links with Israel. Xi Jinping considers Pakistan as a frontline state in the war against terror and is of the view that "its sacrifices can't be forgotten" by China. China expects the CPEC to yield far-reaching economic benefits, and regional security is instrumental for this purpose.

Second, and related to this, is the strategic intent of besieging India. The alignment of Karakoram (land) with Gwadar (sea), both having commercial and military utility, could serve as strategic chokepoints vis-à-vis India. As Andrew Small notes *in his book The China-Pakistan Axis: Asia's New* Geopolitics, "Pakistan is both a Chinese pawn (against India) and platform for power projection.....a long history of secret deals between their two armies – overrides the problems with

Islamic extremism." Third, China is mindful of Pakistan's vulnerabilities and the latter's links with terror that could result in unpredicted consequences. The possibility of the Af-Pak belt becoming a safe haven for Uighur militants once the US troops leave is very much on Chinese minds. Beijing's eagerness for Afghan reconciliation talks explains that. Yet, Beijing will shield Pakistan while trading on terrorism with terrorists (jihadists, the Taliban and al-Qaeda), all of whom receive arms in exchange for refraining from exporting terror into Xinjiang.

Fourth, some analysts view the CPEC in the context of offsetting the growing US-India intimacy as well as China's *quid pro quo* to counter India's "Act East" policy. Although such a comparison is nothing but hyperbole, Pakistan does have utility to China for keeping India always edgy. This is a China's nuanced strategy to deter any possible India-US direct prying in Tibetan and Uighur issues. In reality, China would prefer not to bail out Pakistan in moments of its peril.

Finally, against this backdrop, Beijing is keen to employ its *prêt-à-porter* domestic-external interwoven strategy that had been earlier tested in the Xinjiang-Central Asia frontier to fix problems at home and abroad. Therefore, CPEC is a perfect counter-offensive defence strategy for dealing with threats emanating from the Af-Pak region.

Concerns for India

India needs to be concerned about China attempting to replicate in PoK the well-perfected policy it has applied earlier *in Tibet, Xinjiang and across Central Asia. Beijing would be* seeking a historic opportunity to fill up gaps where India has largely failed. Considering PoK's strategic location as a connecting point of South, West, Central and East Asia, China's move has implications for limiting India's outreach to the critical Eurasian region.

India failed to see the writing on the wall when Pakistan carried out a series of steps to manipulate the legal and demographic profile, the last being a change of nomenclature from Northern Areas to Gilgit-Baltistan under the Empowerment and Self Rule Order (2009). An option for incorporating GB to make it as the fifth province of Pakistan is gaining serious consideration. There is also speculation that Pakistan could lease additional areas of GB to China. The opening a Chinese Consulate in PoK is in the offing. One should not be surprised by Beijing working on a plan to grab the entire GB along with the 5,000 square kilometre Shaksgam Valley held by China since 1963. Academic writings draw historical antecedent for China's claims over the Hunza Valley.

For Islamabad, GB's assimilation would mean quelling popular sentiment while also deflating India's objections to Chinese activities. But this has not gone well with the Kashmiri separatists including the Hurriyat who are against GB's incorporation into the Pakistani constitution.

Meanwhile, Chinese activities in GB are in full swing including the building of hydropower projects at Neelum-Jhelum, Kohala and Chakothi-Hattian that will generate 2,569 MW of power by 2020. The China Road and Bridge Corporation (CRBC) recently completed five tunnels over the Attabad Lake in Hunza Valley. Widening of the Jaglot-Skardu Road is in progress. At the other end, China has taken 923 hectares on lease in Gwadar for developing a special economic zone (SEZ).

None of these developments stirred up an adequate Indian response. In fact, Beijing justified the CPEC as a "livelihood project" when concerns were raised by Prime Minister Narendra Modi during his May 2015 visit to China.

Clearly, India's unhurried stance on PoK explains its unwillingness for changing the status quo. New Delhi has been making sporadic and pro forma protests on the PoK issue only for the purpose of countering Pakistan's raising of the K word at the UN.

And while Pakistan used global forums as the stick to beat India with on Kashmir, India remains loath to play the United Nations Security Council Resolution 47 of August 1948 that implicitly recognised Indian "sovereignty" over J&K and urged Pakistan to vacate territories under its "illegal occupation".

The nature of developments taking place around PoK is too serious for India to ignore. With CPEC coming into effect, Pakistan has gone on a diplomatic spree offering to shape a "New Central Asia" through CPEC, asking the landlocked Shanghai Cooperation Organisation (SCO) members to use Pakistani ports. Pakistan is gaining greater credence in Eurasia as a possible partner. Kazakhstan has already expressed its desire to join the corridor. Renewed efforts are being made to reboot the Quadrilateral Traffic in Transit Agreement (QTTA) with Central Asian states. Pakistan joined the Central Asia Regional Economic Cooperation (CAREC) in 2010 and it separately seeks Transit Trade Agreement (TTA) with Afghanistan for access to Central Asia. To further boost intra-regional connectivity, Pakistan has recently acceded to the TIR Convention.

Involving Iran in the corridor is another ambition. With the current financial down turn in China, it is hard to predict whether CPEC will actually come to fruition. However, the trajectory and even a partial success would be consequential for limiting Indian influence in BRICS and SCO.

Opportunity for India

Modi's government is apt in retrieving the PoK agenda. Placing GB along with Ladakh (82 per cent of J&K) on the political centre stage could easily undermine the Pakistani rhetoric on the Kashmir issue. Mere murmuring is not enough; India needs to start working on Pakistan's domestic resistance i.e. in Baluchistan, Khyber Pakhtunkhwa and GB over CPEC. The "Modi effect" is already working after he offered help to the people of PoK during the 2014 floods. GB is now abuzz with pro-freedom slogans as the people are fed up with decades of Pakistani atrocities, terrorism, and sectarian killings.

Options for India

India should stop making intermittent and tentative overtures and instead adopt a robust policy on PoK. A counter strategy should go beyond building partnerships with the US in the Asia-Pacific. Quite clearly, India's non-endorsement or indifference to China's Silk Road proposal appears to be short-sighted thinking, perhaps stemming from suspicion and insecurity.

In any case, India's options are limited. In contrast to the Asia-Pacific, the US is not alarmed at Beijing's push; instead it has been seeking convergence with China perhaps necessitated by the need to share the burden of containing terrorism in Afghanistan. In fact, Washington's own New Silk Route initiative has fallen short perhaps due to shifting priorities and its inability to commit adequate funds. Geopolitically, China too is not risking a zero-sum game with the US in Eurasia. To be also sure, China also knows that the current priority of the West is to break Russia's ambitions in Eurasia rather than to counter China's move.

Additionally, if Russia moves closer to Pakistan, India's reliance on Moscow for protecting its interests would become less salient. Against the looming threat of terrorism and extremism, any prospect for joining the Silk Route dynamics could open up an opportunity for India to cooperate in soft political areas including greater understanding of the Uighur problem that we know little about. Another equally important challenge is to break the current tight geopolitical spot India finds itself in, wedged between a wall of Pakistani hostility and the fear of cooperating with China.

Also, India can do little to stop OBOR or scuttle the CPEC. Almost all the countries in the subcontinent are excited about the project. India's non-participation would lead to isolation and loss of clout at the regional level.

Being the world's second largest economy and India's largest trading partner, New Delhi is unable to ignore China anyway. To be sure, OBOR may be carrying security undertones but India also requires massive infrastructure investment and only China seems to have the surplus capital.

Without partnering with China, India's integration in Asian regionalisation would be less than smooth. Chinese companies are building infrastructure in India and there is little difference whether one gains by helping or limiting China's influence. It cannot be in India's interest to support the project and not reap all the economic benefits of those projects. It is important to establish a fine balance between economics with security.

India also cannot ignore the significance of the symbolism of history. After all, it was the Silk Route on which Indian trade and philosophy (Buddhism) travelled to the rest of Asia. Modi himself showed an inclination towards and confidence in dealing with China for building an Asian century.

At Ufa, Modi displayed pragmatism by seeking convergence with China and Russia. As China is fast transforming internally, the imperatives of cultural affinity will demand closer propinquity between India and China.

Thus, staying outside cannot be to India's advantage. New Delhi needs to re-conceptualise and seek new realities on the ground. China has called upon India to join the Silk Route and India should respond positively while accepting a trade-off here and there.

A wise approach would be to join the regional networking process just as India joined the Asian Infrastructure Investment Bank (AIIB). There is nothing wrong in exploring OBOR as an alternative as long as India's security interests are not compromised. Remaining disconnected would only instil greater insecurity and fears of Chinese encirclement. What Modi requires is a policy that would help to overcome predicaments that have thus far stymied India's role in Asia.

A Counter Strategy

India needs to work on its own counter strategy by offering a plan for a direct India-China Silk Route Corridor (ICSRC) that could run along the traditional Ladakh-Xinjiang axis. A shift in thinking can no longer be put off, for it would mean not just about breaking the connectivity bottlenecks but about finding interlocking economic interests between its northern states and the Eurasian growth story. The ICSRC could provide an alternate transport, energy, trade, fibre optics and communication highway that could originate from a port in Gujarat run across northern India to connect with Kashgar in western China through the Indus Valley in Ladakh. The initiative would have multiple advantages for both India and China without compromising on their respective security concerns. These include:

1. The corridor could bring massive Chinese investments for building infrastructure in India that would boost the economy and generate greater employment opportunities.
2. India could earn billions as fee from pipeline transit.
3. An energy corridor would help India gain a durable guarantee against any Chinese misadventure across the border.
4. There could be a trade-off here in terms of India possibly getting long-distance transport and energy pipelines from Russia through western China.
5. ICSRC would blunt the impact of the CPEC.
6. For China, ICSRC would be more reliable and less hazardous than risking investments in terrorism-plagued Pakistan.
7. ICSRC would open a historic opportunity for India to physically connect with markets in China, Eurasia, Europe, and beyond. And,
8. India could offer several other alternate outlets for China through the Northeast or Sikkim that are nearer to Chinese growth centres.

If the idea were to be pushed forward, it could become a grand announcement indicating India's willingness to deepen economic engagement with China and would be something akin to how Russia and China started two decades ago. ICSRC could help revive the shared legacy of a common history and culture enriched by the trade in silk and spices. The development could pave the way for strengthening trust between the two countries and eventually contribute to the solution of the boundary problem.

CHINA'S FALTERING STRATEGY IN AFGHANISTAN AND PAKISTAN

The approach China has been taking in Afghanistan and Pakistan is not devoid of successes. Indeed, it has served Beijing well for many years. To date, China has avoided becoming a focus of militant efforts on a scale remotely comparable to that of the West, despite an approach to sections of its own Muslim population, which would attract fierce condemnation were it carried out by any Western state. It has maintained its close relationship with Pakistan military, political parties, and public alike while developing good relations with the Afghan government. Its access to economic projects in both states is also second-tonone. Yet, in many other respects, things are not going according to plan.

The direct threat to China is growing. This year has seen the first kidnappings in Afghanistan of Chinese workers by Taliban guerillas in the Fayrab province. Rocket attacks on the Aynak facility have cooled Chinese willingness to move forward with the project itself as well as with future prospects, such as the Hajigak iron ore deposit, where Chinese companies were again prominently placed in the bidding. But Pakistan has been an even greater concern.

The situation there certainly posed difficulties in the past. In the 1990s, until Beijing exerted considerable pressure, Pakistan was viewed as a haven for Uighur refugees, a number of whom were given training by an array of jihadi groups. Chinese workers have been targeted directly by insurgents in Baluchistan, where several have been killed in recent years, as well as by local groups in the FATA. China has also been prompted to close the border and move troops to its vicinity on different occasions. But the events since 2007 have taken a more dangerous turn.

The June 2007 Lal Masjid incident, in which Chinese "massage workers" were kidnapped and held in the heart of Pakistan's capital, was a watershed. While they were eventually released, the subsequent Pakistani military assault on the mosque complex was seen to have taken place at Beijing's instigation. As an immediate reprisal in the North-West Frontier Province (now known as Khyber Pukhtoonkhwa), three Chinese engineers were executed in July 2007,26 along with a suicide attack on a convoy of Chinese workers in the same month in a market town near Karachi, indicating a more systematic targeting of China throughout Pakistan. Pakistani politicians have expressed concerns that militant groups will look to "drive a wedge" between Beijing and Islamabad. An extensive set of security measures have since been put in place, with a joint task force established in August 2007 at the national and provincial levels to address the threat to the 10,000 Chinese in Pakistan, including providing direct military protection.

But subsequent attacks and kidnappings have led to continued tension in the relationship. At the time of President Asif Ali Zardari's maiden visit to China in 2008, the failure to gain the release of Chinese telecommunications workers in Swat resulted in threats to withdraw all Chinese personnel from the country. While these have been made before, and are seen by some on the Pakistani side as a bluff to extract concessions, the personal involvement of President Hu Jintao and other senior Chinese leaders in statements about the kidnapping incidents have added a level of seriousness to the Chinese threats.

This focus on personnel security has been coupled with Chinese political pressure, as one former Pakistani military officer put it "of a kind that there has not been before," on Islamabad to crack down on Uighurs based in the country. At points, this has leaked into the press when Chinese behind-the-scenes lobbying has not delivered results, such as 2009 pressure ahead of supposed threats to the 60th anniversary celebrations for the People's Republic. Despite a number of high-profile extraditions, Chinese analysts have described counterterrorism cooperation as falling short of expectations, criticizing ISI warnings to Uighur groups to disperse ahead of some of their operations and questioning their motivation to eliminate the threat.

The strength of the TTP has also been a concern to China. While initially sanguine about the Pakistani government's deals in Swat and Buner, they became increasingly worried that the writ of the Pakistani state was running out in a territory that runs dangerously close to the principal Sino-Pakistani trade route, the KKH. While never as worried about the "Talibanization" of Pakistan as some of the more alarmist accounts suggested they should be, the Chinese ultimately took a clear position encouraging the Pakistani government not just to mount the operation, but to bring it to a decisive conclusion. Since the campaign started, China has provided aid to assist with massive numbers of internally displaced persons as well as counterterrorism equipment, ranging from scanners to night-vision goggles, to the Pakistani army. The army, in turn, has provided additional security for the KKH, placing troops along its length to protect it from being used as an escape route for militants fleeing the Pakistani army's campaign.

The deterioration in the general security situation and the fracturing of the Pakistani military's relationship with various militant groups has posed broader problems for Beijing. China is particularly exposed when it comes to groups seen to operate under the authority of elements of the Pakistani state itself, such as the LeT and the Jaish-e-Mohammed (JeM), which have the capacity to precipitate conflict in the event of another major attack on Indian territory.

China will inevitably be pulled into any potential Indian-Pakistani crisis diplomatically, and has even attempted to send signals which convince few that it could be engaged militarily in the event of any Indian retaliation. Since China bears significant historic responsibility for Pakistan's nuclear program, it is also notably culpable in the event of any diversion of nuclear materials, a scenario most likely to occur in just such a conflict situation.

Managed tension has been in China's interests, but Pakistan's capacity to maintain control is essential. While China continues to express faith in Islamabad, doubts have inevitably been creeping in as militant groups have become stronger and the lines between them have become less cleanly delineated. The capacity of the jihadi groups to hijack policy is a major risk to Chinese strategy in the region, not least because the ramifications are so unpredictable.

Many of these problems escalated under General Pervez Musharraf, but China is far more skeptical about the political direction in which Pakistan has been headed since his fall in September 2008. As a general principle, Beijing is more comfortable with Pakistani military than civilian rule. Although it can work with Pakistan People's Party governments, it sees them as the most pro-Western of the possible political constellations. Zardari's relationship with Beijing has been particularly poor from the very start, when he bypassed the traditional practice of paying the first presidential visit to China, and instead took trips (albeit classified as private) to the United Arab Emirates, the United Kingdom, and the United States.

Zardari's quarterly visits to China since then have not notably remedied this, and Chinese officials have been privately disparaging about the weakness of the civilian government. While any problems on the civilian side are traditionally trumped by the Sino-Pak military relationship, China has also been uncomfortable with what it sees as closer U.S.-Pakistani military-to-military ties. Chinese officials have sought assurances that their interests will remain a protected class.

The common thread across all of these issues is that the principal guarantor of China's interests, the Pakistani military, is growing less capable of securing them. But Beijing at present lacks a Plan B. The People's Liberation Army is resistant to rethinking the level of Chinese reliance on Rawalpindi, and as a group they are unusually influential over this bilateral relationship. Even among the Chinese military though, while the basic tenets of the Sino-Pakistani relationship are not in doubt, there is reportedly a broader debate about the competing imperatives of geopolitics and the more pragmatic desire to improve the stability of China's Western periphery. The first school of thought sees the overriding regional objectives as keeping India down and the United States down or out. The latter position sees greater strategic advantage in being able to minimize the risk of major contingencies in Pakistan, weaken the external support base for Uighur militants, and embed Xinjiang in a secure and economically thriving environment. This stance still does not inherently result in any greater cooperation with the West per se, but it does imply a more active and nuanced set of Chinese policies, especially in a context where Beijing increasingly expects Washington to draw down its presence in the coming years and is starting to feel the need to prepare for the aftermath.

There have certainly been some modest tweaks to China's approach. The weakening of the military channel in dealing with militants has led China to seek more direct methods. The most potent recent successes against Chinese targets have come not from the Pakistani military which was responsible for the 2003 operation against ETIM's leader but from U.S. drone strikes, which have killed numerous TIP militants in the province of Baghdis in Western Afghanistan, along with its leader, Abdul Haq al-Turkistani, in North Waziristan. China has also courted parties with their own routes to extremist groups, the MMA as well as the Jamaat-e-Islami (JI) in particular, being wooed in the past two years. Various members of the MMA have been invited on public relations visits to China, with one of the most recent culminating in a memorandum of understanding between the JI and the Communist Party of China's international department, in which JI "fully backed China's stance on Taiwan, Tibet and Xinjiang issues," and pledged cooperation on "justice, development, security and solidarity," as well as stating that the agreement "makes us accept finally and formally that China's internal affairs are not our business."

Crisis-management scenarios for Pakistan, along the lines of those for North Korea, have even been drawn up by groups affiliated with Chinese military intelligence, even though these are not part of any formal contingency planning process. Looking at case studies such as nuclear weapons falling into the hands of terrorists, another potential conflict between India and Pakistan, and the failure of efforts to contain militancy in the region they suggest that in various worst-case scenarios, Chinese interests can only effectively be secured through closer coordination with other major powers, principally the United States.

CHINA'S APPROACH STRATEGY TO PAKISTAN

Pakistan is a tremendously important country in China's foreign policy calculations. China sees Pakistan as its primary partner in South Asia, with a 50-year history of political and military ties. Pakistan serves as a conduit for China into South Asia and the Indian Ocean and, most importantly, as a foundation of its regional strategy to counter to Indian regional preeminence. For Pakistan, China has been a steady and (mostly) dependable provider of money and weapons and a deterrent against Indian regional domination. It should be noted that China's interest in Pakistan is purely strategic, and not economic. In 2005, bilateral trade was $4.26 billion. By October 2008, annual trade between Pakistan and China had already surpassed $7 billion, and the two sides set the target of $15 billion in trade by 2011. To put these numbers in perspective, the target 2011 trade level between China and Pakistan ($15 billion) is 4% of US-China trade in 2008 ($333.8 billion).

China's military relationship with Pakistan is deep and robust, including joint exercises, arms sales, and defense industrial cooperation. Beijing transferred equipment and technologies to Pakistan's nuclear weapons and ballistic missile programs throughout the 1980s and 1990s. China is currently Pakistan's largest weapons supplier, and Pakistan is by far China's primary customer for conventional weapons: 36% of China's arms sales from 2003 through 2007 were directed to Pakistan (the next-largest customer was Sudan with 7%). Sales include the co-developed JF-17 multi-role combat aircraft and related production facilities, F-22P frigates with helicopters, jet trainers, tanks, the F-7 fighter, anti-ship cruise missiles, missile technologies, small arms, and ammunition. The JF-17 program has important geopolitical ramifications beyond providing Pakistan with an improved combat aircraft. Pakistan has a longstanding, yet unfilled, order for American F-16s. The U.S. decision to not fill the order, while prudent, hurt our ability to cultivate closer relations with the Pakistani military. More important for this discussion, however, is that the JF-17 would primarily be useful to Pakistan in an India contingency. China's continued selling of the JF-17 reinforces Pakistan's focus on India, which the U.S. has been attempting to shift to the insurgents in Pakistan's West.

For China, the relationship with Pakistan is also important because of its easy access to the Indian Ocean. China is building a major port in Gwadar that would enable support of a military presence closer to the Middle East and along vulnerable sea lanes of communication. Road and rail links would need to go through Afghanistan. Pakistan is interested in exploiting its geography as a Trade and Energy Corridor (TEC) for China. In February 2008, Pakistan's then-President Musharraf told an audience at Tsinghua University in Beijing that "Pakistan is very much in favor of a pipeline between the Gulf and China through Pakistan and I have been speaking with your leadership about this. I am very sure in the future – it will happen".

A CHINA-PAK NUCLEAR AXIS AGAINST INDIA

The issues involved in China's sale of two more nuclear reactors need to be better understood. Arguments that India, as a non-NPT state, has itself secured a nuclear deal with the US and therefore has little ground to oppose a China-Pakistan nuclear deal, or that two additional reactors for Pakistan is not going to enhance the nuclear threat to India, miss the point. That Pakistan has acute energy shortage and needs to tap nuclear energy as a source, more so as it is environmentally cleaner, is not sufficient reason to justify the Sino-Pakistan deal in the way it is being considered at present. The argument that China and Pakistan will in any case go ahead and therefore it makes little sense for India to oppose the deal is a defeatist position. A further one that, given this reality, it might be better to engage China and Pakistan diplomatically on this question in a conciliatory mode does not take into account the deeper strategic and political intentions behind China's nuclear cooperation with Pakistan and this specific deal.

China has engaged in strategic nuclear proliferation in the subcontinent by transferring nuclear materials and weapons design to Pakistan, and even testing Pakistan's weapon in 1990 at its testing site in Lop Nor. China's objective has been to strategically neutralize India through Pakistan, give it the muscle to continue its confrontation with India and the capacity to deter serious Indian military reprisals for its adversarial policies. China has manoeuvred to blur the reality of any direct China-India nuclear rivalry, transferring such rivalry to the subcontinent, making India appear as the initiator of a nuclear arms race in the region, and creating in the mind of the international community a dangerous India-Pakistan nuclear equation with the potential of a nuclear conflict erupting between two "historical enemies".

The US has overlooked errant Chinese nuclear conduct vis a vis Pakistan for several reasons. Pakistan became central to US effort to counter the Soviets in Afghanistan, and, therefore, despite evidence that Pakistan was pursing a nuclear weapon programme with Chinese assistance, the Pressler Amendment was devised to allow military and economic assistance to Pakistan debarred under US law for a proliferating country. For Cold War considerations, the US was unwilling to apply any serious sanctions on China which had by then become a strategic partner against the Soviet Union. The US, opposed to India's nuclear ambitions and wary of the perceived India-Soviet axis that had successfully broken up Pakistan in 1971, has long backed a "strategic balance" in South Asia, which explains its remarkable tolerance of Sino-Pak nuclear collaboration. US unwillingness to expose the A.Q.Khan affair in full, in which the the Pakistani political and military establishment has been involved to the hilt, is consistent with US equivocation on China-Pakistan proliferation infractions.

The Indo-US nuclear deal marked a strategic "de-hyphenation" of India and Pakistan in US policy, evoking anguish in Pakistan and distrust in China. The US was seriously disturbing the hitherto tacit entente between it and China to contain a nuclear India. Pakistan, obsessed with parity with India, has vociferously opposed the deal and also asked for one for itself.

For China, making an exception for India to the current nuclear rules could only mean building up India as a potential counterweight to it. By signing up for two aditional nuclear power reactors for Pakistan, China wants to send several messages to the US, India and the wider world. Its warning that if the US made an exception for India, other countries may do likewise for their friends is being translated into action. What the US has done for its protege, India, China is doing for its protege, Pakistan.

If the US is disturbing the nuclear balance in South Asia- as China has alleged- China is restoring it. If the US will not accord parity of treatment to Pakistan, China will do so. China is signalling that the US cannot set the nonproliferation rules for all others, or use its clout to break the global consensus on the nonproliferation regime to suit its strategic needs, and that China will take autonomous decisions to suit its own interests. China is occupying space being ceded by declining US hegemony and setting itself up as a rival power to the US. China no doubt calculates that a militarily and financially embattled US will avoid a frontal conflict with it on this issue, keeping in mind also that the US needs its political support in dealing with the nuclear defiance of Iran and North Korea, problems of higher strategic priority for the US.

Finally, China is declaring to India that it will continue to build up nuclear Pakistan against it, deny India any advantage, counter any potential India-US axis with a countervailing China-Pakistan axis. That China is willing to extend its patronage to Pakistan in disregard of its non-proliferation obligations and the NSG guidelines implies high stakes on both sides: need for the facade of civilian nuclear cooperation to continue Chinese technological and material support for Pakistan's military programme with its suspected extra-regional linkages.

India must therefore oppose the envisaged China-Pakistan nuclear cooperation. If this passes through an open, widely debated process, with legislative underpinning and imposition of stringent nonproliferation conditions on Pakistan, India would have no reason to object. If, as the Chinese argue, both sides are respecting their international obligations and the new power plants will be under IAEA safeguards, why was India, with a clean nonproliferation record, no A.Q. Khan type baggage, no religious extremism, terrorist groups and clandestine proliferation networks blotting its landscape, required to separate its civilian and military facilities, shut some reprocessing units, accept the "right to return" if it tests, legally commit itself to a testing moratorium, agree to cooperate with the US on FMCT negotiations, establish a special reprocessing facility according to US dictated specifications for reprocessing US spent fuel, put its future fast breeder reactors under IAEA safeguards etc.

We too could have obtained nuclear cooperation by simply agreeing to put internationally assisted reactors under IAEA safeguards. Why was cooperation with India by others opposed by the US until it cleared the way? If China does not have domestic legislation on nuclear cooperation like the US, the NSG can stipulate the conditions under which Pakistan would become eligible for civilian nuclear cooperation as a non-NPT state. We struggled hard to get a "clean waiver" from the NSG, and didn't quite get it.

There cannot be different standards for China/Pakistan and India. The US, so far subdued, must insist on the projected China-Pakistan deal being presented to the NSG for approval. If China ignores the NSG, the intended cooperation should be blocked in the IAEA where the issue of safeguards will have to be addressed and decided. Our strategic partnership with the US will lose meaning if the US once again overlooks nuclear cooperation between our two adversaries avowedly intended to counter the strategic advantage India has ostensibly obtained through the India-US deal. If the US sacrifices India's interests to protect its China and Pakistan equities, the India-US nuclear deal would look most invidious.

PAKISTAN, CHINA AGREE TO PROPEL LEVEL OF ECONOMIC COOPERATION

Pakistan and China Thursday agreed to propel level of economic cooperation in diverse sectors on fast trajectory as an important plank of comprehensive strategic partnership. The two countries also agreed to make continuous efforts to strengthen good-neighbourly relations and friendship, develop mutually beneficial cooperation and deepen strategic partnership of cooperation which serves the fundamental interests of the two peoples and contributes to peace and development in the region, said a Joint Statement issued on the first state visit of Pakistan's President Asif Ali Zardari to China. Both sides opposed to all forms of terrorism, extremism and separatism, resolved to cooperation with each other to fight the above-mentioned three forces, said the Statement adding, China conveyed its complete support to Pakistan's commitment and efforts to fight terrorism and appreciated the sacrifices made by the government and people of Pakistan in this regard.

The two sides agreed that economic cooperation is an important part of strategic partnership and both sides enjoy great economic complementarity and should fully tap the potential and comprehensively deepen mutually beneficial cooperation in the economic field. The two countries agreed to fast track the implementation of the Five Year Development Programme on Economic Cooperation and make full use of the Free Trade Agreement in Goods and Investment and Pakistan-China Joint Investment Company.

In this regard, the statement said, they agreed to convene a meeting of Pakistan-China Economic Cooperation Group under the Five Development Programme on Economic Cooperation at an early date. Both sides agreed that the Treaty of Friendship, Cooperation and Good-neighbourly Relations between the

People's Republic of China and the Islamic Republic of Pakistan (Treaty) signed in April 2005 is of great historic and immediate significance, laying a solid legal foundation for the long-term stable and health growth of China-Pakistan relations.

Both sides decided to abide by the policies and principles enshrined in the Treaty, earnestly implement the bilateral legal documents signed since the two countries established diplomatic ties and further intensify cooperation in the areas of economy, defense, science and technology, people to people contact, thus constantly advancing the China-Pakistan strategic partnership of cooperation. China stressed that Pakistan is China's good neighbour, close friend, dear brother and trusted partner. China will continue to view China-Pakistan relations from a strategic and long-term perspective, and make joint efforts with Pakistan to lift China-Pakistan Strategic partnership of cooperation to a new height, the statement said.

Pakistan stressed that Pak-China relationship is the cornerstone of its foreign policy, and friendship with China represents the common desire of all Pakistani people, the statement observed continuing, Pakistan appreciated the strong support and assistance provided by the government and people of China to Pakistan in its economic development. Pakistan remained committed to continuing its policy of friendship towards China and making unremitting efforts to promote the healthy and steady growth of relations between the two countries.

According to the statement, President Asif Ali Zardari extended invitation to President Hu Jintao to visit Pakistan once again at his convenience and President Hu Jintao thanked President Zardari for his kind invitation. The statement said Pakistan unequivocally upheld the one-China policy and considers Taiwan as an inseparable part of the Peoples Republic of China and supports all efforts made by the Chinese government to realize national reunification. China, the statement added, appreciated Pakistan's long term and staunch support to China on issues concerning China's sovereignty and territorial integrity, reaffirmed its support for Pakistan's efforts to uphold its sovereignty, independence and territorial integrity and appreciated Pakistan's important role in promoting regional peace, stability and security and strengthening international counter-terrorism efforts.

The two sides agreed to enhance cooperation to further develop and boost Pakistan's Mineral and Energy sector as well as broaden financial and banking sector cooperation.

They agreed to further enhance "connectivity" by developing new communication and links including fiber optic links and also agreed to explore the concept of Integrated Border Management, overland trade and development of trans-border economic zones. Both sides agreed to maintain communication and coordination on major international and regional issues to safeguard their common interests besides continuing to cooperate closely on issues such as the reform of the United Nations, climate change and energy and food security to promote world peace and development.

President Asif Zardari offered congratulation to the Chinese government and people on the successful hosting of the Beijing Olympic Games and the successful completion of Shenzhou VII's mission. According to the Statement, President HU Jintao congratulated President Zardari on his election as the President of Pakistan and thanked Pakistan for its valuable assistance in the wake of the devastating earthquake in Wenchuan, China. He also appreciated Pakistan's support to ensure the success of the Beijing Olympics and Paralympics Games.

Pakistan applauded the outstanding achievements China has made in the 30 years of reform and opening-up and believes that China's development will contribute to world peace and prosperity. On the invitation of President Hu Jintao, President Asif Ali Zardari paid four-day long state visit and during the stay held talks with his Chinese counterpart. Mr Wu Bangguo, Chairman Standing Committee of the National Peoples Congress, Mr Wen Jiabao, Premier of the State Council, and Mr Jia Qinglin, Chairman of the Chinese Peoples Political Consultative Conference met the visiting president. Talks between the two Presidents and President Zardari's meetings with other Chinese state leaders were characterized by traditional warmth, friendship and mutual understanding. The two leaders reached broad agreement on strengthening China-Pakistan strategic partnership of cooperation and on international and regional issues of mutual interest under the new circumstances. The president of Pakistan also held wide ranging discussions with the leaders of the Chinese corporations and financial institutions.

The leaders of the two countries reviewed with satisfaction the growth of China-Pakistan relations over the past 57 years since the two countries established diplomatic ties. They agreed the friendship between China and Pakistan has withstood the test of time and practice, notwithstanding changes in the international, regional and domestic environments. The all-weather friendship and all-round cooperation have become the distinctive features of China-Pakistan relations.

Both sides inked twelve agreements/MOUs during the visit in the fields of economic and technical cooperation, free trade, minerals, petroleum and natural resources, environmental protection, radio and television, space technology, agriculture sector, properties exchange between foreign ministries of the two countries, museum of natural history, cricket field and project of X-Ray container/vehicle inspection system.

CHINA-PAKISTAN NUCLEAR REACTIONS

Chinese Pakistani nuclear cooperation began in 1971. Pakistan Prime Minister Zulfiqar Ali Bhutto had famously remarked in the aftermath of the Indian nuclear test that "If India builds the bomb, we will eat grass or leaves, even go hungry, but we will get one of our own." Zulfikar Ali Bhutto's last testament reveals that 1976 was the inaugural year for China Pakistani nuclear cooperation, with American concerns about this cooperation following suit. Talks between US Secretary of State Henry Kissinger and Bhutto during this period, discussed the nuclear cooperation between the two countries, however, the focus was on nuclear reprocessing; uranium enrichment was not yet a concern. In 1986, a formal treaty outlining the nuclear cooperation between the two states was signed. 1986 is also significant, since it came at the height of the Cold War conflict in Afghanistan, and therefore, an ideological battle for influence in the region was being fought by the two superpowers. Pakistan recognized its frontline role in being the vanguard for the Islamic world against Communism, following which President Zia ul Haq rhetorically declared the following about nuclear weapons: "It is our right to obtain technology. And when we acquire this technology the Islamic world will posses it with us."

The 1986 treaty, as mentioned, was the formalization of a robust nuclear transfer which was already underway between the two countries. According to letters written by Dr. Abdul Qadeer Khan, the father of Pakistan's nuclear program, serious nuclear cooperation between the two countries is documented as early as 1982.

In his letters, he cited the case of a Pakistani military C 130 which left the Chinese city of Urumqi with enough weapons grade uranium for two atomic bombs. The yield for these weapons is estimated at 20 25KT. The official patronage given to this relationship can be established when he wrote "Upon my personal request, the Chinese Minister... had gifted us 50 kilograms of weapon grade enriched uranium."(sic) Additionally, transfers included blueprints to develop the nuclear weapons. These letters are corroborated by American journalist Bill Gertz, who in 1996, wrote that Chinese diplomats refused in 1982 to give an "unequivocal answer" to queries about nuclear weapons aid to Pakistan.

Cooperation between the two countries steadily increased in the years following, with substantial transfers occurring in the decade of 1986 1996. According to media reports during this period of time, in addition to assisting with the Kahuta nuclear reactor, the Chinese also transferred tritium gas, which is used in the manufacture of a hydrogen bomb. Beijing also supplied heavy water (D_2O) to the safeguarded Kanupp reactor (originally supplied by Canada) at a rate to make up heavy water losses of 2 to 4 per cent a year. It is also believed that China offered its test facilities at Lop Nor in 1989, to conduct a Pakistani nuclear test. While the international community was increasingly aware of such transactions, the response to them was limited owing to a variety of geo strategic and diplomatic considerations. One of them was economic; in 1985 the Chinese and US governments signed a Nuclear Cooperation Agreement (NCA) that, when enacted, would allow American firms to apply for licenses to sell nuclear reactors to China. Implementing the agreement on the US side required the president to certify to Congress that China was not proliferating nuclear weapons. Additionally, the Pressler Amendment was passed which required the US government to certify at the start of each fiscal year, that Pakistan did not possess a nuclear device. The government did so, since Pakistan was a frontline ally, against the Soviet forces in operation in Afghanistan.

On 30 May 1989, American officials questioned Chinese diplomats over Chinese cooperation with Pakistan; an unidentified Chinese diplomat denied the allegations, instead stating that Beijing's accession to the IAEA in 1984 required all its transactions to be conducted under safeguards. It was largely owing to Chinese efforts that Pakistan was nuclear weapons capable by 1989 itself. A partial admission was provided by Former Pakistan Prime Minister Benazir Bhutto in an interview, when she admitted that a cold test had been conducted in 1989. Despite international scrutiny, in 1991, China agreed to build the Chashma 300 MW nuclear power reactor for Pakistan. In order to lend international credibility to this exercise, Pakistan was asked to sign an IAEA safeguards (limited scope) agreement for the reactor at Chashma. Significantly, while these proliferation rings were being strengthened, China was not a part of the Nuclear Non Proliferation Treaty, and therefore not violating its principles. China signed the Nuclear Nonproliferation Treaty in 1992 and the Comprehensive Test Ban Treaty in 1995.

China's tactics to violate their international obligations were evident during the immediate period after the end of the Cold War, with Chinese firms acting as fronts for transferring

European technology to Pakistan. This was highlighted in an American cable, outlining a Chinese ploy to buy German cooling equipment for reactors to supply Pakistan, for use in its Chasma reactors. A similar attempt earlier was rebuffed by Germany, when it was disclosed that Pakistan was to be the end recipient. Similarly, further attempts at proliferation were seen in 1995, when 5,000 specially designed ring magnets from the China Nuclear Energy Industry Corporation (CNEIC), were sold to an un safeguarded Pakistani nuclear facility.

China denied any such transfers, with a Chinese Foreign Ministry spokesman calling the reports "groundless", in talks with US officials, China eventually privately admitted that the sale had taken place, but argued that China should not be penalized for two reasons. First, China insisted that CNEIC had arranged the sale without the knowledge or consent of the central government. Second, China argued that the ring magnets were not magnetized, and the Nuclear Suppliers Group (NSG) Trigger List only covers ring magnets magnetized at a specific tolerance. China escaped punitive measures with a warning, after it publicly reiterated its commitment to the Non Proliferation Treaty.

It can be argued that the mid nineties, should have seen a shift in China's focus towards genuine non proliferation, especially since it was the period of time when North Korea's nuclear ambitions were coming to the fore, however, while China expressed concern over its Eastern neighbour, its proliferation activities continued Westwards. According to a report by the CIA Director, published in June 1997, "China was the primary source of nuclearrelated equipment and technology to Pakistan, during the second half of 1996."26 This cooperation continued into the late 1990s, culminating with alleged assistance to Pakistan in its response to the Indian nuclear test of 1998.

According to former US Air Force Secretary Thomas Reed, suspicions surround the Chinese role in Pakistan's tests in May 1998. He pointed out that the United States itself took over two weeks to retaliate to a Soviet nuclear test, despite having the weapon for years. Therefore, the Pakistani device was a pre engineered one, which their scientists had great confidence in. Chinese proliferation has not seen periods of low activity, even during periods of tumultuous developments in the region, including the Kargil Conflict of 1999, during which China maintained a neutral position. In the years 2000 2004, Chinese entities have been sanctioned by the United States, a total of 50 times. In 2004 alone, 14 Chinese entities were sanctioned a total of 23 times, most of which are related to the Iran Non proliferation act, which indicates an upswing of proliferation activity, corresponding with increasing American presence in West Asia and South Asia. In what was intended to be a corrective measure, China joined the NSG as a full member in 2004, despite revelations of A.Q Khan's dealings with the country in the preceding year. This followed a whitepaper on non proliferation which the Chinese government released, which strengthened its case to an international audience. Since the initiation of discussions on the Indo US nuclear agreement began in 2005, China took an active interest in the regional implications for its strategic partner, and opposed the agreement on grounds that it is not equitable, and favoured a similar NSG exemption for Pakistan. When the international community expressed their reservations on Pakistan's non proliferation record (based on inputs that Dr. Khan had further proliferated Chinese designs to Libya, North Korea and Iran), China took it upon itself to strengthen its nuclear relationship with Pakistan. It was here that the grandfather nuclear clause was invoked.

UNDERSTANDING CHINA'S NON-PROLIFERATION VIEWS

China has traditionally viewed multilateral control regimes to be discriminatory and a means of control over third world states by western powers. "Even as it criticized international non proliferation regimes, however, the Chinese leadership professed an opposition to nuclear weapon states sharing the bomb with non nuclear weapon states and proclaimed that

China would assist other countries' nuclear energy programs but not weapons programs." China's progression into accepting these multilateral regimes, and gaining membership to them in contemporary times reflect its progression in policy, wherein it accepts some of the elements of the international order which gives legitimacy to its status as a great power Its interest in maintaining non proliferation double standards is linked to its great power status, especially one as being the sole accepted nuclear power in Asia. It also ties into the strategic outlook of China, on what it deems to be its interests and what it views as inconsequential irritants. For example, it is argued by T.V Paul, that "South Asia and Middle East are less vital to China than is East Asia. China has been uncomfortable with the North Korean nuclear efforts and Beijing shares the desire of the US and Japan that the Korean peninsula remains non nuclear." Former US Air Force Secretary Thomas Reed articulates China's thinking on proliferation in the following words, "China in about 1982, under Deng Xiaoping, decided to proliferate nuclear technology to communists and Muslims in the third world. They did so deliberately with the theory that if nukes ended up going off in the western world from a Muslim terrorist, well that wasn't all bad. If New York was reduced to rubble without Chinese fingerprints on the attack, that left Beijing as the last man standing. That's what the old timers thought." He adds that, while this represented the old school of thought, the new generation of Chinese leaders realizes the limitations of such a policy, and has therefore tempered their nonproliferation views.

Chinese Vice Foreign Minister, Wang Guangya in an op ed dated October 16, 2002, elucidated China's 'non proliferation policy and practice', stating "China has consistently stood for the complete prohibition and thorough destruction of all kinds of WMD and firmly against the proliferation of WMD and their delivery systems. For this, China has over the years been an active participant in international non proliferation efforts." He adds "we have steadfastly pursued a policy of not advocating, encouraging or assisting any other country in developing weapons of mass destruction and made our contribution with concrete deeds to the international non proliferation process." Furthermore, in closed door interactions with senior Chinese scholars and former military officials, the Chinese have continued to maintain their deniability in supporting Pakistan's nuclear weaponization program.

However, proliferation links to China have allegedly influenced major international policy matters in the international stage. One of the regions in addition to South Asia is West Asia. This can be attributed to the China US rivalry for resources in the region, especially since China's growing economy becomes increasingly dependent on fossil fuels in addition to alternative energy resources. By proliferating, nuclear and missile technology, it seeks to leverage against the United States in these regions. The expectation in Beijing is that the supply of these materials to the Middle Eastern countries will increase Chinese influence, thereby reducing American influence.

Why Proliferate to Pakistan?

China's proliferation to Pakistan achieves twin strategic objectives of encirclement of India, and a proliferation buffer, wherein Pakistan in turn further proliferate Chinese nuclear technology, giving China leeway in investigations.

According to Robert Ross, China continues its support for Pakistan by supplying nuclear and missile technology because "China views a credible Pakistani deterrent as the most effective way to guarantee the security of its sole ally in Southern Asia against Indian power." This argument is also postulated by T.V Paul, that "China wants to limit India's power capabilities to South Asia and thereby constrain New Delhi's aspirations to become a major power in Asia. India's emergence as a peercompetitor in Asia would upset China's predominant position in the region. However, if acute conflict and an intense arms race between India and Pakistan persist, India would continue to be bracketed with its smaller regional rival Pakistan and not with China." Proliferation to Pakistan, also offers China a certain leeway in their doctrinal stance of No First Use, since

Pakistan does not subscribe to that element. China can make use of its proxy in instigating a nuclear conflict in South Asia, wherein the affected parties would be Pakistan and India, with China attempting to emerge unscathed. For China, using Pakistan as an extended deterrence proxy was much more practical than merely extending its nuclear umbrella onto Pakistan. This would likely explain the Chinese aversion to Pakistani Foreign Minister, Shamshad Ahmed's request in 1998, to guarantee nuclear protection should India attack. While growing Indian aspirations in the region are clearly opposed by China, the original reason for the Sino Pak relationship was largely economic.

According to Mao Zedong's calculations, Pakistan was nothing but China's easy access to the Atlantic and the Indian Ocean It was to be the route for Chinese access to Middle Eastern oil, and resources to Africa, and therefore there was a need to build upon an economic and military relationship with the country. This argument is bolstered through the fact that China has been deeply involved in building of a deep water naval port at Gwadar, Balochistan, and has consistently advocated Pakistan as a trans national corridor for Middle Eastern energy transport to its mainland. The nature of the China Pakistan military/nuclear alliance makes it beneficial for China to extend its nuclear proliferation tentacles worldwide through proxies; thereby holding a level of plausible deniability in international forums. This is exemplified in the case of proliferation rogue states of North Korea, Iran and Libya, wherein Chinese nuclear components have been found, courtesy the proliferation ring run by A.Q Khan Laboratory's. Therefore, China can use Pakistan as a scapegoat for any eventual international sanction, gambling on Pakistan's geo strategic importance for furthering its own interests beyond the region.

International Implications of the Alliance

A consequence of the China Pakistan nuclear trade has been further proliferation from Pakistan to additional states, thereby weakening the non proliferation regime, and indirectly furthering Chinese strategic interests in these countries. The implications for regional peace and stability in South Asia are also critical, since Pakistan continues to hold ambiguous red lines on its nuclear doctrine, allowing it to extend a nuclear umbrella over terrorist groups based in Pakistan, operating against India. Pakistan's nuclear links to North Korea were first reported in October 2002, when press reports suggested that nuclear materials and technology for uranium enrichment were transferred to North Korea since 1997.44 In July 2011, A.Q Khan made further revelations on the nuclear trade between Islamabad and Pyongyang, alleging that $3.5 million was paid to senior Pakistani officials to facilitate the agreement. Collaboration with North Korea for missiles was acknowledged by Benazir Bhutto, who said "When I went to North Korea, AQ Khan told me we could get their (missile) technology (so) that we can compare (it) to our own. So I took (it) up with Kim Il Sung...December '93 I talked to him, he agreed...and it was in cash, they needed money and so it was done for cash, with no exchange of nuclear technology. Exchanging nuclear technology for missiles was never even discussed during my visit."

It remains unclear whether the government was in the know about nuclear transactions. However, the spread of the network to countries including Libya, Iran and allegedly to Myanmar, make it difficult to accept that the Pakistani government or Army headquarters was completely unaware of these transactions. Especially in the realm of nuclear transfers to North Korea, as pointed earlier, China would have been aware of the ongoing transfers, owing to the sensitivity of its interests there. The fact that China did not broach this topic with Pakistan, and on the contrary continued its nuclear relationship with Pakistan, leads this author to believe that China tacitly approved of these transfers. Similarly, the implications of Pakistan furthering Chinese products to West Asia can be seen in how Pakistan is trying to play both sides of an ideological divide, by having contributed to the Iranian nuclear program, and having a suspected tie up with Saudi Arabia to arm them with nuclear warheads too.

In an interview, A.Q. Khan lauds Iran, saying "If Iran succeeds in acquiring nuclear technology, we will be a strong bloc in the region to counter international pressure", adding that "Iran's nuclear capability will neutralize Israel's power." Khan, having been associated with the nuclear program, would be well aware of the strategic implications of the ideological divide between Saudi Arabia and Iran. It is alleged that Saudi Arabia also played a role in supporting Pakistan's nuclear ambitions, in return for an extended nuclear umbrella against Iran. This is the reason argued for Pakistan's rapid fissile material productionto cater for its own demands, and those for West Asian deterrence. The Chinese ambivalence in pushing for sanctions on Iran, and its missile transfers to Saudi Arabia, add to these suspicions of collaboration.

5

Pakistan-China: Strategic Encirclement of India's Core Interests

Having failed to constrict India within South Asia with its "String of Pearls" (an American euphuism) Strategy, China has now embarked on a new initiative to trip India's growing comprehensive national power (CNP) and influence beyond South Asia. India's neighbours swam with China periodically, depending on the government in those countries. For Example, the Mahinda Rajapksa government in Sri Lanka jumped into China's lap for their own political reasons. The Mathiripala Sirisena government has restored the balance.

The BNP led four party alliance government (2001-2006) in Bangladesh brought relations with India to the lowest ebb. The alliance had parties like the Jamaat-e-Islami which were beholden to Pakistan and actively complicit in the savage rape and attempted extermination of the pro-liberation Bengalees in 1971. They were natural allies of not only Pakistan but also China which supported Pakistan. The return of the Awami League to power changed this policy drastically. The Awami League government, due to practical necessity and real politics, crafted a friendly relationship with China, but not at the expense of their relationship with India. China, however, is trying to entice Dhaka, but this does not worry India because India-Bangladesh relationship has more than political market imperatives. There is a cultural and historical conjunction. Nepal has been vacillating between India and China. Lodged between the two giant countries, they are trying to get the best out of the two. China recognises India's influence in Nepal, but has been consistently trying to weaken the India-Nepal relationship.

Pakistan has emerged as China's mainstay in the region and extends to the Gulf, the Central Asian region, and now they are trying to draw in Russia in this ambit. Weakening India-Russia relations is one of its aims. With its promised 46 billion investment in Pakistan for the China-Pakistan Economic Corridor (CPEC), Control of the Gwadar Port (a military project), primary arms and defence equipment supplier and recent acquisition of 40 percent of the Pakistan stock market by a Chinese conglomerate, Pakistan is fast emerging as a country under Chinese suzerainty. Evidence suggests Pakistan may soon become a platform for the projection of both soft and hard power for being along the route envisaged for the "One Belt, One Road" (OBOR) project. China is unlikely to declare Pakistan as one of its "core" interests, but it is already acting as such.

Lately, China has been expressing concerns about achieving the full potential of the CPEC. In an article in the Communist Party affiliated newspaper *Global Times* (Dec. 28, 2016), Wang Dehua, Director of the Institute of Southern and Central Asian Studies, Shanghai Municipal Center for Internal Studies, wrote that the CEPC was facing challenges. He went on to describe the project as having "Significant economic, political and strategic implications for both China and Pakistan".

Wang wrote this in the context of a spat between the Chinese Charged Affaires in Islamabad Zhao Lijian and a journalist of the Pakistani newspaper *Dawn*. The concerned journalist asked Zhao some uncomfortable questions including use of Chinese prisoners as labour. The senior Chinese diplomat lost his cool in a public place, which is very uncharacteristic of the Chinese.

Wang Dehua revealed that Chinese investment was raised to \$51 billion from the initial \$46 billion. The Chinese party media have extolled the virtue of the CPEC not only for China and Pakistan but other countries of the region including India, Iran, Afghanistan and Russia. The emphasis has been more on India, suggesting that India joining the project could help reduce tensions between India and Pakistan. Simultaneously, there is a suggestion to link Gwadar and Chabahar ports as sister ports and sister cities.

The CPEC is the flagship project of the larger OBOR strategic conception of extending China's circulatory system far and wide. It has political and strategic penetration as significant benefits. Most important is the fact that it is Chinese President Xi Jinping's prestige project. It cannot be allowed to fail at any cost. It is also part of China's great power signature.

At the same time, Beijing is ramping up pressure on India in a shower, trying to destabilise India's emerging foreign policy. Beijing's stand will have serious negative implications especially on the biggest threat to the world at this moment, terrorism. In the last week of December, China vetoed India's move to designate Masood Azhar, head of Pakistan-based terrorist organisation Jaish-e-Mohammad as a "terrorist" at the UN Committee 2167 on terrorism. This, when the organisation itself is designated as a terrorist organisation by the same committee.

This one move by China has hit at the very roots of the global movement against extremism and terrorism. Read plainly, China will use terrorism as a political weapon against perceived enemies, in this case India. It also encourages Pakistan to use terrorism with impunity against India, Afghanistan and even, perhaps Bangladesh. India is determined to continue its efforts to bring other Pakistani-based and backed terrorists in front of the 2167 committee. China is the only member of their 15 member committee to oppose the move against Azhar. In a manner China stands isolated.

China took umbrage and accused India of interfering in China's internal affairs after the Indian President met His Holiness the Dalai Lama at a function which was totally non-political. Their official media threatened India of retaliation of the kind they subjected the tiny country of Mongolia after Dalai Lama's visit to Mongolia that was a purely religious one. Mongolia is a Buddhist Country, mostly of the Gelugpa sect of Buddhism which the Dalai Lama heads spiritually. This is a stupid threat. Mongolia a tiny land locked country, with a population of around two million is dependent on China for outside access. Such threats do not impress the Indian government and the Indian people. The Chinese threat appears to be an act of frustration.

Nevertheless, Tibet is a declared core interest of China, hence the Dalai Lama. The 80 year spiritual leader has withdrawn himself from politics, but his influence and reverence among Tibetans inside China and outside is palpable. The Chinese have not been able to come to a firm conclusion whether the living 14th Dalai Lama or deceased 14th Dalai Lama will be to their interest.

The Chinese leadership has tried to denigrate the Dalai Lama in all possible ways, calling him a 'splittist' (separatist), 'devil', 'wolf in sheep's clothing among other things, but these have not impressed anyone. Beijing suspects India is using Dalai Lama as a 'card' against China.

India has accepted Tibet Autonomous Region as a sovereign part of China (2003). The Tibetan refugees in India are not allowed political activities. Successive governments in New Delhi have bent over backwards to accommodate China's concerns. But if China continues to attack India on this issue, India will be forced to fight back. Allow the Dalai Lama and the generally accepted Kargyupa head Ughen Thinley Dorjee freedom to move around India including Tawang and the rest of Arunachal Pradesh.

China is trying to push the OBOR to and through Nepal and Bangladesh. They hope that through persuasion from these two countries India may succumb and agree to join the OBOR in the interest of its good neighbourhood policy. If India does not relent China may seek alternative policies in India's neighbourhood to constrict India. The *Global Times* has already hinted at this. Beijing remains determined to keep India out of the Nuclear Supplies Group (NSG). It has now objected to India's successful testing (Dec. 16, 2016) of the 5000 kms nuclear capable ballistic missile Agni V. In a sharply worded statement Chinese foreign ministry spokespersons threatened to take this issue to the UN Security Council resolution 1172 after the 1998 nuclear tests by India and Pakistan. The resolution passed at the heat of the moment and engineered by China and the US calling on the two countries to stop further nuclear tests, cap their nuclear weapon programmes, cease all fissile material production, and end development of ballistic missiles capable of carrying nuclear weapons. The resolution, however is non-binding. China's threat falls through the floor.

Since then, India has come a long way on the nuclear issue. It issued a moratorium on nuclear testing, announced no first use of nuclear weapons policy and signed the India-US nuclear deal. India, however, will have to counter Chinese pressures in several such areas in the future.

The Chinese spokesperson also said that "China maintains that preserving the strategic balance and stability in South Asia is conducive to peace and prosperity of regional countries 'and beyond'. Basically, the statement implied that India may have disturbed the strategic balance in South Asia and beyond, without counting its own intercontinental nuclear capable ballistic missiles and other weapons. As China its military development is defensive and not aimed at any country, so is the official India position.

But things between India and China may get worse if the CPEC and OBOR falter seriously. This is closely linked to Xi Jinping's politics and stature of "core" leader of the Chinese Communist Party. The 19th Congress to the party will be held in autumn this year and major leadership changes will take place. Xi cannot have any chinks in his armour.

IMPLICATIONS, OPTIONS FOR INDIA

It will span the entire extent of Pakistan and is planned to connect Gwadar port in Pakistan to Kashgar in China's western Xinjiang province through road infrastructure, railways and oil and gas pipelines passing through Gilgit-Baltistan (GB) region of Pak Occupied Kashmir (PoK) covering a distance of 3,000 km. Also included is development of Gwadar into a deep water sea port.

A major geopolitical challenge that is engaging Pakistan is about the constitutional status of GB through which CPEC passes. India has objected to CPEC passing through GB which is an integral part of India by virtue of having been part of the princely state of Jammu & Kashmir. The feeling in Pakistan is that China may be concerned to invest $46 billion on a corridor passing through disputed territory lacking legitimacy. However, China is trying to overtly downplay such concerns.

None the less, Pakistan is mulling over various options to overcome this legal tangle ranging from fully integrating GB as the fifth province of Pakistan to raising the constitutional status of the region while keeping it short of a regular pro-vince with representation in parliament.

In effect, both amount to the same and is a complete reversal of Pakistan's historical stand on Kashmir. Any efforts on the part of Pakistan to integrate GB constitutionally into its federal structure or its parliament will amount to violation of UN Resolutions and forfeiture of its demands for a plebiscite, and acceptance of de jure control of India over the parts of Kashmir it holds.

Ipso facto, it implies, legitimising the present Line of Control (LoC) as the border between the two countries. India may not be averse to such a prospect given the background of previous discussions on the subject and back channel chatter. The Kargil Review Committee of India, in its report of 1999, mentioned that such a possibility was reported to have been discussed during the Shimla talks of 1972 between India and Pakistan.

The CPEC is one component of Chinese "One Belt, One Road" (OBOR) initiative and the other being the "21st Century Maritime Silk Route". Disguised in the OBOR initiative is the Chinese vision of political expansion and economic ambition though China is quick to add that the initiative is aimed at integrating the whole of Asia as "One Economic Continent" due to the benefits that accrue to all of the entity of Asia as opposed to China alone. Towards this end, China's endeavour is to bring all nations of Asia under the umbrella of OBOR; more importantly India.

The CPEC and the access it provides to the Arabian Sea through Gwadar are very critical for China to meet its geostrategic and economic needs in the changed geopolitical context. With the withdrawal of United States presence in Afghanistan, China seized the opportunity presented by the power vacuum to expand its regional sphere of influence and further its economic and strategic interests to Pakistan and Persian Gulf built around the linchpin of Gwadar.

Once Gwadar is fully operational, China will be able to ensure that a large share of its oil needs are secured via Gwadar, saving time and billions in costs apart from ensuring security to its oil routes.

More importantly, the new route would circumvent the potentially vulnerable Strait of Malacca and growing US naval presence in South China Sea as part of the US pivot to Asia. Gwadar, though being developed as a commercial port, has the potential to be transformed into a military facility for China's navy with capability to threaten India's energy routes from Gulf and as well impinge on India's naval operations in the Arabian Sea and the Indian Ocean.

India cannot be oblivious to such strategic changes taking place in its neighbourhood with far-reaching regional and global ramifications. While integration with OBOR initiative may be important for New Delhi to serve its national interests and to realise its concept of South Asian integration, Indian participation is equally important to China for its successful implementation. China is aware of this reality.

'Asian Century'

From a bilateral perspective, the joint statement of May 15, 2015 between India and China, released during Prime Minister

Narendra Modi's visit to China, does enunciate "Asian Century" and recognise the emergence of India and China as 'two major powers' in regional and world politics, and their cooperative relations will be key to the realisation of an 'Asian Century'.

India must leverage the advantages of such bilateralism and pressurise China to stop CPEC passing through India-claimed territory. Considering the inevitability of CPEC from Chinese strategic perspective, whether such leverages have enough traction is debatable.

Alternatively, India may also consider the option of legitimising the present LoC read in conjunction with Kabul Agreement as the international border subject to unconditional acceptance by Pakistan to withdraw all its claims over Siachen and cessation of proxy war in J&K and acts of terrorism directed against India. Given the irreconcilable geometrics of South Asia, such an option may raise many hackles both in India and Pakistan.

Statesmanship is more about dynamic ability to respond to situations recognising the ground realities and seizing the opportunities presented by history. India today is at the threshold of an opportunity which has never before been offered by history.

For sustained economic growth and development, India certainly needs peace and as well infrastructure connected to markets in the region. The CPEC offers such a platform and engines for growth. If India is to become a reckonable power, it is but incumbent for the nation to ensure robust economic growth for the next decade or two and strengthen itself militarily.

BEHIND CHINA'S GAMBIT IN PAKISTAN

The China-Pakistan Economic Corridor (CPEC) is part development scheme, part strategic gambit. Although Beijing and Islamabad have been close partners for decades, the CPEC is a reflection of intensified and expanded bilateral cooperation at a time of rising Chinese geopolitical ambition and persistent concerns about Pakistan's security and development.

The CPEC is intended to promote connectivity across Pakistan with a network of highways, railways, and pipelines accompanied by energy, industrial, and other infrastructure development projects to address critical energy shortages needed to boost Pakistan's economic growth. Eventually, the CPEC will also facilitate trade along an overland route that connects China to the Indian Ocean, linking the Chinese city of Kashgar to the Pakistani port of Gwadar.

Pakistan and China formalized plans for the CPEC in April 2015, when they signed fifty-one agreements and memoranda of understanding on Chinese investments, totaling $46 billion over the next ten to fifteen years. Some projects are already underway, including highways and energy projects where completion is expected by the end of 2016.

CPEC developments are part of a grander Chinese agenda of regional economic connectivity: the One Belt, One Road (OBOR) initiative outlined in March 2015 by China's National Development and Reform Committee (NDRC). The highly ambitious plan calls for new state-directed investments in roads, railways, pipelines, ports, and information networks to deepen economic integration and connectivity across Asia and into Africa and Europe.

Because OBOR consists of a continental Eurasian "Silk Road Economic Belt" and a Southeast Asian "Maritime Silk Road," Pakistan has the potential to serve as a nexus for the two routes, and Beijing describes the CPEC as a "flagship project." Although Beijing is quick to downplay geostrategic motivations behind the CPEC, many commentators have noted that over the long run, an overland link across Pakistan to the Arabian Sea could help alleviate the "Malacca dilemma," China's vulnerability to the fact that roughly 85 percent (PDF) of its oil imports travel through the single chokepoint of the Strait of Malacca.

Security Through Development

Understanding the CPEC requires an appreciation for China's security concerns, especially those stemming from its restive western region of Xinjiang. Beijing has sought to clamp down on Xinjiang's ethnic Uighur community and has met political violence with an expanded security presence and push for economic development schemes. These efforts implicate Pakistan because Uighur militant groups, like the East Turkestan Islamic Movement (ETIM), have sought refuge in the Pakistan-Afghanistan border areas, where they have established links with al-Qaeda and the Taliban in Afghanistan and Pakistan. China perceives the ETIM as a persistent threat, committed to targeting China and attacking Chinese interests (PDF) inside Pakistan.

The CPEC represents an international extension of China's effort to deliver security through economic development.

In this context, the CPEC represents an international extension of China's effort to deliver security through economic development. Investments in Pakistan are intended to create jobs, reduce antistate sentiment, and generate public resources for additional improvements in law and order. By tackling the threat of jihadi organizations in neighboring Pakistan, China hopes to better secure its own territory. Consequently, while the CPEC is often portrayed as a transportation corridor, security concerns will likely impose limits on the cross-border flow of people and goods, at least in the short to medium term.

Pakistan's ruling civilian and military leaders also appreciate the economic, political, and security opportunities that the CPEC offers. Pakistan needs direct investment to spur economic growth, but investors have generally shied away over the past decade. If delivered, China's investment plan represents more than double all foreign direct investment (FDI) in Pakistan since 2008.

China's investments in energy infrastructure are especially welcome. National demand outstrips supply by an average of 4,500 megawatts. Supply shortages and distribution problems lead to frequent blackouts and cost as much as 2 percent GDP growth (PDF) a year. These troubles will worsen as Pakistan's population of nearly two hundred million expands at a rate of almost 2 percent (PDF) annually. Without the creation of new jobs, however, the nation's youth (over half of Pakistanis are under the age of twenty-four) will lack productive outlets for their energies. In a state riven by sectarian, ethnic, and political cleavages and populated by networks of extremism and militancy, the need for a growing economy takes on special significance.

Politically, Pakistan's ruling civilian government recognizes that by delivering a range of "early harvest" projects, it will have a better chance of winning national elections slated for 2018. From a security perspective, Pakistan's military leaders believe that if Chinese investments can turn around the nation's sagging economic fortunes, they will also strengthen the state against challengers, both foreign (India) and domestic (antistate insurgents).

Plans and Realities

In Pakistan, CPEC projects are being managed primarily by the Ministry of Planning, Reform, and Development in partnership with China's NDRC. The two sides have established a Joint Cooperation Committee with working groups focused on four main areas: the Gwadar Port, transport infrastructure, energy, and industrial cooperation.

Operations at Gwadar, a warm-water, deep-sea port in Balochistan near the Strait of Hormuz, were handed over to a Chinese state-owned enterprise in November 2015. Gwadar remains a work in progress, with total traffic of only half a million tons in 2016, but traffic is expected to double in 2017. Planners estimate that eventually it will process three hundred to four hundred million tons annually and that the surrounding city will grow from eighty thousand to two million residents.

The physical "corridor" of the CPEC consists of an interconnected highway, railway, and pipeline system. In May 2015, the Pakistani government unveiled three highway routes for the project: a western route through Balochistan and Khyber Pakhtunkhwa provinces; an eastern route primarily through Sindh and Punjab provinces; and a central route crisscrossing the country. A northern highway route connects to Kashgar, via the Karakoram Highway, itself a major symbol of China-Pakistan cooperation and their only ground linkage. Other transportation projects include the construction and improvement of existing railways, including laying more than 1,200 kilometers of new track and upgrading another 3,100 kilometers.

The lion's share of China's investment—roughly $35 billion—is expected to go to energy projects, including coal, solar, hydroelectric, liquefied natural gas, and power transmission. If all goes according to plan, twenty-one new projects will generate nearly 17,000 megawatts of energy and nearly double Pakistan's installed capacity.

Of those twenty-one projects, Pakistan expects fourteen "early harvest" projects to add 10,400 megawatts to the national grid by 2018. To take advantage of new infrastructure and power capacity, the government has identified more than forty sites for new and upgraded industrial parks and special economic zones, designed to encourage investment and boost local employment.

CPEC projects are being negotiated on a government-to-government basis, with Chinese firms selected by Beijing. The projects are covered by low or zero-interest concessional loans that include financing from China's Export-Import Bank and Silk Road Fund. To date, Pakistan's wider public has had little access to the specifics of these arrangements, and the closed bidding process makes it difficult to assess whether contracts reflect fair market costs, accounting for Pakistan's difficult security environment.

Unlike their Pakistani counterparts, Chinese power plants will benefit from protections against the "circular debt" (PDF) crisis that has plagued Pakistan. Pakistani power purchasers will be required to fund a revolving account covering 22 percent of monthly costs, and Pakistan's Ministry of Finance will back those funds with sovereign guarantees to ensure uninterrupted payment. In early 2016, these arrangements were expanded from coal-fired power plants to all CPEC energy projects.

Challenges

The primary obstacle to the CPEC's full implementation is security. To address Chinese concerns and ensure the safety of these projects, Pakistan announced in early 2016 the creation of a dedicated CPEC force of ten thousand security personnel, but even a force of that size will be stressed by the task at hand.

In Pakistan's northwest frontier, road networks are planned to run near or through territories where the Pakistani Taliban and other antistate militant groups could attack construction crews and disrupt the flow of goods. In ongoing military operations targeting those groups, the Pakistani military has placed a special emphasis on the ETIM due to Chinese pressure and is concerned that attacks could delay or derail the CPEC. In October 2015, the military claimed to have eradicated the ETIM from Pakistan, but the threat of other groups remains. Islamist militant groups have already attacked Chinese targets, including kidnapping construction personnel, and hinted that their campaigns could expand to include more targeting of Chinese interests.

In a state riven by sectarian, ethnic, and political cleavages and populated by networks of extremism and militancy, the need for a growing economy takes on special significance.

A decades-long insurgency simmers in Balochistan, where a number of important CPEC projects are underway. Baloch insurgents have attacked Chinese projects and workers. To protect Gwadar's port town, one proposal includes the construction of a perimeter security fence with entry checkpoints. Such schemes threaten to further alienate local communities.

The CPEC also faces domestic political opposition in Pakistan, with infighting between provinces and the central government over the allocation of investments. Opposition parties have leveled accusations of preferential treatment along the eastern route, claiming the government's proposals for the distribution of services, industrial parks, and special economic zones denies some provinces access to investment opportunities and only benefits Punjab. The lack of transparency surrounding the negotiated deals has heightened concerns and skepticism that only a select few, if any in Pakistan, will benefit from the investments.

Addressing these concerns will require more than additional troops to protect the projects. Unless Pakistan's federal government works with provincial and local authorities to convince communities that these projects are in their best interest, the CPEC's viability will remain in doubt.

China's own tolerance for attacks is difficult to anticipate, but because the CPEC is a flagship of the OBOR initiative China may be willing to weather more violence. Yet if Pakistan is unable to provide sufficient security or address the concerns of domestic opponents, projects will have trouble getting off the ground and will fail to prompt follow-on investments or deliver commercial success.

Implications

If successful, the CPEC could provide important benefits to Pakistan's economy. Economic growth is vital to political stability, and therefore the project should be considered a welcome development and encouraged by the United States.

That said, the initiative will also raise concerns, especially from India and other neighbors worried about growing Chinese assertiveness. Indian analysts question the implications of Chinese investments and worry about Beijing's ambitions in South Asia. Gwadar Port is perceived in India as less likely to become a vibrant economic hub than to serve as a naval base for China's expanded blue water fleet and operations throughout the Indian Ocean.

Additionally, Indian Prime Minister Narendra Modi and other officials have lodged complaints with Beijing, protesting current and proposed projects because they run through territory claimed by India. To reduce the likelihood that Chinese activities in Pakistan exacerbate regional tensions, Washington could raise the issue in bilateral dialogues with New Delhi and Beijing, or even play host to a trilateral discussion.

The CPEC will have the best chance of transforming Pakistan's economic outlook if it also sparks a wave of foreign investment from other countries, including the United States.

The United States will also have its own long-term concerns about the CPEC, as it represents the leading edge of China's expanding access to, and likely influence within, Eurasia. As Pakistan grows closer to China, there may be temptation in Washington to compete for influence in Islamabad. This competition is best avoided, as it would be costly, unwinnable, and almost certainly counterproductive to other U.S. goals in Pakistan and the region. Pakistanis will reach their own conclusions about how best to pursue relations with Beijing and Washington, and are likely to pursue distinct ties with both sides. U.S. officials should seize the opportunity provided by Pakistan's intense focus on the CPEC to advance its own set of politically sustainable goals in Pakistan, paying particular attention to U.S. concerns about terrorism, nuclear proliferation, and the war in Afghanistan.

Finally, though Chinese and Pakistani officials are wary of U.S. overtures, the CPEC should be appreciated as an opportunity for closer trilateral cooperation. The United States could redirect a portion of current civilian assistance funds into projects that are aligned with CPEC goals—such as technical improvements to Pakistan's national power grid—to help create jobs, spur economic growth, and provide incentives for additional outside investment. U.S. aid can and should continue to play a constructive role in Pakistan, and if harmonized with Chinese efforts could enhance the efficacy of both. This would require opening a new, detail-oriented dialogue with both Pakistani and Chinese officials. In addition, U.S. officials, including from the State Department and Export-Import Bank, should use their conversations with Pakistani counterparts to ensure that CPEC-style protections for Chinese corporations and investors are also applied to U.S. firms. The CPEC will have the best chance of transforming Pakistan's economic outlook if it also sparks a wave of foreign investment from other countries, including the United States.

ECONOMIC EMERGENCE AND POLITICAL CHANGE

Seeds of economic change have long been embedded in the liberal system that North America and Europe together constructed after the Second World War. Indeed, as more of the world adopted liberal market-oriented strategies, the club of developed countries widened, and the international system evolved as a result.

This has not always been a seamless process; shifts in the economic balance of power invariably alter relations among states, and in so doing generate no small degree of friction. China's explosive economic emergence, however, promises the greatest shake-up ever of the reigning post-war economic order. It will invariably alter international relations and, by extension, North American-European relations in profound and perhaps unanticipated ways.

China, however, is hardly a new economic power. Prior to the closing of its borders in 1500, its emperors presided over the world's largest and most sophisticated economy. Although modern Europe moved quickly to catch up and ultimately surpass China over the ensuing centuries, it still generated 32% of the world's wealth in 1820. (Hale and Hale) The forced reopening of its borders at the hands of colonial powers marked the beginning of China's return to the world stage; yet colonialism, anarchy, warlordism, nationalist reaction, world war, occupation, civil war and communist revolution rendered this an exceedingly fitful and terribly painful process.

It was only with the 1978 reforms launched by Deng Xiaoping that Communist China began to develop in a more organic fashion. Oddly enough, this reform commenced in the countryside when the state suddenly allowed peasants to adopt market structures in order to encourage production and boost income. Since 1994, however, China's economic revolution has been largely an urban and industrial phenomenon. Growth along the Eastern coast has far outstripped development in the countryside. Between 1978 and 2003, China's per capita GDP grew by 6.1% a year, registering a 337% increase over that period. (Wolf) Large swathes of China's vast hinterland have however been left behind in this process.

China has very quickly moved from a communist ownership model, in which the state possessed virtually all the means of production, to a far more complex system in which private ownership increasingly overshadows state ownership. It has also advanced rapidly up the production scale, moving from very simple assembly to ever more complex manufacturing processes.

The area for autonomous action by the individual in China generally has also been expanding, despite persistent, regrettable and ultimately counter-productive limitations on political freedom.

The Chinese people now enjoy unprecedented freedom of movement, information flows are far more developed and open today, and young Chinese possess ever-greater control over their destiny despite the real political constraints they confront. In the words of one western analyst, the Chinese at least enjoy the freedom not to engage in politics. This is hardly the same thing as democracy, but it suggests an important evolution away from the totalitarianism of the Cultural Revolution when the Chinese were compelled to live and breath politics.

Yet, within parameters defined largely by the Communist leadership, China's economic boom is providing an outlet for the country's long pent-up commercial energies and the aspirations of its people for a better life. The possibility of achieving this has certainly diverted some of the political passions that spilled onto Tiananmen Square in 1989, (Hutzler) although repression has done its part as well. China's huge student population certainly has its share of aspirant democrats, but many have simply abandoned politics to focus on their careers. Recent polls suggest that the Chinese are tremendously optimistic about the future; particularly the well educated, who are best positioned to benefit from China's economic expansion and global integration. (Giles)

China's civil society has grown more complex and articulated since 1989 and this too is shaping both the aspirations of its people and the likely manner in which future political change will unfold. Many people today recognize their growing stake in the preservation of civil order. This does not mean that democratic reform will not come, rather it points toward new modalities for pushing for these changes-strategies in which pressure comes from both within the governing elite and from an ever-more articulated civil society.

In the words of the historian Lanxin Xiang, the Chinese have embraced Perestroika (restructuring) but have no desire to push for glasnost (openness). (Meeting with Lanxin Xiang) The great threat to the current order may come not from the kind of students who were targeted during the Tiananmen crackdown, but rather from the millions of disenfranchised Chinese, many living in the country's vast interior, who have not benefited from economic reform and growth.

China's elite is aware of this and clearly hopes that by easing conditions in the vast hinterland, the regime will be better positioned to defend the political status quo and the stability needed to generate economic growth. But even this offers only a temporary solution to the longer-term problem of China's lack of democracy.

Several years ago after the high technology stock bubble, American economists were ringing their hands over the question of which country might possibly serve as the engine of a global economic recovery. Europe, it was said, was hopelessly over-regulated and increasingly uncompetitive; the United States was heading down a path of rising government and consumer debt, corporate accounting scandals and investor uncertainties; and Japan's economy remained mired in a deflationary recession. Two bright spots, India and China, it was then claimed, lacked the economic weight for their high growth rates to have any significant spillover impact on global growth. Such forecasts, it seems, were made under the old assumption that the global economy and OECD member countries, with a few important caveats, were more or less the same thing.

That assumption proved false. According to a recent Economist survey, China now accounts for 13% of world output in purchasing power parity terms (second only to America's) and will soon be the world's third largest exporter after the United States and Germany. Its domestic demand has been the single greatest factor in Asia's recent recovery, and it is a major underwriter of American deficit spending through its purchase of US treasury bills.

The IMF has suggested that if China proves able to implement much needed banking reform, the country will continue growing over the coming decade at 7-8% per annum, a rate which could push the country's GDP above that of the United States by 2020 in purchasing power parity terms. (The Economist, October 2, 2004.) China is thus crossing a threshold. Its economy can no longer be judged as a mere potentiality. It is now an integral player in the global economy, and its international economic weight has grown extraordinarily consequential.

Over the last year, the world economy grew by 5%. The two engines of that growth were an American economy unleashed by loose monetary and fiscal policies, very low savings rates and a high propensity to import, and Chinese producers, who are orchestrating one of the greatest economic expansions in recent memory. Yet, China remains a developing country. This accords it a rather unique place in the world economy, one that is perhaps rendered all the more paradoxical by the fact that this ever more economically liberal society is still administered by a Communist party.

ECONOMIC INTERESTS OF FOREIGN NATIONS IN BALOCHISTAN

Balochistan has always been influential on local, national, and international politics. As Balochistan borders two very significant strategic countries Afghanistan and Iran, and having majority of Baloch residents in Afghan and Iranian areas, any type of unrest or violent insurgency in Pakistani Balochistan would disturb regional instability affecting the neighboring countries and consequently become a regional dispute. Baloch insurgency may create large problems in Iran and Afghanistan due to the strong demand for greater Balochistan which includes Baloch areas of Iran and Afghanistan. (Javaid, 2010:116). Being located in the middle of the Central, Western Southern and South-western Asia, Balochistan is always under the effects of global geo-politics.

The maritime significance and potential of port Gwadar to connect the landlocked, Afghanistan and the Central Asian states to the Indian Ocean as an international trade route and an energy transit corridor, and mineral resources have heightened geo-political competition among global powers, in the Eurasian region Balochistan provides an ideal profitable aim for global powers.. Plenty of energy resources, trade routes and maritime choke points, Balochistan has attained not only its national interest but can be more important than on international level too.

This unique and valuable situation provides golden opportunity to the global powers to instigate their regional play. The world is increasingly moving towards multi-polarity and economic and military powers are growing in the Asian regions. United States has been at a powerful position exclusively since the disintegration of the Soviet Union. The objectives of Asian states like China and India are to become economically more powerful to get global hegemony by controlling the major portion of world's energy resources.

Demand for energy supply of China, India, and other Asian countries is quickly increasing, so it is the biggest requirement of time to spread their influence over world energy resources, energy transit corridors, major land and maritime trade links. For this purpose, Balochistan has become the focus of global geopolitical manipulation in this region. The resettlement of borders in the name of Greater Balochistan would definitely affect the economic development of China, Iran, India and Pakistan. United States have many times highlighted the geostrategic and geo-political significance of Balochistan and they have presented and supported the idea of free Balochistan which could serve best to secure US geopolitical and geo strategic benefits.

In order to counter Iran, the land of Balochistan is of much importance for America. The natural resources of China and oil of the Arab world are going to eliminate in coming 30 to 40 years (Mazhar, et al. 2012: 120) and then the US will have to rely upon Central Asia, Iran and Afghanistan; and for this purpose, US would have to cross Balochistan and its Coast, due to the interference of China in Balochistan, it would not be possible for US to attain an influential position. America would not be able to extend its economic hegemony for a long time, it will be substituted by China which is going to be influential over Gwadar Port and coastal line of Balochistan. That is the main reason behind US displeasure with the construction of Gwadar Port in collaboration with China.

When the Taliban administration ended in Kabul and rebellious groups of Taliban crossed the Pak-Afghan border to enter into Balochistan and organized revolutionary struggle against the aliened forces in Afghanistan. Moreover, the re emergence of the Baloch nationalist insurgency also complicated the internal situation of Pakistan's security; Balochistan obtained a new geo-strategic significance and became focus of US as a Trans border energy route.

The Baloch insurgency was recharged with the development of Gwadar sea port and their demand to share the benefits of Gwadar Project attracted strong US interest in Balochistan because it has the capacity to convert Balochistan in a main corridor of energy transportation from Central Asia and Iran to other parts of the region in minimum time. The US has to maintain a crucial and essential role in the new great game of resource development in Balochistan and in other parts of Asia. Therefore, all the three prominent factors; the Taliban militancy, Baloch insurgency and future significance of Balochistan as an energy transit route, played a very strong role in attaining and developing serious attention of US to Balochistan. (Aazar, 2010:164) Prior to that, Balochistan due to its defensive proximity with Afghanistan had a significant hand in the early triumph of US war on terror post 9/11. Pakistan provided US the access to airspace and airfields in Balochistan for US aerial bombing on Kabul to destroy the Taliban regime and their network in Afghanistan. (Aazar, 2010:165) Balochistan has been playing a central role in the geo strategic development of South and West Asia long before the US war on terror post 9/11 but during war, Balochistan's territorial proximity to Afghanistan was a great strategic advantage which was fully exploited by US forces.

American involvement in Balochistan is somehow blamed for supporting Baloch insurgents in order to deal with the Chinese influence in Balochistan. It is believed that CIA agents in Afghanistan provide financial support to the Baloch insurgents. it is discovered that the US spy agency CIA is involved in recruitment of local agents in Balochistan to locate the members of Quetta based Taliban Shura. The Quetta Shura is a term used by the Americans for the Mullah Omar-led Taliban commanders. (Waheed, 2011, Apr.27) The incident of the arrest of a CIA Spy Raymond Davis in a murder case of two Pakistani in January 2011 increased the tension in Pakistan-US relationship and also exposed the CIA immoral activities in Balochistan. Above all, CIA's activities in Balochistan are clear sign of US growing interest in this region. In fact, Creation of "Greater Balochistan" is the top most agenda of US, India and Israel cooperation. (Hassan, 2011, May.04) Apparently, US propagate her concerns for the stabilization of Pakistan, but at the same time, she does have a deep interest in delaying projects that would enable China to be strategically present in this region and establish herself as an emerging economic power particularly at the Port of Gwadar. Americans are also interested in increasing their influence in Gwadar and other parts of Balochistan. Therefore, the any harm caused to China-Pakistan joint venture of development of Gwadar port is one of the main US interest in Balochistan. Thus, any type of violence in Balochistan protects US interests in the region because it is helpful in delaying the development projects between China and Pakistan.

The basic objective is to control the increasing Chinese existence in Balochistan. China is an economic rival to US and its presence in Balochistan is not beneficial for the strategic and economic future of US. The Gwadar port can serve as the marine base for Chinese forces which is a matter of great anxiety for US. The Indian Ocean, near the Strait of Hormuz, a route for the export of oil from the Gulf States, will definitely come under the observation and influence of China will create serious problems for US in maintaining its monopoly in the region. The divergence of interests of various powers is also worsening the situation in Balochistan. Under the unstable and insecure circumstances in Balochistan, China will not move forward to provide any further technical or financial assistance to Pakistan for the development and progress of any economic project. (Mazari, 2005, Feb.2)

The clear objectives of US are to deteriorate Pakistan, Iran and Afghanistan to establish a strong hold in Central Asian Region and harming Chinese economic interests in African and Middle East through creating obstacles in the Gwadar project. This can be possible only by supporting Balochistan Nationalist Movement to disturb the situation and creating unfavorable environment for any economic investment by China. "CIA supported elements are using America, United Kingdom, India and Afghanistan as their platforms for organizing, planning and operational bases for execution of the plan of Independent Balochistan. Moreover, some militarily supported political lobbies of America and UK are facilitating anti Pakistan elements to carryout nefarious activities against Pakistan". (Hassan, 2011, May.04) US interests are also intended to counter Iran, The United Sates is not happy with the expansion of Chinese energy and military assets, particularly so close to Iran and the Gulf region. An instable Balochistan is far more preferable to US than a stable and economically flourishing Balochistan. Any disturbance in Balochistan reduces the possibility of development of the IranPakistan oil pipeline. The US has openly shown her discomfort with the proposed pipeline project. (Bansal, 2008:182).

The US is not only interested in Balochistan, but also has strong concerns about the massive resources of Central Asian States and Balochistan is the most convenient available path to these resources. US is much anxious to get control over the whole region for their future security plans and eliminate the influence of their only rival and competitor China.

US interest in Balochistan highlights two long term objectives, firstly, US has to create a secure and reliable route to all the energy resources of Central Asia to USA, and secondly to contain China. Balochistan provides the shortest passage between the Indian Ocean and Central Asia outside of the Gulf. Therefore any unrest in Balochistan directly affects and effectively discourages Trans-Afghan pipeline project that is planned for transferring Central Asian resources to South Asia as the control of economically strong and established states of South Asia over this region will not allow US to flourish economic hegemony.

US and Russia have always focused their interest on Balochistan to exploit the land as a tool to make Pakistan a weaker state. Russia has encouraged the "Secessionist Movement of Sindhu Desh, Pakhtonistan or (Independent) or Greater Balochistan" (Najmuddin, 1984: 60). With the Soviet occupation of Afghanistan in 1979, it was predicted that the Soviet would try to take possession of deep-sea-water port on the Indian Ocean, and the Baloch insurgents and their rebellious activities would be significantly helpful to Soviet attempt. (Harrison, 1981:173) Having controlled Afghanistan, Russia tried hard to convince the Baloch to revolt against central government of Pakistan and the Baloch insurgents were assured by Russia that they would be given autonomy over Balochistan after the Soviet completely conquers Afghanistan. (Ismail, 2014:184) The Russian strategy was to establish full control in Kabul as their base and to raise the issues of Pakhtunistan and Greater Balochistan from the land of Kabul, and try to separate and disconnect Balochistan from Pakistan and to either merge it with Afghanistan or to create a new independent country that should be under full control of Moscow. "Whether Russian loose their interest in Afghanistan, yet in Balochistan and Indian Ocean its interest would not die down" (Ahmad, 1992: 253).

Russia also needs a suitable corridor to the warm waters of the Indian Oceans. Like USA, Russia also wants to preserve its monopoly over all the energy resources of Central Asia. At present all the Central Asian States (CAS) are entirely dependent on Russia for export of their energy projects. Soviet Interests in Balochistan have various aspects which are not much different than that of US. Russia wants to control the Gulf oil, which constitute almost 60 percent of world's known reserves. Any trouble in Balochistan gives Russia a hope to discourage Trans-Afhgan pipeline or any other similar projects.

A Russian influenced Balochistan would bring the natural resources of the Indian Ocean and Antarctica under direct control and pressure of Russia. Fish catch from Indian Ocean and particularly from Arabian Sea, which constitutes almost 1/3rd of total fish catch, will be transported to Central Asia Republics over lands, without any trouble, in less time, thus will be more economical. (Ahmad,1992: 256) Balochistan will provide Russia the shortest route to the world's largest untapped mineral resources which are located at Antarctica. (Mazhar et al. 2012:119). All these future probabilities which can provide economical stability to Russia are related to Balochistan.

Balochistan is the only Province of Pakistan which shares direct border with Iran. The geographical location of Balochistan plays a very significant role in shaping the relations between Pakistan and Iran in the socio-cultural and economic perspectives. Balochistan is the only factor which can directly influence Pak-Iran relations both negatively and positively. Unfortunately, there are certain disappointing and inadequate factors which are creating confusions, doubts and stress and making Balochistan a weakening factor in Pak-Iran relations. Balochistan plays a key role in Pak-Iran economic and social integration. The close relation between the people of both countries on the basis of many religious and cultural similarities significantly increases the economic, cultural and social communication between the people of Iran and Pakistan. Infrastructure projects of roads and railways networks can make possible easy trade within the region and cross border.

The proposed venture of oil refinery in Hub will do a lot for the promotion and betterment of economic cooperation between Pakistan and Iran, which has been going through a tensed situation in the past few years because of political misunderstanding over Afghanistan issue. (Khan, 2012:137)

The project will provide an economic momentum to this least developed province Balochistan and will help to meet the increasing demand of high speed diesel. It will also make possible the exploration of oil and gas in Baloch region. The construction of gas pipeline between Iran-Pakistan is the most positive aspect of economic relationship. The proposed gas pipeline project would bring economic and political profit to both the countries equally.

The ongoing insurgency in Balochistan has badly affected the friendly relations of the two countries as the Iranian government blame Pakistan's involvement in the Balochistan based Jandullah Organization which is a group of Baloch nationalist militants which is also creating political disturbances in Iranian areas with the active support and cooperation of USA. (Khan, 2012:137) Moreover, the growing competition between the Pakistani sea port at Gwadar and the Iranian Port Chabahar, and strong rivalry between India, China and Pakistan to increase their influence in Central Asia through these ports, have already disturbed economic and political relations of Iran and Pakistan.

Chabahar seaport is situated at about 70 kilometer distance from Pakistani seaport of Gwadar, developed with Chinese assistance. Both these ports are great competitors as both are constructed with the same objectives in a same region. The difference between the two lies in the fact that Gwadar port is facing many issues like the bad security situation in Balochistan and lack of proper infrastructure of connecting links to main highways.

The project is not making progress due to slow and process of development. While there is no such situation at Chabahar which is being developed rapidly and also has gained attention and interest of China successfully. Not only China but also Iran, Afghanistan and India are equally emphasizing at Chabahar Port ahead of Gwadar as regional trade and commerce center.

The Chabahar seaport is located outside the Strait of Hormuz, in Iran's Free Economic and Industrial Zone. This port is away from the passage of heavy seatraffic in the Persian Gulf waters and provides more easy entrance to ships besides connecting it to Afghanistan and Central Asia. A road and rail communication system is also being constructed between Chabahar and Herat to connect with Central Asian States. India is seriously interested in the development of this seaport just to avoid Pakistani route to Iran, Afghanistan and Central Asian States. (Hussain, 2015:146)

Chabahar is somehow is an Indian financed Port and a part of the Indian plan to develop another mean of transportation in eastern Iran to counter and reduce the emerging influence of Pakistani port of Gwadar. India intends to connect Chabahar port with Central Asian countries through roads and railway to avoid Pakistan, and to reduce the dependency of Central Asian countries on the port of Gwadar. (Khan, 2012:135) As Gwadar port is expected to improve not only Pakistan's but also Chinese influence in Central Asia and beyond. Gwadar can be a potential trade route for the landlocked Central Asian States and this new trade route would have tremendous economic impetus to Pakistan in the form of new and great investments as the CARs will rely upon Pakistan for their trade and commerce.

Chabahar is providing India with an easy access to Afghanistan through the Indian Ocean. An agreement between India, Iran and Afghanistan has been signed according to that, Central Asia and Afghanistan are bound to give special preference and tariff reduction to Indian trade goods. (Khan, 2012:135) Therefore, Gwadar port is a threatening factor to

Indian trade through Indian Ocean. Being so close to the Straits of Hormuz, Gwadar would create negative impact on India's commercial interest by enabling Pakistan to implement vast control over entire energy routes. Gwadar will also enable China to observe and examine Indian naval activity in the Persian Gulf and Arabian Sea and any future maritime cooperation between India and Iran will be easily monitored by China. Similarly, Iran has clear apprehensions about the use of Gwadar port by the United States as a base to monitor activities inside Iran. (Asia Times, 2005,April.29).

India also is trying to secure energy routes to counter the growing Chinese influence in the Arabian Sea, Persian Gulf, and the Indian Ocean. So India chose Iran as her economic and strategic ally. India has spent huge amount on the construction and development of Iranian Port of Chahbahar. Iran is already working on Chahbahar port in sistan Baluchistan, which will facilitate Indian trade activities to Afghanistan and Central Asia through roads and rail links. The Chinese involvement in Pakistani Gwadar and Indian influence on Iranian Chahbahar has resulted not only in economic competition and strategic rivalry between India, Pakistan and China but also has increased risk of controversy for the economic and natural resources of Central Asia.

The growing competition between China and India has an unfavorable impact on the Pak-Iran relations. Gwadar and Chahbahar are the main causes of geostrategic and economic competition. China is largely alarmed by the growing Indian growth in the Indian Ocean and the Arabian Sea. Moreover, the progress and warmth in Indo-US relations since the conclusion of US-India civilian nuclear cooperation and mutual aid between India and Iran in Afghanistan and Central Asia became a matter of serious concern for China's long-standing strategic and economic objectives in the region. (Khan, 2013: 79-80)

India is establishing good relations with Pakistani neighbors; Iran and Afghanistan just to contain Pakistan and to counterbalance Chinese emerging power, because China is the only power which is quite capable of competing and suppress Indian hegemony and supremacy in the region. As Indian navy is greater than that of Pakistan, therefore to surpass India, Pakistan needs Chinese support and cooperation in the Port of Gwadar which is in the best welfare of both China and Pakistan. Through the Gwadar, China can keep a strict watch on Indian approach and emergence in the Indian Ocean, the Arabian Sea, and Persian Gulf. (Khan, 2013: 79-80).

So far as Afghanistan is concerned, she has historically been remained a dispute between major powers. Mostly, Afghanistan remains in state of war and process of nation building, so there is no functional type of economy in Afghanistan and mostly depends on limited agriculture which is not meeting the basic food requirements of Afghans and they have to depend upon foreign donated food for survival. (Shah, 2007:65) The Turkmenistan-Afghanistan-Pakistan-Iran (TAPI) pipeline project is a big hope to help restore the Afghan economy as the project could bring in over 300 million dollars royalty to the country and other foreign investments in the project may do a lot to stabilize and revive Afghan economy with the renovation of other infrastructure. Afghan transit trade was earlier handled through the Karachi port, but now the Gwadar port will serve this purpose well. Afghanistan has admitted the significance of Gwadar as a gateway to wealth for Afghanistan and also has offered support for the development of the Gwadar port. (The Dawn, 2003, Aug.5)

CHINA'S SOUTH ASIAN INTERESTS AND POLICIES

China's broad objective in South Asia is to expand multi-dimensional cooperative relations with all the countries of that region. "Multi-dimensional" signifies military ties as well as more innocuous political and economic cooperation. "All" means both India and India's smaller neighbors: Pakistan, Myanmar, Nepal, Sri Lanka, Bangladesh, Bhutan, and the Maldives. India has sometimes objected to China's relations — especially military-security ties — with these countries. Beijing views

South Asian countries as "neighbors" with whom it is especially important to have friendly, cooperative ties both to increase China's own economic and political influence and to lessen the ability of potentially hostile powers (currently the U.S.) to injure China's interests.

Economically, China seeks to draw South Asia's resources into China's development drive. India with its fast-growing, industrialized, and relatively affluent economy has become China's strongest economic partner in South Asia. Two-way Sino-Indian trade in 2003 was $7.6 billion, compared to $2.4 billion for Sino-Pakistan, $1.4 billion for Sino-Bangladesh, and $1.1 billion for Sino-Myanmar trade. During their April 2005 meeting, Wen Jiabao and Manmohan Singh agreed to increase trade to $20 billion by 2008. While that amount is paltry compared to China's trade with countries like Japan, Germany, South Korea, or the United States, it leads China's South Asian trade by far.

The simple fact is that India produces much more that Chinese firms want to purchase than do Pakistan, Bangladesh, or Myanmar — let alone the small countries like Nepal, Bhutan, or the Maldives. In 2003, China imported $1 billion more from India than it exported to it, while Chinese exports to Pakistan were three times the value of China's imports, exports to Bangladesh were forty times the value of China's imports, and exports to Myanmar were over five times the volume of imports. While these figures are based on official statistics and do not reflect smuggling (which is substantial in the case of Myanmar), the broader point is that India simply has more to offer China. From India China imports a wide array of mining and industrial products: steel and iron ore, zinc, aluminum and aluminum products, copper and copper products, acids and alkalines, dyes, colouring, alcohol and other chemical products, rubber, plastics, cotton, wool, thread and yarn, leather, and machinery and machine parts. From Pakistan, in contrast, China buys largely cotton, yarn, and leather.

China also recognizes that in key economic-technological areas it has much to learn from India. Chinese analysts recognize

India's world-leadership position in computer software creation and aspire to learn from India in this area, meshing these strengths with China's existing strengths in computer hardware production to help catapult China to world-class-economy status. There are no comparable inducements in the case of the other South Asian countries. Pakistan and Bangladesh offer attractive markets for Chinese consumer goods and machine tools. But the ability of these poor countries to purchase Chinese goods, and to produce things useful to China's booming industry, is limited compared to India's. China has not been able to forge with the South Asian countries a robust foreign energy-for-Chinese-capital-goods swap such as it has engineered with Iran. The exploitation of Bangladesh's natural gas deposits could conceivably overcome this structural imbalance, with Bangladesh entering into an energy for Chinese capital goods swap similar to that characterizing the Sino-Iranian relation.

Politically, there are interrupted visits between China and the larger South Asian countries at the minister and vice minister level to "exchange views" on various bilateral, regional, and international subjects. Beijing seeks to engage South Asian governments in dialogue and cooperation on substantive subjects of mutual concern: countering narcotics traffic, smuggling, and terrorism; stabilizing the Karzai government in Afghanistan; or dealing with Tibetan presence and activities in various South Asian countries. Beijing also strives to line up South Asian support on the Taiwan subject: to counter Taiwan efforts to expand ties and to guarantee South Asian neutrality in the event of a U.S.-PRC clash over Taiwan.

Friendship with China is often attractive to smaller South Asian countries living in India's shadow. People in those countries often see ties with China as affirming their independence from India and as a way of gaining bargaining leverage with New Delhi. China's voice in the U.N. Security Council is valued by South Asian governments because of Beijing's occasional willingness to say a few words on behalf of smaller South Asian countries, or even to criticize Washington on behalf of those smaller countries. China has expressed a desire for observer status in the South Asian Association for Regional Cooperation (SAARC) where its ability to offset India will be valued by the other South Asian states.

China views military links as part of the normal repertoire of international cooperation and seeks to expand military ties with South Asian countries. Every year China exchanges with Pakistan, India, Bangladesh, and Myanmar two or three delegations at the deputy chief of staff through defence minister level, or from military regions, military academies, or defence industrial agencies. China has recently attempted to institutionalize exchange of views with the larger South Asian countries in the security / military areas. At the political level, there are periodic discussions of regional security subjects of common concern. Bangladesh, Pakistan, and Myanmar have been preferred and heavy customers for Chinese military equipment. Chinese training, maintenance, and parts have come with equipment purchases. Exchange of intelligence between China and Pakistan and Myanmar is routine, with Yangong providing important electronic listening posts at several points in the Bay of Bengal / Strait of Malacca area. Chinese naval squadrons have made friendly port calls to Pakistani (1985, 1993, 2001), Bangladeshi (1986, 1995), Myanmar (2001), and Indian (1993, 2001) ports. In October 2003, the PLA-Navy conducted its first-ever joint exercises with the Pakistani navy in the East China Sea. The next month it conducted joint exercises in the same region with the Indian Navy. China assists Pakistan's missile development and its nuclear energy efforts. Although China's involvement in the latter is under IAEA supervision, the intrinsic fungibility of nuclear materials and know-how makes it likely there is some spill over to Pakistan's nuclear weapons capabilities.

In the past India, has objected to China's military links with South Asian nations. In 1989, for example, a Nepalese attempt to purchase Chinese weapons and initiate an intelligence exchange agreement with China precipitated severe Indian economic sanctions that forced Kathmandu to abandon the objectionable policies. Given New Dehli's opposition to Sino-

South Asian military cooperation, Beijing's insistence on forging such links is testament to its determination to become a multi-dimensional power in the region, and its refusal to cede South Asia to an Indian sphere of influence.

China's response to Indian concerns over China-South Asian military cooperation has been to assert that since China does not have aggressive or malevolent intentions, China's military cooperation with India's neighbors does not threaten India. If India is concerned about China's military ties with the smaller South Asian nations, Beijing argues, the proper course is to increase mutual trust between China and India via security dialogues and other such venues. Or if New Delhi is unhappy with Chinese military cooperation with India's South Asian neighbors, China is quite willing to expand such cooperation with India itself. There is no valid reason to object to these friendly, cooperative relations, Beijing argues. In fact, such objections manifest "anti-China" sentiments and hostility toward China, which will be answer in kind by China.

The sort of punishment contained in this implied threat was demonstrated during the eighteen months after India's May 1998 nuclear tests that New Delhi had justified as a response to threat from China. After the Indian tests with their China threat justification, Beijing cancelled scheduled sessions of the Joint Working Group on the boundary. Chinese media rhetoric became harsher, even resurrecting charges of Indian "hegemony." Beijing urged Washington and the U.N. Security Council to adopt tough measures against India, and to target mainly India, not Pakistan's "response" to India's tests. Beijing hinted it might shift to a more pro-Pakistan position on Kashmir. Beijing's carrot and stick approach seems to have been fairly successful. India has agreed to open-ended cooperation with China, even while China expands military ties with India's neighbors.

INDIA'S CHINA POLICY

Certain scholars believe that India's China policy has undergone three major phases of adjustment since the end of the Cold War: the pre-1998 phase policy of reconciliation; the 1998–2000 phase policy of hostility; and the 2000 to present phase policy of engagement. The second phase around the time of the 1998 nuclear tests featured harangues from the Indian government regarding the 'China threat' and a brief deadlock in Sino–Indian relations. The author, however, believes that two, rather than three, phases of adjustment are applicable to an explanation of the state of bilateral relations between China and India in the post-Cold War era.

When considering India's overall strategic aims at the time of the 1998 nuclear tests and the implications and specific actions of its subsequent China policy, it is difficult to pinpoint two 180 degree-policy shifts in the course of just two years. Facts demonstrate that India named China as a threat at the time of the 1998 tests as a matter of expedience to acquiesce in the anti-China stance of certain parties in the United States and other Western nations; it was a ploy whose purpose was to divert attention from and rationalize the nuclear tests, thereby dispelling any notion of sanctions.

It should be borne in mind, however, that India's understanding of comprehensive national strength deepened after the Cold War, as did its leaders' belief that nuclear arms and credible nuclear deterrence were hallmarks of a superpower. Entering the nuclear club was consequently a stride towards achieving one of the sub-continent's greatest national aspirations. The Rao government, which pursued a China policy of reconciliation and engagement, had made preparations for nuclear tests but stopped short of carrying them out for fear of the potential burden on the newly recovered economy of international sanctions.

Prime Minister Vajpayee and other political leaders repeatedly and publicly expressed soon after the 1998 tests that India had no wish to hold China as an enemy or a threat, stating, to the contrary, their desire for reinforced friendly relations. At no point during this period did diplomatic engagement between India and China cease. Indian External Affairs Minister Jaswant Singh's visit to China in June 1999 demonstrated that the Sino–Indian relationship had recovered in the space of a year from any damage that the nuclear tests had inflicted upon it. That becoming a nuclear power while maintaining stable relations with China were post-Cold War India's strategic goals was also implied by the sub-continent's explicit moves towards repairing its relationship with China. The 1998 nuclear tests constituted no fundamental change to India's China policy and should, within the scope of Sino–Indian relations, be regarded as a minor episode. Moreover, the shift of India's China policy in 1988 was not prompted by any change of security concept; Prime Minister Rajiv Gandhi's trip to China that year was motivated by the fact of Sino–Soviet reconciliation. Changes in security concept explicitly propelled India's; post-Cold War China policy adjustments. This book, therefore, primarily examines developments and changes in India's China policy after the Cold War. It holds that a substantive change indeed occurred; specifically from one of hostility and antagonism during the Cold War (especially 1962–1988) to reconciliation and engagement thereafter. This policy change, however, was by no means instantaneous but characterized by gradual, phased development. Two, rather than three, phases of adjustment tally with changes in India's post-Cold War security concept.

India's China Policy from the End of the Cold War to 1998

Indian leaders believed after 1962 that hostilities between China and India were inevitable, and viewed China as a major enemy. Prime Minister Indira Gandhi considered Sino–Indian antagonism as going far beyond border disputes, and that China was pursuing the more 'complex' policy of pressing India on all fronts and, moreover, displacing the sub-continent by establishing its own dominant position in the Asian power hierarchy. The goal of India's China policy during this period, therefore, was to ensure its supremacy over China in Asia and, in the event of armed conflict, to avoid repeating mistakes that had led to its defeat in the 1962 Sino–Indian conflict. India's policy at the time can be so summarized: strengthen military capability and deployment; seek aid from major powers, respectively, the United States, United Kingdom and USSR; and support Chinese separatist forces. After the Cold War ended, however, changes in India's domestic and international situation brought tremendous challenges, and its position as regards China and its related policy goals showed clear adjustments. India considered China as a nation going through a reflective, 'inward looking' period and, as such, had no intention of attacking the sub-continent. In the short-term, therefore, it constituted no threat. The goal of India's new China policy was to maintain stability in Sino–Indian relations, ensure peaceful borders and create conditions suitable for India to gather its resources and restore economic and military strength. The specific policy adjustments were as follows.

Achieve Simultaneous Progress in Solving Border Disputes

For almost two decades after 1962, India made resolution of border disputes a pre-condition for normalizing relations with China. Its insistence in this regard was the main reason for the longstanding chill in Sino–Indian relations. Although the two nations restored ambassadorial-level diplomatic relations in 1976, and in 1981 agreed to begin talks on the border issue, this principled standpoint did not change. Upon meeting with visiting then-External Affairs Minister Vajpayee early in 1979, Comrade Deng Xiaoping proposed an agreement that would provide 'a package solution' for relevant border disputes. He said that if it were not possible completely to resolve border disputes at an early date, he would consider cooperation in other areas. But it was not until 1988 during Rajiv Gandhi's trip to China that the Indian government accepted this suggestion and formally initiated the process of normalizing bilateral relations which the successive Indian governments pursued and implemented after the Cold War ended. It is notable that during the time the two sides promoted negotiations on border issues they also exchanged high-level visits in which the two nations signed cooperative agreements in such areas as trade, technology, education and culture, and that cooperation between them grew ever greater in depth and breadth.

Shift Strategies on Border Talks

As India needed a peaceful, stable environment in which to concentrate on economic recovery, securing Sino–Indian borders was its primary goal in the early 1990s. Because of India's; pre-1988 insistence on not normalizing Sino–Indian relations until the border issues were settled, there were suspicions that the sub-continent was 'taking improvements in bilateral relations as a bargaining chip through which to force China to yield in border disputes'. India consequently insisted in the talks that began in 1981 on its own position as regards a segmented solution to the issue. India's objective understanding of the complexity of the Sino–Indian border dispute after the Cold War and of realistic strategic considerations and needs prompted an adjusted strategy for these talks. This was manifest in its suggestion of a gradual solution to border disputes: the first step would be to stabilize the Line of Actual Control (LAC) situation and eliminate disagreements over its demarcation; the second to reach agreement on preserving peace and tranquillity along the LAC; and the third to take measures to establish mutual trust along the LAC.

This accomplished, the two nations could then address substantive problems in their border dispute. This tentative plan enabled India and China to approach a consistent position whereby the two sides worked to achieve a solution to Sino–Indian border disputes and create an atmosphere of reasonableness and peace. The two nations made progress, signing in 1993 the Agreement on Maintenance of Peace and Tranquillity along the Line of Actual Control in the Sino–Indian Border Areas, and in 1996 the Agreement Between the Government of the Republic of India and the Government of the People's Republic of China on Confidence-Building Measures in the Military Field Along the Line of Actual Control in the India–China Border Areas. India saw these two agreements as on the one hand ensuring the two sides could resolve border disputes peacefully without resorting to violence, and on the other that border disputes would not inhibit the development of their bilateral relations.

Tibetan Issue and do not Provoke China

Leaders of India's independence movement had at the time of the British Raj followed the British colonialist concept of Tibet as a 'buffer region' between India and China. After winning independence, therefore, the Indian government supported from the very beginning the so-called 'Tibetan independence movement'. At around the time of the founding of the People's Republic of China, India seized the opportunity offered by China's political upheaval to promote the international standing of the local Tibetan government and thwart China's liberation of Tibet. New Delhi continued unremittingly in its efforts to convince China's central government, even during the 1950s heyday of Sino–Indian amity, to give Tibet substantial autonomy and to reduce to the greatest extent possible the size of its garrison there.

After the insurrection of 1959 the Indian government was more overt in its support of Tibet, giving asylum to fugitive rebels and propping up the so-called 'Tibetan Government in Exile' established by the Dalai Lama in 1960 in the Indian city of Dharamsala. India further incited and encouraged Tibetan independence activities after the Sino–Indian conflict of 1962. In truth, Indian leaders considered their support for exiled Tibetans' separatist activities as an effective containment against China. But when Prime Minister Rajiv Gandhi visited China in 1988 he issued the statement: 'The Indian side reiterates the long-standing and consistent policy of the Government of India that Tibet is an autonomous region of China and that anti-China political activities by Tibetan elements are not permitted on Indian soil,' which implied India's change of approach from that of support for Tibetan independence.

Indian leaders reiterated this pledge after the Cold War ended and imposed limits on Tibetan fugitives' anti-China political activities. For instance, Indian officials would generally contact the Dalai Lama and leaders of the so-called Tibetan government in exile before a visit by Chinese leaders to India, requesting that they refrain from Tibetan protests, demonstrations or other anti-Chinese behaviour.

Yet, differences still exist between China and India on the issue of Tibetan autonomy. Although, proceeding from the requirement of preserving stable Sino–Indian relations, the post-Cold War Indian government has been low-key in its support of the Dalai Lama and other Tibetan fugitives, this does not signify a substantial change in its strategic treatment of the Tibetan issue.

Changes in India's China Policy from 1999 to Present

Achieving recovery, contending for the status of global power had been India's ambition for decades. The growth of the sub-continent's comprehensive strength and improvements in the international environment in the late 1990s presented to it a real possibility of realizing this ambition, as well as a number of other unprecedented strategic opportunities. Against this backdrop, reconciliation with China and the unchanged overall direction of the relationship produced several new adjustments to the positions and goals of India's China policy. At this stage, India saw China neither as enemy nor friend, believing that cooperation could coexist with competition between the two nations. India still considered China as constituting no threat in the short term, but began focusing on long-term trends in the balance of power. The emphasis of the goals of its new China policy are on ensuring that future Sino–Indian relations are of benefit to India by making China a positive factor in the process of its rise. Maintaining the stability of Sino–Indian relations remains fundamental. The new policy adjustments are as follows.

Expand Economic Cooperation with China

Trade between the two nations ceased after the 1962 Sino–Indian Border Conflict, and did not resume until 1977. The volume of trade between the two sides in the 1980s wavered at around roughly Us." million. But after the Cold War ended, Sino–Indian trade experienced a seemingly spontaneous phase of rapid development. The trade volume between China and India increased from $264 million in 1991 to $1.988 billion in 1999—a yearly average of 31.2%—or an increase factor of 6.5 over eight years. Indian leaders' concerns about India's economic recovery nonetheless maintained at this point the China policy focus on stabilizing political relations and establishing tranquil borders. Indian leaders' understanding of economic strength and security having becoming more profound since 1999, their enthusiasm for developing bilateral trade soared.

As China and India were the world's two most rapidly developing nations, Indian leaders could see the obvious potential for trade between them and that strengthening bilateral trade would be of great mutual benefit. Also that close economic ties could have a stabilizing influence on their political relationship. Statistics show that bilateral trade since 1999 has entered into a new period of growth. The average yearly growth to 2006 was 44.4%—a rate which exceeded that of the preceeding period and which is being achieved on an ever-stronger numerical foundation. The volume of Sino–Indian trade reached US$24.8 billion in 2006, having increased by a factor of 11.5 over 1999 and one of 93 over 1991. China became India's second largest trading partner in 2006, and India China's tenth largest. It may be said that the role of Sino–Indian trade has grown from one unworthy of mention to a decisive aspect of the overall bilateral relationship.

6

Benefits and Risks of China-Pakistan Economic Corridor

Traditionally, China and Pakistan have cooperated closely at the strategic and political levels. Now the two nations are making efforts to expand their bilateral collaboration economically as well. The construction of the China-Pakistan Economic Corridor (CPEC) is a milestone that signifies this shift. At its core, the CPEC is a large-scale initiative to build energy, highway, and port infrastructure to deepen economic connections between China and Pakistan.

This initiative has been well-received in both countries, although it is not without its problems. Nevertheless, China and Pakistan regard the CPEC as a new source of potential synergy between their respective national development strategies, which may help the two countries translate their close political cooperation into multifaceted economic cooperation, attain mutual benefits, and achieve win-win outcomes. For the economic corridor to reach its potential, however, there are security and political challenges in Pakistan that must be addressed.

China first proposed the corridor project in May 2013. Chinese President Xi Jinping then visited Pakistan in April 2015, and both sides agreed to elevate their relationship to an "all-weather strategic partnership." During Xi's visit, the two countries signed fifty-one agreements at an estimated value of $46 billion.

The CPEC is now moving into the implementation phase. On May 6, 2016, there was an opening ceremony held in the city of Sukkur in Pakistan's Sindh Province, as construction began on a section of highway between Sukkur and the city of Multan—it will be part of a network of highways that will connect the cities of Peshawar and Karachi. This network is a major component of the CPEC's plans for infrastructure expansion, which highlights the progress the two nations have achieved thus far in the area of transportation. In addition, on November 13, 2016, the first large shipment of Chinese goods went through the port of Gwadar, a flagship CPEC project in Pakistan's southwestern province of Balochistan.

China considers these development initiatives a potential source of stability and prosperity for both countries. From a Chinese perspective, cooperation in the areas of security and economics are closely intertwined, and improvements on one side can improve the other.

It is almost as though security and economics are two separate wheels on the same vehicle, and both need to be spinning to move things forward. China believes economic development can strengthen Pakistan's internal stability, thus reinvigorating the latter's economy through investment in infrastructure projects as well as the construction of oil and gas pipelines. China hopes this will create a certain level of stability within Pakistan and in turn stabilize China's western periphery, particularly the province of Xinjiang.

More broadly, the CPEC has to be understood in the context of China's strategic interests in East Asia and the way the United States has challenged them. Faced with such difficulties, China hopes it can expand its strategic space by heading west. Pakistan serves as a crucial bridge between China and Central Asia, South Asia, and the Middle East. Security and stability in Pakistan will make it possible for China to exercise greater influence in these regions and to ensure security at home. This is why China is willing to pour vast amounts of resources into the economic corridor—based on the logic of improving security through economic development.

Likewise, Pakistan has realized that no other country places such high strategic importance in its economic relationship with Pakistan as China does. Pakistan also greatly values the economic corridor and views it as mutually beneficial in terms *of politics and economic development. According to Pakistan* 2025—a blueprint for economic development published in 2014 by Pakistan's Ministry of Planning, Development, and Reform—Pakistan aims to advance from being a lower-middle-income nation to an upper-middle-income nation by 2025. To achieve this goal, Pakistan hopes to attract increasing amounts of foreign investment. The country is working to improve its overall economy by constructing energy projects and other forms of infrastructure, to create employment opportunities for its populace, and to improve its governance.

The logic behind this strategy is that fundamentally improving Pakistan's economy will help alleviate the challenges posed by political extremists, radicals, and jihadists. China and Pakistan share the belief that economic development can help stabilize Pakistan and improve its domestic security situation. However, China also recognizes that the security, political, and cultural risks and uncertainties facing the economic corridor cannot be overlooked.

The first of these risks is terrorism, which has long affected Pakistan's internal security and stability. Although Pakistan has worked hard to strike at religious extremism and terrorist activities, its problems with terrorism have not substantially improved in recent years. Because the CPEC is so important to the Pakistani government, these projects' construction sites and engineering personnel may become targets for religious as well as nationalist extremists. Indeed, there already have been numerous occasions when Chinese engineers working in Pakistan have been attacked or even lost their lives. In May 2016, for instance, engineers in Karachi were attacked by Sindh separatists. Fortunately, no Chinese personnel were wounded or killed. Then in September, Baloch rebels killed at least two Chinese engineers and injured many others. Moreover, several large-scale terrorist attacks in Balochistan have killed dozens of people, which shows that the security situation in this province where China has key projects is far from ideal.

The security threat posed by terrorism remains ongoing, despite the economic benefits that the CPEC can offer Pakistan. The corridor aims to enhance the well-being of people throughout the country and bring long-term prosperity and stability. The Pakistani authorities, meanwhile, have promised China they will do everything possible to ensure the safety of Chinese workers. This is a feasible commitment in the short term. However, over time, it will become more difficult for Pakistan to guarantee the security of the CPEC's growing transportation networks, which will require increasing investments of security personnel and material support. It will likely become uncertain in the future whether Pakistan can maintain a strong enough military presence to ensure the security of all these transportation routes.

Second, Pakistan's domestic politics is also important to the CPEC's success. The country's political system has never been particularly stable. Political power oscillates between military and civilian leaders. General Pervez Musharraf's resignation as president in 2008 ended the latest period of military rule, and from that point onward, the military has been pushed from center stage. In the 2013 election, the Pakistan People's Party lost power after the Pakistan Muslim League Nawaz defeated it. The successful completion of this election, as well as the smooth transition of power that ensued, was the first time in Pakistan's history that a civilian government was able to serve out its entire term. This was a sign of improvement for Pakistan's democracy.

On the other hand, Pakistan's traditional political culture, which is almost feudal in nature, also continues to play an important role. Powerful families based in different provinces, such as the Bhuttos and the Sharifs, have typically held political power. Behind the party politics are local interests groups associated with these families.

Various parties within Pakistan have disagreed a lot about how CPEC transportation routes should be mapped out. The competing parties are primarily interested in how the cake should be divided, so to speak. To strengthen its respective standing among the electorate, each of Pakistan's political parties hopes the CPEC will pass through the region it represents, allowing its local community to enjoy the corridor's benefits. In fact, since the initiative was first presented in 2013, the debate over which route the CPEC would follow has caused substantial delays. The construction of the corridor has just begun. It is expected that competition among Pakistan's domestic political groups will continue to affect its future implementation.

Yet the CPEC will not only serve as a roadway that simply connects point A to point B—the initiative is designed to do more. The corridor also aims to facilitate multisectoral economic cooperation in finance, trade, energy, and industry.

Amid a market slowdown and high unemployment rates, Pakistani Prime Minister Nawaz Sharif came back into office in 2013 with the intent of reinvigorating the economy, and he undertook a series of measures to improve Pakistan's economic prospects. One was lowering barriers to foreign investment. As for addressing energy shortages, Pakistan has been making efforts to restructure its energy industry and increase its electricity production. At the same time, the government has worked hard to strengthen investment in infrastructure, has moved forward with tax reforms, and has focused on increasing revenue and reducing expenditures. In addition, the government has adopted other measures to develop its market economy. It has overseen reforms for state-run enterprises and encouraged market privatization.

These measures are already starting to take effect. The country's GDP is growing at a stronger rate, and the economy is improving. For the time being, however, it will still remain unclear whether these economic advances can actually alleviate Pakistan's serious security and stability problems.

Cultural considerations and public relations should be also taken into account when evaluating the CPEC's prospects for economic success. Ordinary citizens in China and Pakistan are not very familiar with each other. The countries' leaders have built an all-weather friendship and close political relationship over the years, but this is not yet true of the two societies at large.

As China and Pakistan gradually expand cooperation, there will be an increasing number of Chinese corporations investing in Pakistan. Different cultural practices and ways of thinking could cause misunderstandings, and this could negatively affect CPEC projects. For these corporations to be successful, they will need to understand local cultures, norms, and rules. Having information about and services for doing business in Pakistan is also crucial for Chinese corporations.

China should abandon its traditional way of dealing only with the Pakistani government and instead get in contact with local communities to better accommodate local interests so that more Pakistani people can benefit from the CPEC. China and Pakistan need to strengthen their cultural ties and increase people-to-people interactions. This has already begun, due to the increasing economic activity between the two countries, forcing China to become more informed about the complexities of Pakistani society. The China-Pakistan Economic Corridor Council was founded in 2015 to jointly address the challenges arising in the CPEC projects. The council has opened offices in Beijing and Islamabad respectively, and its purpose is to assist with the implementation of CPEC projects.

China and Pakistan have taken positive measures to help set up the CPEC for success. Nevertheless, Pakistan's domestic situation is still decisive. Until the country's political and security conditions turn a corner, it will be difficult to judge the corridor's future prospects. For China, this means neutrality, strategic patience, and caution are needed as the construction of this grand initiative continues.

CHINA: A RISKY BUSINESS PROPOSITION

With a largely untapped market of 1.2 billion people, China has had a magical allure for international capital. In 1995, Canada was China's 5th largest trade partner, and that level of trade is expected to increase with the Chinese takeover of

Hong Kong in 1997. However, investment in China is a high-risk proposition. In 1994, the Chinese national government decided that foreigners could not have a majority ownership of power projects. China has also apparently decided to limit the rate of return for foreign companies investing in power projects ~ limits ranging from 12 to 15% have been discussed. Even well-known power project developers such as Gordon Wu have abandoned China for deals in Pakistan and India that are presumably safer and more lucrative. This is extremely revealing, since through Hopewell Holdings, Wu pioneered power investments in China. There are a number of other danger signs ~ Chinese state enterprises have defaulted on $600 million in loans from Japanese, German and Italian banks; the China International Trust & Investment Corp. (CITIC) refused to pay a $40 million debt to the London Metal Exchange; and two other state companies are refused to pay $100 million in trading losses to Lehman Brothers Inc. In a survey of Canadian businesses with an interest in China, the Conference Board of Canada found that less than half of businesses surveyed that invested in China in the last five years had made money on their investments.

For several years, a serious trade disagreement has been simmering between the USA and China over the copyright protection of intellectual property rights in Chain ~ in particular Chinese pirating of western video's, music recordings and computer software. A trade war was narrowly averted in February 1995. However, the reconciliation was short-lived, as a new trade disagreement was triggered when China failed to live up to a 1992 Memorandum of Understanding to lift import controls, licence requirements and quotas on a variety of products. By May 1996, the US government was again threatening to place 100% tariffs on $2 billion worth of Chinese imports, such as textiles and electronics, to the US. China for its part threatened to place retaliatory tariffs on US exports to China. The US imported about $46 billion worth the US of goods from China in 1995, and exported about $12 billion to China. However, on June 17 1996, the US pulled back from the brink of a trade war, when it announced that sanctions would not be placed on China, since it was taking steps towards cracking down on illegal compact disk manufacturers. Given past history, it seems unlikely that we have seen the last of the "intellectual property" issue. This will remain a concern for potential investors in China, who may see their interests affected by international trade problems with the US.

Adding to the economic and political uncertainty of China's future is the impending death of national leader Deng Xiaoping. The 90 year-old Communist Party leader has been in control since 1978, and has been the architect of China's recent mix of brutal repression and market liberalization. A recent Pentagon report has given only even odds for the maintenance of stability following Deng's demise.

Corruption in China remains an endemic problem. In 1995, almost 100,000 people in China were charged with corruption ~ an increase of 8% from 1994. The German organization Transparency International, has ranked China as the second-most corrupt country, behind Indonesia, among the world's 41 major trading nations. In December 1995, a guide book published by Canada's Foreign Affairs Department warned that Canadian business people "may receive requests for agency fees or kickbacks" in China. The guidebook notes that kickbacks are illegal in China.

CPEC: THE BUMPY NEW TRADE ROUTE BETWEEN CHINA AND PAKISTAN

A new international trade route in Southwest Pakistan opened up on Sunday by a Chinese ship exporting goods to the Middle East and Africa. The route that is being developed by the Chinese in Pakistan is expected to make huge amount of economic gains for the country. When China decided to develop the China Pakistan Economic Corridor (CPEC) in 2015, the idea was to deepen economic ties with Pakistan and ensure security for China's larger 'One belt, one road' project. Involving an investment of $46 billion, the project is the means by which China can ensure the quickest availability of energy resources from the Middle East by avoiding the Malacca straits and the South China sea.

Over the year, however, the project has witnessed a large number of obstacles, especially resulting from the poor economic conditions in Balochistan which forms the bulk of the area in which the CPEC is being developed and the opposition to the project meted out by the locals.

What is the CPEC?

The CPEC is one of the most important projects of the 'one belt, one road' project initiated by China that aims to connect the Asian economic giant with Europe and Africa, thereby making the country a bigger player in world economic affairs. Consisting of a number of road, rail and pipeline ventures, the CPEC connects Xinjiang in Northwestern region of China with Pakistan's Gwadar port on the Arabian sea, going over the Pakistan occupied Kashmir territory of Gilgit-Baltistan and the disputed region of Balochistan.

Reportedly, the port at Gwadar will have the capacity to manage 19 million tons of crude oil which will be directly transferred to China.

The project had been conceived much earlier in the 1950s, but failed to achieve completion over the years due to political instability in Pakistan. Its present form was announced by the Chinese government in November 2014 and work started off in April 2015. As a multi-million dollar project, the CPEC is reported to have brought Pakistan twice the amount of foreign investments the country received since 2008.

How does it benefit Pakistan?

In the words of Pakistani leaders, their relationship with China is "higher than the mountains, deeper than the oceans, stronger than steel and sweeter than honey". For Pakistan, the Chinese investment in the south-western region of the country is a game-changer for the economy, especially considering the fact that despite the high concentration of mineral resources in the region it has remained the poorest district.

The $46 billion promised by China will be used in generating close to 17,000 megawatts of electricity at a cost of $34 billion through coal, nuclear and other renewable energy projects. The rest of the money would be utilised in building up transport infrastructure. According to Pakistani Prime Minister Nawaz Sharif the development of the Balochistan province could make Pakistan a regional hub of economic activities.

Why is it opposed by Balochistan?

All of Pakistan is not unanimous in its claims of high gains being made from the Chinese initiated project. The strongest opposition to the investment comes from the disputed territory of Balochistan that has historically had strained relations with the government of Pakistan.

The province of Balochistan is the largest district in the country and its importance lies in the high concentration of natural resource. Despite this, it has remained the poorest province in Pakistan. The conflict with the Pakistani government is rooted in a feeling of nationalism that stretches back to the 1948 when the province was allegedly made a part of Pakistan on unfair terms. That apart, there is also a feeling of political and economic isolation that the government of Pakistan has not been able to erase in all these years.

The strongest grievance of the Baloch nationalist groups against CPEC is that benefits from developmental projects like these are almost always, unfairly distributed, majority of the employment opportunities and profits going to non-Balochs, especially Punjabis. The Baloch Republican Party, a separatist group, recently made its opposition to the CPEC very clear, stating that an economic pact between China and Pakistan would lead to both countries utilising the resources of Balochistan that belong to the locals. They further believe that an increase in military operations and abductions are a direct result of the pact between Pakistan and China. There is also the fear that the initiation of the project would lead to the influx of a large number of non-Balochs, thereby demographically outnumbering the Balochs in the region.

Abductions of activists and even civilians have for long been a problem in Balochistan. Allegedly, they are carried out by Pakistan's military forces in order to subjugate the separatist movement. As per the International Voice for Baloch Missing Persons (IIVBMP), a protest group formed by families of missing people in Balochistan, between 2001 and 2013, about 18,000 people have gone missing in the area, out of which around 2000 have been killed.

In the wake of the thriving separatist movement in Balochistan, the Pakistan government has vowed to increase military surveillance in the area in order to quell Chinese fears. Reportedly, a sum of $250 million has been promised by the Pakistani government for the sake of building a new security force in the region.

A result of these new arrangement has been a strengthening opposition to the project by the Baloch nationalist groups. Protest movements are being held outside Balochistan as well. In August this year, separatist groups staged a protest outside the Chinese embassy in London. Baloch activists have been particularly reaching out to India, asking the country's media and bureaucracy to raise the issue of atrocities against Baloch nationalists onto the international stage. In September, a group of Balochis along with Indians held a joint protest outside the United Nations headquarters in New York asking for UN intervention in order to protect the Balochis.

What are the challenges being faced by China?

For the Chinese, security in the province of Balochistan has been the biggest concern. Reportedly, Baloch separatists, especially those from the Baloch Liberation Army, have been abducting and killing foreigners, particularly the Chinese. In May 2014, a Chinese tourist had been kidnapped from Dera Islmail Khan, close to the balochistan border. In March 2015, five oil tankers carrying fuel from Karachi, reportedly for a Chinese company was set on fire. The Balochistan Liberation Army was accused for the attack. Further disruptions to the infrastructural projects are being anticipated by other Islamist groups and splinter factions of the Pakistani Taliban. The prime motive of these acts is to make the Pakistan government appear incapable of providing adequate security measures.

However, the Pakistani government has been continuously assuring the Chinese state of security to their personnel and assets in the region. Although the CPEC is being funded by China, at the initial stage of the project, only Pakistani personnel would be involved in the construction. Chinese personnel are expected to come in after the first stage, by which time the Pakistani government has promised to take requisite measures to curb militancy.

How is India responding?

India is not exactly welcoming towards the Chinese funded project, mainly because of the fact that it crosses through the Pakistan occupied part of Kashmir. Earlier in September, PM Modi expressed his concerns over CPEC to President Xi Jinping of China at a bilateral meeting between the two leaders. He is reported to have told the Chinese president that both countries need to be 'sensitive' towards their respective strategic interests. A response to the Chinese development of Gwadar is the bilateral agreement between India and Iran to develop the Chabahar port.

In the recent past though experts on South Asian politics have been ringing alarm bells that any act on the part of India that explicitly opposes CPEC might lead to strained relations between India and China.

PAKISTAN ON THE VERGE OF COLLAPSE AND DISINTEGRATION

Attempts by the Pakistani government to micro-manage the economy have failed. The ill consequences of government economic control have been exacerbated by political instability.

In fact, foreign investment has completely collapsed. Unemployment and inflation are high; economic infrastructure is decrepit; even Islamabad suffers routine power outages. The practice of democracy has been consistently corrupt, incompetent, and disillusioning.

The political system is essentially authoritarian with a democratic veneer. The government is ineffective, discouraging individual and communal action.

Moreover, the elections are formally but not practically free. Even when civilian politicians formally ruled, they could not control the military and especially the Inter-Services Intelligence Agency ISI, which long aided the Taliban and various terrorist groups against the elected government in Kabul.

A nuclear-armed military and ISI have sponsored Islamic extremism as an intrinsic part of their foreign policy for nearly four decades. That's why it is extremely difficult for Pakistan to give up its self-destructive and double dealing policy after 9/11 under the watchful eye of CIA. Islamabad cannot be trusted to confront the problem of terrorism and extremism because , the military and ISI have too many ties, both formal and informal, with these terrorists and extremists.

The Al Qaeda and the Taliban supported by ISI have destroyed the culture of Pakistan and rendered it into a state of turmoil and despair where no one can say when a suicide bomber will appear and blow himself up .There are everyday shoot-outs between Islamic factions .Both the Taliban and the Al Qaeda have changed the character of Pakistan forever making it one of the most dangerous countries in the world.

Often described as the most dangerous place on earth, Pakistan's semi-autonomous tribal region serves as a haven for Al Qaeda operatives, Pakistani militants, and Jihadists from across the Islamic world. Muslim radicals from the United States and Europe who come for ideological instruction to Pakistan and to plot terrorist attacks in their home countries. Al Qaeda is gaining strength. A flood of recruits from Pakistan's well-educated urban middle class—young people, professionals, and retired military officers—have flocked to its strongholds in the tribal areas. This new generation of militants, committed to global jihad, act as a magnet for Muslim radicals from across the world. They are part of a new Al Qaeda that has taken root in Pakistan.

The economic and political costs of the spreading militant violence have been huge, threatening to destabilize the country. Meanwhile, high inflation and growing unemployment have fueled discontent among Pakistanis, providing an even more conducive environment for religious extremism.

The recent blow-back from these policies is now threatening the state, undermining the Army , decapitating the political elite and drowning the country into a sea of blood.

That's why The fragmentation of the country has become a real possibility. At this stage the Army may have not wanted to be stuck attempting to govern the ungovernable. The Afghan-Pakistani border is an artifact of history, artificially dividing one nation the Pukhtuns. The mapmakers of Durand line sowed the seeds of endless conflict. Predictably, the tribesmen despised the artificial divide, and continued to move freely across the border as if it did not exist.

So the best solution is to remove the Durand line as soon as possible and Pukhtuns living in Pakistan should be integrated to their motherland Afghanistan. Ralph Peters, a retired army officer, had speculated that the khyber Pukhtunkhwa, long the scene of ethno nationalistic movements, would break away from Pakistan as soon as possible and join their motherland Afghanistan.

Islamabad does not like the U.S. supports a government in Kabul, that's why Islamabad is going to meddle, often against American objectives. Since 1947 Kashmir has been a running sore between India and Pakistan, over which the two countries have fought four wars in 1947, 1965 , 1971 and in 1999. Kashmir is still a festering sore between India and Pakistan.

Pakistan Army and its Intelligence unit, the Inter Services Intelligence (ISI) tried its best to rouse the people to rebel against India , but all these attempts failed. The Haqqani network has perhaps 10,000 fighters battling U.S. and other

NATO forces in Afghanistan. Its strong connections with Al Qaeda have made the network the most dangerous insurgent faction in Afghanistan.

The Pakistani military and establishment plan that after 2014 , there will be civil war in Afghanistan , then they will use the Haqqani network and Taliban group as proxy forces to protect Pakistan's interests in Afghanistan against other tribes and the much-feared Indian influence. However , India has never been responsible for initiating any of the wars with Pakistan.

"The Haqqani network acts as a veritable arm of the ISI," charged Admiral Mike Mullen. Pakistan is potentially dangerous to itself, the region, and the world. So Hussian Haqqani former Abassador of Pakistan believes Pakistan's threat to itself and the world, is essentially a failure to come to terms with itself as a nation. It would make it even harder to deal with the country's sectarian divide ,the ethnic tensions, the insurgency in Baluchistan; and the spread of the "Pakistani Taliban" out of the border tribal areas into the heartlands.

Pakistan is on the verge of collapse and disintegration due to internal political turmoil , terrorist threats,export of terrorism, economic problems and territorial disputes with Afghanistan and India. But even then Pakistan still has the energy and gumption to promote proxy wars in Afghanistan, Kashmir and India. Pakistan hates India and Afghanistan , because it realizes that Pukhtunkhwa , Balochistan and Kashmir may slip from its grip at any time.

Without the elimination of Pakistan, "India,Afghanistan and the remaining world may never become secure nations". The civilized world wishes peace and economic prosperity against a threatening climate, growing population, an oncoming oil crisis, and worldwide economic woes, then for how long the world community will tolerate the negative and spoiling behavior of Pakistan. Pakistan is more dangerous as an independent state than a disintegrated state. Because Pakistan can be taken over by terrorist elements supported by a manipulative ISI at any time. which will be then a huge disaster for the whole world community. Although this whole reorganization will change the boundaries of the region, but one thing that has to be undertaken that it will be a welcome change to the current bloodshed, turmoil, and export of terrorism.

Very often, major change is needed to change the status quo when minor changes don't succeed. The central Asian states to the North of Afghanistan with a lot of untapped oil and gas deposit are land locked. The world community can easily has approach to central Asian state through Afghanistan but again Pakistan is a problem. So the best solution is to get rid of Pakistan that will make not only that region but the whole world safe and economically prosperous. It will create the mechanisms in which the rule of law and civil society would grow and flourish. Otherwise then Alqaeda and other terrorist groups can exploit the gap to make the situation worst in that region. Time is ripe for action at this current time where Pakistan is reeling under internal imbalances. If a boxer will not knock out his opponent when the opponent is dizzy and imbalanced, then other opportunities are only guesswork.

Eventually, for India , Afghanistan and the world community to succeed, Pakistan must be out of the picture and cease to exist for the peace on earth. Therefore, throughout the world community must actively work towards that objective rather than waiting passively in spectator stands. "superpower Soviet Union collapsed because it was built on an idea that did not work. This is the biggest danger to Pakistan which also rests on the idea .

Asking whether Pakistan will exist in the future is actually a "trick" question: Pakistan already does not exist. The "illegal creation" ceased to exist in 1971. Pakistan itself remains unsure about why it exists. Pakistan will collapse because of no governance, problematic relationship with its Islamic Identity, history of military rule, struggle of power between army and political parties, incompetent leadership, President Ziaulhaq Islamization reforms, territorial dispute with Afhanistan, Kashmir problem , geopolitical insecurities, and support of ISI with the Jehadies and other militants. And when the end comes, it tends to be all over fairly quickly. India sees itself as a major rising Asian state and Pakistan is a drag on it.

Poverty, terrorism, corruption and Jihad are four pillar of Pakistan state. Pakistani nuclear weapons are not safe. Paksitan was never a viable nation idea. Nation created on religious identities and anti- indianness itself was denial to one's own identity. The leaders of Pakistan are distorting the history of Pakistan. They are international lairs including Jinnah

In any case, time will only tell that how long Pakistani leaders and Army can fool the civil society by their distorted history. Pakistan is collapsing and disintegrating as soon as possible, because its all departments and institutions are failed . Once an American who said we assumed that with all our aid and alliances we believed that Pakistan would emerge as an independent democratic state. However, it turned out that India, which did not get our military assistance and partnership, has emerged as that kind of country.

In India, the military has a legitimate role but still remains under the government's control.Once cheif of Army staff of India called Indra Gandhi , the then prime minister of India , to discuss some political issues. She told him come tomorrow to my office, When he came to her office, she handed over termination letter to the general and told him that Politics is our job not yours. You have to protect the borders of India.

But in Pakistan government is controlled by the military. When government does some think which the Army don't like, they convene the core commander meeting just to warn the government. In Pakistan, the military has identified enemies among its own fellow-citizens. If you demonise your own people, you are in deep trouble.You can't treat the Pukhuns , the Baloch, or other ethnic or religious minorities the way you treat foreign enemies. That's the route to catastrophe.

China can not teach pakistan the democracy because in China itself there is no democracy . There is one party totalitarian government in China. Also Pakistan, like North Korea, uses its nuclear asset and its political fragility as a means to extract concessions from other countries. In Pakistan where people are not able to afford bread for two times a day, then how some one can talk about science and technology. Now the entire world agrees that the right to an education is a first prerequisite to the development of any sector. Education gives people the skills they need to help themselves out of poverty and move into prosperity. But in Pakistan budget for education is negligible. Because they think the educated people threat for their power, influence and survival. In addition to holding political power, the Pakistani army controls vast commercial and industrial interests and owns massive rural and urban properties.

As a result the curse of illiteracy in Pakistan is at its peak. Catastrophic failure of this nuclear-armed state is surely a possibility. In the worst case, Pakistan would simply come apart, spewing nuclear technology and terrorists in all directions. which will be then a huge disaster for the world.

And the problem is that there is no savior ahead: all models have failed; leaders have failed; religious Parties have failed; capitalism has failed; socialism has failed; political parties have failed."

Every institution has failed. Target killing, suicide attacks are very common now a days. People are no more afraid of these things they are getting use to it. Office worker in Pakistan has a fear , will they return home after a hard day at office. Students have fear will they return home safely after school. Everyone from a child to grown up carries this fear.In Pakistan from a bus driver to a president each and everyone thinks about themselves, it doesn't matter what happens to Pakistan.

7

China Pakistan Economic Corridor and China's Approach-India's Response

The hype surrounding the China Pakistan Economic Corridor (CPEC), to be built through Gilgit Baltistan, resurfaced with the recent visit of Chinese President Xi Jinping to Pakistan. The visit yet again generated an animated discourse in the global media about the corridor's future. The long-gestated CPEC project received initial traction during Nawaz Sharif's visits to China in the year 2014. Subsequently, on his maiden visit to Pakistan in April 2015, the Chinese President reaffirmed the previously announced commitment, worth $46 billion, towards the CPEC. The CPEC is considered a significant project that seeks to cement Sino-Pakistan bilateral ties and further consolidate their strategic ties. The corridor will run through India's periphery, more significantly, Gilgit Baltistan, claimed by India as part of the erstwhile princely state of Jammu and Kashmir (J&K). In due course, this geographical reality of the CPEC could potentially impinge upon India's geopolitical calculations and pose a strategic challenge.

CHINA'S APPROACH, INDIA'S RESPONSE

In December 2014, the Chinese state-run *Xinhua* published a statement announcing the closure of the strategic Khunjerab Pass and in the process referred to Gilgit Baltistan as part of

Pakistan. Until then, China had maintained that J&K was a bilateral problem/dispute between India and Pakistan. Whether terming Gilgit Baltistan as part of Pakistan reflected a possible shift in the Chinese position on the J&K— a change from its previously held neutral position – was debated in the Indian media for a while.

A section believes that by taking up a long term project such as the CPEC, the arteries of which will originate in Gilgit Baltistan, China has yet again tacitly approved Pakistan's claim and control over this region. There was no reaction from the Indian official sources to the *Xinhua* statement. In the past, a similar statement was withdrawn after India registered a protest to the Chinese news agency.

Responding to a query in the Lok Sabha in December 2014, Minister for External Affairs Sushma Swaraj noted:

"Government has seen reports with regard to China and Pakistan being involved in infrastructure building activities in Pakistan Occupied Kashmir (POK), including construction of China-Pakistan Economic Corridor. Government has conveyed its concerns to China about their activities in Pakistan Occupied Kashmir, and asked them to cease such activities."

But somewhat contravening the above is a recent statement by India's High Commissioner to Pakistan, who noted: "India has no worry over the construction of Pakistan-China Economic Corridor as an economically strong Pakistan would bring stability in the region."

India is yet to comprehensively articulate its approach towards the CPEC despite the fact that the corridor bodes strategic implications for India. As stated, the corridor will pass through the Gilgit Baltistan region where China has invested in the past in infrastructure and hydropower projects. In the Gilgit Baltistan segment, the CPEC project design includes a major expansion of the Karakoram Highway, establishing industrial parks in special economic zones, constructing hydropower projects, railway line and road building. The project also entails building hydropower projects and motorways/highways in the so-called Azad Jammu and Kashmir (AJK). India has occasionally raised objections to Chinese infrastructure investment in the region.

The origin of the CPEC could be traced to the Border Agreement of 1963, considered a milestone in China-Pakistan relations. The agreement ceded the 5000 plus square mile Trans Karakorum Tract to China and served as a precursor to the Karakoram Highway, conceived later as a strategic link defining China and Pakistan's 'all-weather friendship'. The then Defence Minister of India, Krishna Menon, elaborately enunciated India's position on the issue at the UN, condemning the agreement as illegitimate. Besides, India lodged an "emphatic protest" to China and conveyed its concerns in a letter of protest. Decades down the line, while India's policy orientation and broader claim on Gilgit Baltistan remains unchanged, its stance on Chinese investments in the Karakoram Highway, and Chinese efforts to leverage this territorial link to build a strategic corridor, is perceived to be weakening over time.

India's Dilemma

Is it because of a realization that in a changed strategic landscape, the options for India vis-a-vis a project like CPEC are limited and complicated? Is India conflicted about whether to engage itself in the mega connectivity network project or stay out of it in accordance with its stated positon on Gilgit Baltistan and the so-called AJK? Participating in the project would require a major alteration in India's policy. Overlooking the territorial dimension could be interpreted as a massive climb-down from its stated position. It may even be construed as acquiescing to the China-Pakistan alliance in the region and beyond. Thus, the CPEC poses a policy challenge to India on how best to strike a precarious balance between securing its strategic/territorial interests without at the same time being confrontational.

Be that as it may, India would need to take a clear positon on the CPEC sooner or later. Domestically, there has been, till now, no serious political or public debate on how India should approach the issue. In the absence of a rational public discourse, India is yet to articulate a clear stand or position on the CPEC. This is also owing to the fact that public debates in India on issues concerning China and Pakistan are often emotive and devoid of a rational evaluation of policy options. Charting a policy course is essential since China has, of late, through stray remarks extended an invitation for India to participate in the Silk Route 'one route one belt' project. The onus now lies on India to respond to such overtures. India has to take a call on whether it would like to be a party to the CPEC, sit on the fence, or convey its concerns more emphatically in a bid to discourage China.

CPEC may materialize despite scepticism

Ironically, in Pakistan itself, there is growing cynicism about the CPEC's prospects and feasibility because of security-related concerns and inter-provincial political discord on route preferences. Nevertheless, given the Chinese determination to find a route to oil-rich West Asia through Pakistan, and the Pakistani desperation to provide every possible assurance to China about safeguarding its investments, the project is likely to be implemented, even if its scope may be limited. The Chinese decision to strike deals worth US$ 22 billion out of a total of $28 billion with private players rather than the Pakistan government has been touted as an indication of Chinese seriousness in investing in Pakistan. One has to remember that China and Pakistan have weathered geographical and logistical extremes in the past to build the highest metalled road on one of the toughest terrain, i.e. the Karakoram Highway. Moreover, the Pakistani decision to raise a special security division to protect Chinese workers and interests in Pakistan, consisting of 10,000 security personnel, including 5,000 from the elite special services group (SSG) of the Pakistan Army who are specially trained for counter-terrorism and security, indicates its resolve to implement the project in all earnestness.

While India's overall stance on PoK remains understated, the commencement of the CPEC warrants more serious attention than what has been accorded so far. There is a need to carefully weigh the situation and devise a suitable and sustainable approach that could serve India's long-term interests. It is imperative that some of the explicit strategic concerns regarding the CPEC figure in the bilateral round of talks during the Indian Prime Minister's forthcoming visit to China.

INDIA, CHINA NEED TO BE SENSITIVE TO STRATEGIC INTERESTS: MODI ON CHINA-PAKISTAN ECONOMIC CORRIDOR

Prime Minister Narendra Modi expressed concerns over terrorism emanating from PoK. India raised its concern with China on Sunday over the CPEC which runs through PoK and terrorism "emanating from the region" as Prime Minister Narendra Modi told Chinese President Xi Jinping the two countries need to be "sensitive" to each other's strategic interests. Asserting that fight against terror should not be motivated by "political considerations", Modi said it is of "paramount importance that we respect each other's aspirations, concerns and strategic interests" to ensure durable bilateral ties.

During the bilateral meeting with Xi on the sidelines of the G20 summit Hangzhou, Modi raised India's concerns over the US $46 billion China-Pakistan Economic Corridor (CPEC) being laid through Pakistan-occupied Kashmir (PoK). Besides a host of energy-related projects, the CPEC consists of rail, road and pipelines to ferry oil and gas from Gwadar port on Arabian Sea to Kashghar in China's Muslim-dominated Xinjiang province through PoK.

Replying to a question whether the terrorism emanating from the region where the CPEC is being laid through has been discussed, External Affairs Ministry spokesperson Vikas Swarup told reporters the issue has been raised during the meeting. In his candid comments reflecting India's concerns, Modi said both India and China need to be "sensitive" to each other's strategic interests and called for specific actions to "prevent growth of negative perception".

"As a matter of principle, both countries would have to be sensitive to each other's strategic interests," Swarup said while touching upon broad themes that Modi stressed upon during his 35-minute bilateral with Xi, their eighth meeting. "In order to promote positive convergence, we would also need to prevent growth of negative perception. For this, the specific actions by both countries would play the major role," he said. In particular, Modi highlighted that "we have succeeded in maintaining peace and tranquillity on the border", he added. Condemning the recent suicide bomb attack on the Chinese Embassy in Bishkek, capital of Kyrgyzstan, Modi said it is yet another proof of the continuing scourge of terrorism.

"The Prime Minister reiterated that our response to terror must not be motivated by political considerations," Swarup said. On his part, Xi said China is willing to work with India to maintain their "hard-won sound" ties and further boost bilateral cooperation.

What does Xi Jinping have to say?

"China is willing to work with India to maintain their hard-won sound relations and further advance their cooperation", state-run Chinese *Xinhua* news agency quoted Xi as saying. "China and India should respect and care for each other on issues of major concern, and handle differences in a constructive way," Xi told Modi.

Xi said both sides had seen healthy, stable and speedy development of their relationship, and that as neighbours and developing nations they should continue high-level exchanges. About the bilateral relations, which experienced turbulence due to differences over a raft of issues, Modi said in order to make the Asian century a reality, the countries of the continent would have to take responsibility.

On his part, Xi said China and India should continue dialogues at various levels and in various areas, and frequently exchange views on major issues of common interest to enhance understanding and trust. Their meeting came at a time when the bilateral ties have witnessed turbulence over a raft of issues involving Pakistan including China's technical hold on UN ban against Pakistan- based Jaish-e-Muhammad chief Masood Azhar and its attempts to block India s entry into Nuclear Security Group.

With these issues involving Pakistan, the perception in India is gaining that carefully developed ties by the two countries in the last few years were being allowed to slide to further the interests of Beijing's all weather ally Pakistan. Asked whether Prime Minister Modi raised the issue of China blocking India's bid for the membership of the Nuclear Suppliers Group (NSG) during the bilateral, Swarup declined to get into the "nitty-gritty" of the issues discussed.

"I am not going into the nitty-gritty of each and everything that was discussed. Everything is not meant for public consumption. There are certain things (which) need to remain between the two governments," he said.

On yet another question on the NSG issue, he said: "I will not go into the specifics, if you read between the lines, you pretty much understand when you we talk about strategic interests, concerns and aspirations, it is not as if China is not unaware of our strategic interests, aspirations and concerns or we are unaware of their concerns. So, it is something both sides are well aware.

"This was a meeting at summit level between the two. They are meant to provide high-level guidance and direction to overall relations." Citing that India has not signed the Nuclear Non-Proliferation Treaty, China had opposed its bid to join the elite 48-member bloc during NSG's meeting in Seoul in June.

Modi said he always had a strategic vision for India- China ties. The India-China partnership is important not only for the two countries but for the entire region and the world. "India has worked to make progress in the closer, developmental partnership with China. Cultural and people-to-people ties have also been increasing," Swarup said.

Asked to comment on the Chinese state-media quoting Xi as telling Modi that China is willing to maintain "hard-won sound" relations with India, Swarup said, "it would not be appropriate for me to characterise President Xi's remarks. "After all we are in his country and it is for the Chinese side to amplify and clarify whatever he said. Not appropriate for me to characterise what the other side said," he said.

"In the context of India and China, he said that our peoples also have the expectation that we make every possible effort to fulfil their dreams of progress, development and prosperity," Swarup said. Ahead of the 8th BRICS Summit next month, Modi, who is here to attend the two-day G20 Summit, extended a personal invitation to Xi to come to Goa which the Chinese leader said he was very happy to accept.

MODI'S BALOCHISTAN PLAN: FROM MORAL ASCENDANCY TO SMART MIND GAMES

Prime minister Narendra Modi's Independence Day address to the nation with references to Balochistan, Gilgit-Baltistan and Pakistan-Occupied Kashmir (PoK) set the cat among the pigeons. Ever since, there are as many opinions as the number of reviews, analyses and articles on the issue. It helps prove just how little the strategic community of India and the world had earlier focused on these contentious issues, especially Balochistan. It has created a strategic turbulence of sorts in Pakistan itself, has got exiled Baloch people in the US and elsewhere gingered up, and produced strategic literature in reams. An issue so volatile has been smartly and adroitly been kept under wraps by Pakistan away from international focus. Even India, fully aware of this Achilles heel of Pakistan, has desisted from raising the issue to embarrass Pakistan despite all the intimidation the latter has done in and on Jammu and Kashmir.

Balochistan is a complex issue with an emotive, political and strategic connection. It has rarely been discussed in India or elsewhere, and knowledge on it is largely deficient even among those who regularly comment on strategic issues. The remarks have got Pakistan so riled that it has booked a couple of Baloch leaders for having supported the Indian PM's remarks.

Former Afghanistan president Hamid Karzai has come out in support of human rights in Balochistan. Bangladesh, which has an awkward connect to the issue, too has supported the call for greater human rights for the Baloch people. However, in India there has been divided opinion with the political opposition questioning the need for raising the issue when India does not even enjoy the benefit of a common boundary with Balochistan. Others objected to the raising of the issue when India itself had an ongoing internal problem with the turbulence in Kashmir. The Balochistan issue has also become important because of the China Pakistan Economic Corridor (CPEC) in which Beijing is investing $46 billion. A major part of this corridor lies in Balochistan as does the port of Gwadar which connects the corridor to the sea. The entire issue needs analysis to arrive at any conclusion about the intent of PM Modi in including Balochistan in his speech.

The PoK and Gilgit-Baltistan (GB) issues are well known because India has claims over those territories. The 1994 Joint Resolution of the two houses of parliament was the strong reiteration of India's claims over the entire territory of J&K, partially under occupation of Pakistan and China. The construction of infrastructure through the disputed territories by a third party, China, has been objected by India but no change of status on that is likely. The state of human rights in GB and PoK will always be of a lower order, affording us opportunities.

India has no claim over the territory of Balochistan and does not contest Pakistan's rights over it. So what is Balochistan all about and how does it enter into the India-Pakistan equation? Without entering into too much detail, it perhaps suffices to know that much like Hyderabad and Junagadh's integration with India, Balochistan also did not have a smooth integration with Pakistan in 1947. There have been a series of uprisings at intervals of a few years. The Baloch people want greater autonomy, increased royalties from provincial revenue and natural resources which are in abundance in their region, and an independent nation-state status. It is Pakistan's largest state (47 percent of the land mass) but also its poorest, with a population of 13 million. The Baloch people exist in a region which is spread across three countries – Pakistan, Afghanistan and Iran. The problem is almost akin to former East Pakistan (now Bangladesh) except that East Pakistan was physically far away from West Pakistan. The alienation that exists among the people is almost akin to that which existed in East Pakistan, a result of ham-handed domination of the Pakistan narrative by the West Punjabis.

Balochistan has the disadvantage of direct and physical connect but large parts of the province are not under full Pakistani control. Hussain Haqqani, the well-known Pakistani diplomat, sums this up by saying, "Some Baloch leaders say Balochistan's integration into Pakistan was done forcefully. But more important than that is the neglect. This is a resource-rich province, and instead of the people benefitting from those resources, they end up in other parts of Pakistan." The one event in recent history which probably raises the Baloch sensitivity by many notches was the killing of Nawab Akbar Bugti by the Pakistan army on direct orders of Pervez Musharraf.

For all these years Balochistan has never had any nation taking up cudgels on its behalf and human rights concern for its people has never emerged primarily because of Pakistan's geo-strategic importance to nations that matter. It has been a frontline state for the US through much of its history and for China it remains a strategic asset. India's relationship with Pakistan, though thorny, has also been about non-interference in its internal affairs. This was especially since the period of prime minister Inder Kumar Gujral (1997-98) whose doctrine was all about a benign policy towards the neighbours. Thus, despite Pakistan's active support for the Punjab separatists and terrorists through the 1980s and the switch to even more active interference amounting to a proxy war in J&K since 1989, India considered two things as anathema. First was the issue of water; never did it consider using threats relating to the Indus Waters Treaty of 1960 even when it was subjected to heinous terrorist attacks such as 13/12 and 26/11. Second, it never mentioned a word about Balochistan even though the potential for exploitation always existed. This strategy placed India on a high horse of morality which has assisted it in attaining much respect in the international community. It is this moral ascendancy which is being referred to by many analysts with the deduction that a carefully crafted international image may receive a hit due to Modi's sudden turnaround in mentioning the 'B' word.

There are other objections from the analyst community which perceives that Iran may be unhappy with India supporting the human rights cause in Balochistan. Such support is many times taken as backing for separatism and separatist tendencies of Pakistan's Baloch province will have its spinoff effects on Iran's people of the same ethnicity. Then there is Kashmir; there is this thought that by raking up Balochistan we in India were making ourselves vulnerable to international inquisitiveness about our human rights record too.

For many years and more emphatically now, Pakistan has been using every possible propaganda tool to colour India black with accusations of our interference in its internal affairs. The home-grown terror campaign by the Tehreek-e-Taliban Pakistan (TTP) and the high-intensity contestation of the Pakistan security forces by smaller groups is once again placed at the doorstep of India in the blame game. So with the demonisation of India at every stage it had become almost routine, a virtual force of habit, to castigate India for imaginary intervention in Pakistan's affairs. Nawaz Sharif's recent remarks immediately after the suicide attack on the Quetta lawyers and follow-up on Pakistan's Independence Day did not hold back anything.

So, if Modi decides to mention Balochistan and focus on the human rights situation there, how should this be taken by his domestic constituency? The first thought; it is testing the waters, getting the feel by forcing the adversary to respond, bring irrationality in his utterances and just unnerve him and the entire security establishment. Very used to the customary transactional responses from India, this one which is slightly below the belt nevertheless gets a standing count. It riles the

Pakistani psyche which for many years has got used to India's defensive stance.

Those who perceive that when Kashmir is unstable this wasn't the time to play quid pro quo also say that our moral standing has taken a beating. They need to consider whether one should instigate the adversary when one's house is stable or when the adversary is pressurising you. You actually have to do it to force the adversary to pull back from his intent.

India's routine response to Pakistan's diatribes against it has been denial. It obtains no advantage. However, when a single word is spoken at the right time its effect is electric. Pakistan is already worried about India's second coming in Afghanistan after Ashraf Ghani's turnaround.

The signing of the Trilateral Chabahar Agreement opens another avenue for strengthening India-Afghanistan relations. It is from that direction that Pakistan fears India's interference since no physical boundary between Balochistan and India exists. The mention of the 'B' word would have created devils of imagination in the minds of the Pakistani establishment; the more the better for India. It is not helpful towards building future India-Pakistan relations but the probable intent of Modi was only to signal that two can play this game and that in future India would meet Pakistan's attempts at interference in Kashmir.

In India's security domain one of its weakest links is information warfare; the ability to play mind games, keeping the adversary on tenterhooks about the next move and taking the battle into the domain of smart warfare.

Since for the umpteenth time Pakistan could raise the temperatures in Kashmir, after the recent killing of Burhan Wani, perhaps a little experiment is what the Modi mind is attempting. Remember Pakistan's chaotic internal security situation and obsession with seeking its space in Afghanistan leaves it little time for Kashmir. Cornering it by imposing caution and giving enough signals about the future intent being in the same domain as that of Pakistan in Kashmir could force a rethink. However, a one-off smart move which has had strategic overtones needs sustenance for continuing effectiveness. We will have to wait and watch how Modi takes this game forward.

TENSIONS MOUNT BETWEEN INDIA AND PAKISTAN OVER BALOCHISTAN

On March 24th, the Pakistani security officials, backed by the civilian authorities, said they had arrested an Indian national somewhere in Balochistan and now they describe it as the "evidence" of Indian involvement in the restive province. The Indian Ministry of External Affairs has also confirmed that Mr. Kulbhushan yadhav, a former Navy officer, has been arrested. While Islamabad says Mr. Yadhav worked for the Indian intelligence agency, the Research and Analysis Wing (RAW), on a high position, New Delhi has denied his affiliation with its premier intelligence agency.

The circumstances surrounding the arrest of the Indian national are still elusive. Nobody knows how and where he was arrested and who arrested him. Likewise, the Pakistanis have leveled all kinds of allegations on him soon after the news about his arrest broke out. They say he was involved in providing training and weapons to the Baloch insurgents and engaged in promoting unrest in Karachi. One wonders how much time it took the Pakistani officials to extract so much information from Mr. Yadhav when they are saying that he has been moved to Islamabad for further investigation. Regardless the authenticity of the Pakistani charges, the arrest of Mr. Yadhav will significantly help Islamabad in embarrassing India and discrediting the Baloch nationalists for what they bill as a homegrown liberation movement.

For the past several years, Pakistan has been accusing India of interfering in Balochistan, but it never brought in public any evidence to substantiate its claims. The alleged Indian involvement in Balochistan has become an integral part of the talking points the Pakistani officials use whenever they meet with the Indian officials. The meeting between former prime ministers Manmohan Singh and his Pakistani counterpart Yousuf Raza Gilani at Sharm-el-Sheikh in Egypt in 2009 was the first occasion when Balochistan was mentioned at a high level. Afterward, the Pakistani officials also provided dossiers to the United Nations — which were not made public — in October 2015 to prove the Indian hand in fomenting trouble inside Pakistan. The Indians, on the other hand, say they have no interest in destabilizing Pakistan.

No matter what the Pakistani and the Indian authorities say, this episode will somewhat benefit the Baloch nationalists who have been marching in world capitals and meeting with leaders and activists desperately seeking international support for their liberation movement. The Baloch leaders have expressed anguish and frustration over the lack of support from the international community amid the slow motion genocide of the Baloch people by the Pakistani security forces. All the Baloch leaders and activists need at this point is more and more international attention. Unlike their vocal support for the Bengalis in 1971, the Indian politicians and the media have not demonstrated any serious interest in the Baloch matter. The episode embroiling Mr. Yadhav would at least help the Indian authorities to have a serious briefing about the conflict in Balochistan and what is actually going on. Likewise, the row between India and Pakistan in the backdrop of this episode is unlikely to escape the attention of the United Nations, the European Union, the American and the British diplomatic corps in Islamabad and New Delhi. The more noise is made on Balochistan, the better it is for the Baloch because beneath this incident lies a mountain of human rights abuses, repression and exploitation of the Baloch people committed by the Pakistani authorities.

This incident will also richly benefit the Pakistani security establishment in justifying its tight grip over the province. Similar to the 2011 Raymond Davis episode when an American citizen and a contractor for the Central Intelligence Agency (CIA) was arrested in Lahore for killing two Pakistani nationals, this event will also tremendously feed the conspiracy theorists in the Pakistani military and the media. Even if Mr. Yadhav had no connections with the Indian government, his arrest from Balochistan (if that actually happened) is still an extraordinary development because the Pakistani authorities do not normally allow foreign nationals to travel to Balochistan. The alternative routes are the borders with Iran and Afghanistan. According to the initial reports, the Indian national sneaked into Balochistan via Iran.

This incident coincided with the first visit to Islamabad of Iran's Hassan Rouhani since becoming the President. Iran has suddenly become an active player in the region after the lifting of the sanctions because of the successful deal with the P5+1 nations. Tensions between Tehran and Riyadh have also skyrocketed in the recent months because of differences on Syria and Yemen. The Pakistani officials have reportedly mentioned Mr. Jadhav's case with the visiting Iranian leader and sought Iran's cooperation on border security. (The Iranian leader denied discussing the matter with the Pakistanis). The Iranians, on their part, have even a worse record than the Pakistanis when it comes to treating the Baloch people. For instance, last month Shahindokht Molaverdi, Iran's vice president for women and family affairs, concededthat "we have a village in Sistan and Baluchestan (province) where every single man has been executed."

When Pakistan and Iran treat their Baloch population as third class citizens, it seems obvious why the latter reaches out to the international community for support. They are willing to facilitate the entry and lodging of anyone who is willing to get the word from Balochistan out to the rest of the world. It is not only foreign "spies" who are eager to know the truth about Balochistan but even foreign journalists, human rights activists and researchers want to have access to Balochistan. When the Baloch people have no objections to anyone coming from anywhere in the world to visit Balochistan, why should Islamabad have a problem? Islamabad should be more transparent and accountable about its policies and actions in Balochistan.

The row over the arrest of the alleged Indian spy now provides the Baloch nationalists an opportunity to demand an international investigation into the matter that is ideally led by the United Nations, the United States or the European Union. After all, the Baloch people should not be sandwiched in a war of words between India and Pakistan. The Baloch conflict has its own history, context and significance. It cannot afford to be overshadowed by the Pakistan-India rivalry. The Baloch leadership should come forward and assert its position on this matter because neither Islamabad nor New Delhi are entitled to speak on the behalf of the Baloch. The Baloch should speak for themselves and they should be heard because Islamabad is the aggressor, certainly not the victim, when it comes to Balochistan.

PAKISTAN INDUCTS CHINA INTO BALOCHISTAN TO COUNTER INDIA

Despite its continuing concerns over the freedom struggle of the Balochs which shows no signs of letting up, China, which originally constructed the languishing commercial port of Gwadar on the Mekran Coast of Balochistan, is reported to have agreed in principle to take over the responsibility for the operation of the port.

The 40-year-old contract awarded by the Pakistan Government in 2007 to Singapore's PSA international for the operation of the port has been a non-starter due to disputes between the Pakistan Navy and the PSA International over the free transfer of land to the PSA international for the construction of warehouses for containers and other infrastructure facilities and over the failure of the Pakistani authorities to improve the road and rail connectivity of the port as promised in the contract.

The Pakistan Government agreed to the request of the PSA International to withdraw from the contract. Islamabad has now approved in principle the signing of a contract with the Chinese Overseas Port Holdings giving it the responsibility for operating the port.

The problems created by the Pakistan Navy in the transfer of land for the PSA International indicated a lack of enthusiasm in the Pakistan Navy for the operation of the port by a Singapore company and its preference for handing it over to the Chinese company.

In the eyes of the Pakistan Navy, the Chinese taking over the responsibility for the operation of the port will have two advantages. Firstly, the Chinese, with their reputation for the timely construction of projects, will be able to get the languishing operations revived quickly. Secondly, it could prove to be the first step towards China agreeing to a Pakistani request for upgrading the port into a naval base, available for joint use by the Pakistani and Chinese navies.

Taking over the responsibility for the operation of the port, will have strategic advantages for China. It can bring oil and gas from Saudi Arabia and Iran to Gwadar and have them transported to Xinjiang through pipelines. Secondly, it will provide a port of call for ships of China's Indian Ocean fleet for refitting and other purposes. At present Beijing has not shown any open interest in helping Pakistan by upgrading the existing Chinese-aided commercial port into a Naval base for joint use by the two navies.

The Chinese took nearly two years to make up their mind as to whether they should get involved in the operation of the port due to the deteriorating security situation in Balochistan because of the on-going freedom struggle of the Balochs. The Balochs are opposed to a Chinese presence in Gwadar because they look upon the area as their traditional homeland over which the Pakistan Government has no right to negotiate with any foreign power. Moreover, the Balochs fear that the Chinese taking over the responsibility for the operation of the port would result in an induction of a large number of Punjabis into the Gwadar area to work.

The Pakistani authorities are hoping that the Chinese agreement to take over the operation of the port could act as a deterrent to India whom they suspect of helping the Baloch freedom-fighters.

Beijing's agreement in principle to take over the operations of the port speaks of its confidence that they could meet any security threats from the Baloch freedom-fighters. Whether their confidence will be sustained or belied has to be seen. The Pakistan Army will not be able to assure the security of the Chinese working in Gwadar. Unless the PLA decides to post its own security contingents in Gwadar as it has done for the security of its nationals working on the upgradation of the Karakoram Highway in Gilgit-Baltistan, security for the Chinese in Gwadar will be uncertain.

What the Pakistan Government announced on January 30, is an agreement in principle for the Chinese company to take over the responsibility from the Singapore company. The details of the final agreement are still to be worked out.

There is a case regarding the security situation in Balochistan presently pending before the Pakistan Supreme Court. The Gwadar project is also linked up in the case. The Supreme Court has to agree to the Gwadar agreement with China being treated as a stand alone issue before the final agreement with China is signed. This should not pose any difficulty.

'BALOCHISTAN WILL BE MAIN BENEFICIARY OF CHINA-PAKISTAN ECONOMIC CORRIDOR'

The China-Pakistan Economic Corridor (CPEC) is not a single road, it's a network. It will spur the growth of industrial zones supported by energy plants, connecting Kashgar in China to Gwadar. Balochistan should be the primary beneficiary of the project. Khyber Pakhtunkhwa will also benefit from it as there's no discrimination against any province.

These were some of the points raised by Masood Khan, director general of the Institute of Strategic Studies, Islamabad and Pakistan's former permanent representative to the United Nations in a lecture titled 'Pakistan: security challenges and opportunities' in the library of the Pakistan Institute of International Affairs on Wednesday.

Before his talk, Mr Khan expressed his sadness at the tragedy that had taken place in the city in the morning in which 43 members of the Ismaili community were murdered in a bus. He termed the dastardly act "a sad day in our history".

Mr Khan commenced his lecture by focusing on national security underlining four important things — ideology of Pakistan, sovereignty and territorial integrity, social and economic development and development of democracy.

Drawing parameters for that he said, "National security is human security," a synthesis of aspirations and intentions of the people of Pakistan where "people are the centre". National security, he said, depended upon internal and external environments.

Highlighting the internal factors, he said terrorism was an immediate and existential threat while extremism, ethnic and religious violence, insurgency in some parts of the country and syndicates of transnational and regional crimes too fell into that category. He raised the question whether Pakistan's ideology was under threat and replied himself, "Yes". Validating his answer, he mentioned the sources from where the threat was imminent — countries that had not accepted Pakistan and forces within Pakistan who either did not want its ideology as it was conceived before 1947 or wanted a different interpretation of it. The latter included violent extremists as well as ultra liberals. Sovereignty was also under threat, from time to time, as drone attacks were one manifestation of it, he added.

Speaking on the external elements, he touched upon neighbouring countries. He said volatility along the Line of Control was an issue; Jammu and Kashmir was a disputed territory and India and Pakistan had different opinions on it. There was conventional asymmetry between India and Pakistan, but Pakistan's "nuclear deterrent is effective". He called Iran a conundrum as there was a "simmering-down" when it came to the nuclear issue, but "heating-up" vis-à-vis Yemen. He claimed operation Zarb-i-Azb was succeeding because security forces were taking on extremists throughout the country. However, he admitted, the success was partial. Democracy, he commented, and democratic institutions were yet to take root. Mr Khan said Pakistan's relations with China were strengthening, and referring to the 'one belt, one road' project he called it a "grand plan".

Expanding on the friendly ties between the two nations, he remarked, "Poetry is as important as prose." Describing poetry he said "our friendship was higher than mountains and sweeter than the sweetest honey, etc" and explaining the latter identified economic and political transactions as its components. He said the China-Pakistan Economic Corridor was going to happen and Pakistanis should prepare themselves for it. He described it as a win-win partnership. In order to remove other nations' misgivings, he asserted, "We want to steer nations away from competition to cooperation." He stressed that the corridor was not one road, but a network, which would enhance Pakistan's capacity in different sectors of development. "It would have a profound impact on the economic growth of Pakistan," he said, calling it a destination and a pathway for many services.

On the subject of India, Mr Khan said since 1971 Pakistan had made many overtures to India most of which had gone wasted. By and large, Pakistan had been proactive but India had never wanted Kashmir as an item on the (negotiation) table. He mentioned the impression was that Pakistan was guilty. Hypothesising, he argued even if Pakistan capitulated on Kashmir, India's hostility would remain. "Modi will continue with his aggressive posture against all his neighbours," he said and advised "Pakistan should deal with India with dignity. Don't go back on Kashmir even if India is reluctant or evasive about it."

With reference to Pakistan-Afghanistan relations, Mr Khan said they had entered a new phase. Pakistan reciprocated president Ashraf Ghani's warm gestures, making a fresh beginning because now there were "no good or bad terrorists".

He also briefly talked about the positive economic indicators suggesting it was a good time for Pakistan, adding that owing to the CPEC confidence of the world in Pakistan's economy had grown. Drawing the audience's attention to Pakistan's strengths, he said it had a geo-strategic importance, operation Zarb-i-Azb was succeeding which had made a major difference and democracy was taking root. He said some people believed that terrorism should be eliminated from society first after which efforts should be made for economic growth. In his opinion, it could happen simultaneously.

After the lecture the floor was opened for a question-and-answer session. Replying to a query on provinces' reservation about the CPEC, Mr Khan said it's not a single road or one link but a network; an access was being developed which would cause a mushroom growth of industrial zones, connecting Kashgar to Gwadar. He clarified that Balochistan would be the primary beneficiary of the project; KP would too benefit from it. "Some would be early harvest projects while others would reap dividends later."

On Narendra Modi's intended cricket diplomacy, Mr Khan said, "If he makes an overture it's bound to succeed. To what extent, I don't know."

Responding to the question on Pakistan's involvement in the current Middle East crisis, he said it was a millstone around our neck. We should have invested in economic policies there. It's our prerogative to pursue a balanced foreign policy in the region. He predicted, "The situation in the Middle East is likely to deteriorate."

INDIA'S RESPONSE OPTIONS TO PAKISTANI NUCLEAR FIRST USE

In the event, India's conflict strategy for its western borders would unfold as per options selected. One among other options is possibly in accord with the much written about Cold Start doctrine. Nevertheless, the conflict strategy can be expected to be offensive, taking advantage of the changed mindset and organisations enabling this over the past decade. The services are conscious that these operations would be under the nuclear overhang. No doubt this would find reflection in the manner political aims are translated into strategic and in turn operational objectives.

Reflection in the early part of last decade on Limited War doctrine indicates that proverbial nuclear thresholds would be respected. In effect Pakistan's nuclear deterrent would have worked but only partially. Its leveraging of the nuclear deterrent to deter conventional war would have failed. But, the nuclear backdrop would help preserve it from any expansive Indian war aims. Since, as Peter Lavoy informs, Pakistan would largely rely on conventional forces to counter Indian offensives, the nuclear card would have political utility. Brandishing the same for nuclear signalling so as to bring war termination pressures from the international community can be expected.

This may be in the form of rhetoric, nuclear tests or a demonstration strike. A hypothetical case of highly provocative nuclear first use with the purpose of nuclear signalling for war termination is defensive use on own territory against insignificant tactical targets. A favoured example in strategic literature is a solitary nuclear strike on an advancing column in the desert. It has been estimated that such a strike would cause just a few Indian casualties. Such a strike would be twin edged for Pakistan. One is that it would breach the professed Indian nuclear threshold of 'any Indian casualties any where' resulting in 'assured retaliation' of proportions exacting 'unacceptable damage'. The second, in Pakistan's favour as intended, is in focussing international attention on to restricting the manner of Indian reaction.

India's nuclear deterrent doctrine is explicit that the counter would be 'massive'. Since this is for deterrence, in case of deterrence breakdown, response strategy could well be different. 'Unacceptable damage' can be caused by less than 'massive' levels of nuclear retaliation. In the event, the political leadership would have its nuclear decision making informed by doctrine, but not restricted by it. In effect, nuclear employment doctrine may be different from nuclear deterrent doctrine. The latter is known, while the former is not known. India's conventional offensives are likely to exploit the existing space between sub-conventional and perceived nuclear thresholds. While Pakistan can be expected to self-servingly project these thresholds as 'low', a realistic appreciation may indicate that enough space exists for measured force application.

This being within the capability of Pakistani conventional counter action, risk of war escalation is minimised. Nevertheless, contingency planning being the measure of a professional military, India's counter options to Pakistani nuclear first use can be expected. This commentary makes some suggestions in this direction. Firstly, in the pre-conflict stage, India needs to make its military doctrine transparent. It needs to indicate a pronounced inclination towards the Limited War concept. This has not been explicitly spelt out thus far in the Army doctrine in the open domain.

The Navy doctrine is somewhat hazy. It takes General or Total War as 'involving nearly all resources of the nation, with few, if any, restriction on the use of force, short of nuclear strike/retaliation.' Two problems arise. One is that this formulation appears to suggest that Total War aiming for 'annihilation or total subjugation of the opponent' can yet occur below the nuclear threshold. Second, there is no category in the 'Spectrum of Conflict' in the doctrine in which it accommodates nuclear use, since the definition of Total War recounted here seems to place it outside into some separate, undefined, category. The issue that arises is that minimalist resort to nuclear weapons such as in the example given does not automatically place the war into the Total War domain since 'annihilation' is not being sought. The overall impression is that the military is undecided to weigh in on the side of Limited War unambiguously. It needs to do so in order to raise the nuclear threshold.

Maintaining the threshold at a high level during conflict so as to gain military objectives without flirting with it requires explicitly conveying to Pakistan at the outset of the conflict through multiple channels that war aims do not seek regime change or state extinction. This would require not only information operations but also be conveyed by the threat perception in Pakistan stemming from its reading of troop deployment and dispositions. There is a paradox that requires to be lived with here. Operational transparency to indicate limited war aims is to the detriment of the heightened threat that serves to deter conventional conflict escalation. In case the enemy gets to know that limited aims are to be achieved, he can throw in much more than he otherwise would to deny these. But the problem of withholding from transparency is that in case the enemy is not able to match professions of limited war with actions on the ground, he may be inclined to a 'worst case' judgement.

This builds in avoidable dynamism in lowering the nuclear threshold. In the hypothetical case of lower order nuclear first use, the first consideration for retaliation is consequences for political aims of the conflict. The original limited political aim is threatened with expansion since nuclear weapons have been introduced into the conflict changing its nature and dimensions. In which case can original limited war aims be sustained? If not, is revision necessary? Such thinking needs be done prior. That an expanded nuclear war needs to be avoided is selfevident. This can at best be in order to degrade a continuing nuclear threat under the logic of 'limiting damage' (Hermann Kahn) that may be sustained in further nuclear exchanges. The logic informing 'massive' nuclear retaliation seems to be precisely this. Taking out enemy nuclear capability along with punishing it would preserve oneself from his counter strikes. Nevertheless, this is ruled out by the second strike capability available with Pakistan in terms of an expanded arsenal. Since both sides share a common interest in limiting damage, continuation of the nuclear threat would be dependent on the counter.

Therefore, the considerations on the nature of the counter would need to factor in the implications of escalation. It being undesirable, retaliation would be designed not so much to punish but also to enable exchange termination. Doing so at the lowest levels of nuclear retaliation would place the onus of escalation on the enemy. Since the exchange can get out of hand and result in spasmic retaliation, in-conflict deterrence based on Schelling's concept of 'threat that leaves something to chance' is heightened. Such deterrence also exists to deter first use, but it is now more consequential since a nuclear war is an entirely new environment and would serve to focus minds more acutely on the threatening possibilities.

Limiting Options

Firstly, the mistaken impression that Indian resolve may be weak, needs to be dispelled in Pakistani thinking. The propensity towards this may be more in Pakistan corresponding to the levels of ideological penetration by extremism of the Establishment and the military mind there. The Army can generally be reckoned as a rational organisation and its nuclear decision making system more so. Transparency has been resorted to over the last decade by Pakistan to influence perceptions that its nuclear capability lacks safety and control. It has taken steps in streamlining systems and these contribute to rational decision making. Irrationality projected is for deterrence purposes.

This circumstance lends itself to Indian planning for conventional war, albeit a limited one. However, in case a mistaken impression on Indian resolve were to inform Pakistani thinking then, the propensity to lower the nuclear threshold would be greater. Therefore, either tests or better still a demonstration strike may both reinforce Indian resolve and impress Pakistani decision makers of its credibility. The action would require prior communication to Pakistan in order that it is not mistaken for a nuclear strike. Unstated possibilities this evokes would bring the international community to bear down on events compelling Pakistan to concede India's reasonable self-evidently demands without further 1 affray. Secondly, as discussed, nuclear first use by Pakistan may be with the political aim of conflict termination through influencing both Indian minds and the international community.

Despite this intent and the low provocation levels of such a strike, this would place Pakistan inevitably and irreversibly on the political defensive. Nuclear resort may be sustainable in international law in the extreme case of threat to existence of the state. This would patently not be the case in light of broadcast limited war aims of India and the progress of the war. Therefore, India could profit politically from a measured response including a non-nuclear one. Such responses could be more violent conventional strikes against value targets of Pakistan that were originally kept off the scope of the war due to the intent of limitation. These could include political and military leadership, symbolic targets such as politically significant structures, expanded infrastructure degradation and heightened attrition on conventional forces.

The nuclear threshold having already been crossed, restrictions would no longer apply. Therefore, keeping going conventionally would enable greater attrition on the Pakistani state and it's military. This would have political dividend post war in that the military not only would be blamed for provoking the punishment but would be too weak to regain its political salience in internal politics. Indian restraint in contrast to military adventurism in Pakistan would heighten calls for accountability, both internally in Pakistan and externally in a war crimes court. Therefore, a better peace post-conflict is possible through negotiations with a civilian regime.

The point is that a non-nuclear counter deserves to be considered. Continuing restraint has advantages that current calls for scaling down Indian restraint and prudence seem to neglect. The counter argument would be that restraint at this stage of a war gone nuclear may give the impression of pusillanimity to the enemy and embolden further, possibly more provocative, strikes. This is based on the logic that deterrence requires capability, resolve and communication of possession of both to the enemy. While capability exists, resolve may require communication. This can only be through striking back, deterring him from further strikes and limiting damage thereby. It would be useful for in-conflict deterrence, broadcasting unambiguously worse to come in case of continuation of the exchange by Pakistan. Internally political pressures would only be satisfied by nuclear punishment for Pakistan's temerity.

The sustainability of the argument can best be seen in light of the changed conflict environment; one that has transited speedily from a limited war to a nuclear one, but has not acquired Total War portents. What would be the mental condition of decision makers in a nuclear war scenario? Would they be amenable to being deterred as this logic indicates or would they be emotionally so charged as to be incapable of the self-restraint on which deterrence is predicated? Here, an answer is not attempted, but it is suggested that any risk of the latter is enough to bring the non-nuclear response route back into the reckoning, particularly in case of militarily inconsequential, non-provocative lower order nuclear use by Pakistan. The promise of 'massive' nuclear retaliation may prove inadequate in staying Pakistani nuclear hand in face of Indian offensives.

Inflicting 'unacceptable damage' may appear disproportionate to its leadership if in response to lower order nuclear first use. Therefore, nuclear retaliation could well be of quid pro quo or quid pro quo plus levels with damage not amounting to an 'unacceptable' order. Nevertheless, there is a case for considering the non-nuclear measures covered here since the advantage would be a better post conflict peace and at a lower cost.

8

The Strategic Importance of Chinese-Pakistani Relations

Of all China's neighboring countries, China-Pakistan relations are the closest and friendliest. The two countries established diplomatic relations in 1951, making Pakistan one of the first Islamic countries as well as the second country in South Asia after India to establish diplomatic relations with China. The two countries have remained strong allies ever since. The closeness of the relationship between the two countries can be seen from major bilateral interactions over the years. For instance, in the Indo-Pakistani wars of 1965 and 1971, China took the side of Pakistan against India.

In addition, China supported the alliance between Pakistan and the United States against the Soviet invasion of Afghanistan in 1979. China also provided assistance for Pakistan to become a nuclear power in 1998, and used its Security Council veto power for the first time in 1972 to block the entry of Bangladesh into the United Nations.

Pakistan played a crucial role in the ice-breaking visit of U.S. National Security Adviser Henry Kissinger to China in 1971, and was one of only two United Nations member countries (along with Cuba) to support China following the Tiananmen Square incident of 1989. The two countries enjoy close cooperation in areas such as trade, borders, and their militaries, meaning that Pakistan has a unique status among China's many diplomatic allies.

How can we understand the special relationship between China and Pakistan? Why have the two countries enjoyed such friendly and stable diplomatic relations across a whole range of areas over the past 65 years? If we can accurately answer these two questions, we can more fully understand the strategic importance of Pakistan both in the region and worldwide. As one of the world's major powers, China's development across a range of areas has been the subject of increasing international attention in recent years. China is widely considered to be an "emerging power" that may threaten the United States in the future. Therefore, China's strategic relationship with Pakistan must be understood from an international strategic perspective, specifically the interlocking geopolitical relationships between China, the United States, India and Russia. In addition, the struggle between Western and Islamic civilisation in the context of developments in the Middle East following the 11 September attacks, in particular the global spread and diffusion of terrorism, are also crucial factors in China–Pakistan relations.

The Regional Context and Players

After the Second World War, in the context of the U.S.-Soviet Cold War, China and India took a more prominent role in East Asia and South Asia. Although China is not a member of the "Non-Aligned Movement", while India is one of its three founding countries (along with Egypt and Yugoslavia), both China and India took independent foreign policy positions outside of the U.S. and Soviet power blocs. As a result, bilateral relations between China and India, as well as their diplomatic relations with the U.S. and Soviet blocs have had an important impact on the strategic relations between China and Pakistan. In simple terms, although India pursued a policy of nonalignment during the Cold War, it had close military and diplomatic relations with the Soviet Union. In addition, the tension in relations between China and India mainly arose from long-term territorial disputes along the two countries' shared border. At the same time, friendly relations between India and the Soviet Union were a thorn in the side of the Chinese whose own relations with the Soviet Union deteriorated from the 1960s onwards. Therefore, within the South Asia region, China pursued a policy of alliance with Pakistan to balance against India. Even after the collapse of the Soviet Union, China has continued to maintain this policy, even as China and India tried to improve relations with each other and establish a degree of mutual trust.

During the Cold War, relations between the Soviet Union and India were friendly. In addition, following the 1979 Soviet invasion of Afghanistan, together with the normalisation of relations between China and the United States, the United States and China followed consistent policies towards Pakistan, offering it political and military support in hopes of containing Soviet influence in Central and South Asia.

In this case, with the Taliban's rise to power in Afghanistan in 1996, and the 11 September attacks, there was a structural change in the strategic situation. The main effect of this was that U.S. policy in Central and South Asia changed from its previous supporting role to a dominant role in the regional order in order to carry out its post-911 global anti-terrorism policy. In recent years, there was a radical change in the roles of Russia and India from their previous animosity towards the United States and China, as both countries to some extent became partners of the United States in the fight against terrorism.

The role of China was even more subtle, in particular after the 2008 global financial crisis as China's overall power advanced substantially and it's political, military, economic, and even cultural influence expanded, thus changing the regional power relations in Central and South Asia. These changes can be understood on the following three dimensions. First, although relations between China and India are still defined by competition in the context of great power politics, China regards India as a potential overseas market for future expansion, and therefore China-India relations have been quickly normalised. Second, the above changes have not undermined the importance of Pakistan to China. This is because Pakistan has an important role in ensuring a stable regional order in Central and South

Asia and preventing the spread of terrorism to China. Third, even more importantly, after Xi Jinping's rise to power, China proposed the grand strategy of "One Belt and One Road." India has not offered its support, while China has announced plans to invest 46 billion US dollars in Pakistan, focused on core projects in railway construction, highway construction, energy, and infrastructure with the goal of accelerating the modernisation of industry in Pakistanand connecting China's Xinjiang to Gwadar Port in Pakistan.

This "China-Pakistan Economic Corridor" will continue the expansion of China's political and economic influence in Central and South Asia.

The Current Status of China-Pakistan Relations

Although China-Pakistan relations have always been friendly, past cooperation between the two countries was mostly at the political and military level and had not extended to the comprehensive social, economic, and cultural exchange relations of today. This new phase in relations started in May 2013 with the visit of Chinese Premier Li Keqiang to Pakistan and the official proposal of the concept of the "China-Pakistan Economic Corridor." Subsequently, there was an exchange of visits between leaders and officials from both countries, including the visit of Pakistani President Mamnoon Hussain to China in February 2014 and Pakistani Prime Minister Nawaz Sharif's subsequent visit in April 2014 which involved intensive consultations over the proposal.

Finally, during Chinese President Xi Jinping's visit to Pakistan in April 2015, the proposal was officially finalised, including the signing of 51 Memorandums of Understanding between the two countries, the inauguration of eight projects, and the launching of five joint energy projects. Aside from the familiar infrastructure and energy projects, this new phase of relations between the two countries also included social, economic, technological, and even cultural cooperation. For example, the two countries have organised bilateral exchanges in radio and television. The Industrial and Commercial Bank of China set up a branch in Lahore, Pakistan's second city; the ministries of science and technology in the two countries jointly established the China-Pakistan Joint Cotton Bio-Tech Laboratory; Pakistan's University of Modern Languages (NUML) and Xinjiang University jointly established the NUML International Center of Education, and the China Culture Center in Pakistan has been established.

If these initiatives are successful, relations between the two countries will become more closely intertwined at all levels, from high-level political and military relations, extending to the full range of contacts and relations at each level of society.

What will be the ultimate effect of the 46 billion US dollar China-Pakistan Economic Corridor? According to an interview given by China's ambassador to Pakistan Sun Weidong last month (June 24) to the Xinhua News Agency, at present achievements from China-Pakistan cooperation projects are focused on four areas: energy projects, transport infrastructure, Gwadar Port, and industrial cooperation.

Major energy projects include construction of a 300 megawatt solar power plant by Chinese company Zonergy, and work has already started on more than half of the remaining sixteen planned energy projects. In terms of transport infrastructure, reconstruction and upgrade works of the Karakoram Highway (KKH) within Pakistan are underway, and the construction of the Karachi-Lahore Motorway also started this March. For the development of Gwadar Port, on November 11, 2015, Pakistan handed over 280 hectares of land use rights to a Chinese company for a term of forty-three years, and construction on new facilities is already underway. Finally, Chinese projects in Pakistan under the China-Pakistan Economic Corridor already employ more than 6,000 Pakistani workers, showing that the close relationship between China and Pakistan has already moved from the policy announcement to the project implementation stage. The amount of funds involved, the depth of the exchanges, and the number of people participating are unprecedented in relations between the two countries.

Issues with China's Muslim Minority

However, the relationship between China and Pakistan is not without worries. First, in the past the Chinese government held suspicions that Uyghur terrorists were operating in Pakistan and running terrorist training camps in the country, and that these terrorists had a direct relationship with terrorist incidents in Xinjiang. Second, in recent years, fundamentalism has spread very quickly within Xinjiang, and a large number of terrorist incidents have occurred. As a result, the Chinese government has been extremely concerned about Pakistan's willingness, ability, and determination to fight Islamic terrorism. Finally, China is also concerned about the continued failure of the United States to successfully rebuild Afghanistan's political order, especially the ambiguous role played by Pakistan in the country, which in theory supports the political order constructed by the U.S.-led alliance, but is also surreptitiously supporting the Afghan Taliban and Al-Qaeda. Therefore, China has recently expressed a desire to participate in peace talks between the Afghan government and the Taliban, meaning that due to its powerful influence over Pakistan, it may be better qualified than the United States to play the role of mediator in delivering peace to Afghanistan.

The above concerns stem directly from the serious issues that the Chinese government is facing with its Muslim minority. These problems mainly originate from the Islamic consciousness of the Uygur population, and the creation of a national identity separate from "Chinese identity," which has led to a growth in Xinjiang separatism. The Chinese government has been unable to prevent the occurrence of violent resistance to Chinese rule by the Uygur population for three main reasons. First, the Uyghurs are generally less educated, and receive most of their education in the Uyghur language, causing serious linguistic and cultural barriers with the Han majority. Second, while Uygur Communist Party cadres often claim to support the central government's restrictions on the Islamic religion and Chinese nationalism, in reality they are opposed to the repressive rule of the Han over the Uygur people. Third, in recent years, Islamic fundamentalism has spread rapidly though pilgrimages, the Internet, and underground religious schools; and there are signs that these developments have been influenced by international Islamic terrorist groups such as the Turkistan Islamic Party, Al-Qaeda, and the Islamic State. As a result, attacks against government office, the military and law enforcement have become regular occurrences. In response, the ruling party has adopted both hard and soft measures, combining repressive measures to maintain stability and prevent the occurrence of violent incidents with other measures to strengthen economic assistance from other provinces and cities to Xinjiang. However, these approaches offer no possibility of penetrating Uygur grassroots networks or resolving the estrangement of the Uygur group from the Han and the Hui, or promoting the incorporation of the Uygur population with its Islamic identity into Chinese identity centered on Han Chinese culture.

Although they are also Muslims, the problems faced by the Hui minority are much less significant. An important reason is that the Hui also speak Chinese Therefore, Chinese Communist Party organs can more easily penetrate into the grassroots networks of the Hui people, while also carrying out more comprehensive training and management of Imams. More importantly, the Islam adhered to by the Hui has incorporated the cultural elements from various Chinese dynasties, for example the replacement of religious denomination with menhuan (meaning faction) and the appearance of Taoist architectural features in mosques as well as the exclusive use of Chinese versions of religious texts for preaching. The characteristics described above closely match the Chinese Communist Party's movement to "Sinicize religion," which attempts to incorporate all religions under a larger Chinese identity. This is true for Islam as well as other religions such as Catholicism, Protestantism, Buddhism, and Taoism. Finally, among other Islamic minorities, due to the small numbers, the Chinese communist party is still capable of using party-state mechanisms to stabilise the social order, which means that violent terrorist incidents of the type found in Uyghur areas are extremely rare.

How China Views Pakistan in the International Context?

To understand China's view of Pakistan from the perspective of international politics, we must take into account Pakistan's interlocking relationships with the United States, China itself, and the Arab world. Following the military interventions in Afghanistan in 2001 and Iraq in 2003, the efforts of the United States to reestablish the regional order in the Middle East suffered a major setback. The financial, material, and human costs gradually eroded domestic support for military intervention in the region and, following the rise of Islamic State in 2014, there was a strong wave of public opinion in the United States advocating withdrawal from the Middle East with U.S. peacekeeping efforts in Afghanistan and military and political support for Pakistan coming under increasing scrutiny. For this reason, the United States has played the role of mediator for Chinese involvement in Afghanistan, generally welcoming China's enhanced role. This trend reflects U.S. concern that if efforts to reconstruct the order in Afghanistan are not sustained, there will be a power vacuum in Afghanistan, causing the Taliban, the Islamic State, and even pro-Pakistan militants to carve up political power. Therefore, if China can effectively share the burden with the U.S. and exert influence over Pakistan, it should be sufficient to stabilise the current political situation in Afghanistan.

China and the United States are both aware that Pakistan hopes to hold influence over the regime in Afghanistan for the long term, and are also aware that Pakistan tries to use its influence over the Taliban, Al-Qaeda, and other Islamic militants to extract political, military, and economic benefits from the West. However, China and the United States have quite different expectations. For the latter, withdrawal from Afghanistan without the threat of Pakistani blackmail, while also maintaining stability in Central Asia and containing the spread of Islamic extremism is the ideal outcome. From China's perspective, Afghanistan and Pakistan act as a geographical hub between Central and South Asia, representing a strategic location for the development of "One Belt and One Road" as well as a route to the Indian Ocean and Arabian Sea that is not constrained by India. More importantly, the Chinese government can use its influence over Pakistan and Afghanistan to contain the penetration of Islamic extremism into Xinjiang. This illustrates that China and the United States both have an interest in allowing China to participate in the reconstruction Afghanistan and constrain opportunistic moves from Pakistan.

The calculations of China and the United States also affect the thinking of neighboring countries. For example, China has always taken a supportive position towards Iran. In fact, after Iran was subject to international sanctions in 2006 due to its nuclear weapons programme, China was Iran's main ally in breaking the sanctions. Therefore, Iran does not view the Chinese government's influence over Pakistan and Afghanistan in entirely negative terms.

For Arab countries, in particular the Gulf states led by Saudi Arabia, Pakistan is viewed as a close political ally particularly for its role the joint fight against the alliance between the Soviet Union and India during the Cold War. As a result, the Gulf States have offered long-term political, military and economic support for Pakistan. However, there is a perception that these favours have not been returned by Pakistan. This perception reflects subtle changes in recent years in relations between Pakistan and Saudi Arabia. In many international issues, Pakistan has not offered unreserved support for Arab countries. For example, after the Yemeni civil war broke out in March 2015, Pakistan refused an invitation to join a Saudi-led coalition to intervene in the conflict. In addition, Saudi Arabia has also sought to form an alliance with Pakistan against Iran. However, this request did not produce a positive response from Pakistan. On Syria, Pakistan has taken a different position to Arab countries, advocating a negotiated political solution to the civil war as opposed to the Arab countries' support for the Syrian opposition. This also explains the previous efforts of Arab countries to strengthen cooperation with India, which they hoped would provide a reminder to Pakistan that Arab support for Pakistan should not be take for granted. If Pakistan chooses to turn away from the Arab countries, the latter can respond by withdrawing their support from Pakistan and transferring it to its old enemy, India.

MUTUAL INTERESTS UNDERLIE STRONG CHINA–PAKISTAN RELATIONSHIP

China seems to have abandoned its cautious approach to relations with Pakistan and has adopted a policy of active and deep engagement. This new approach will most likely increase Beijing's influence in Islamabad.

During Chinese President Xi Jinping's visit to Pakistan in April 2015, China announced US$46 billion worth of investment in the China–Pakistan Economic Corridor (CPEC).

This ambitious mega-project intends to link China's Kashgar to Gwadar Port in Pakistan through a network of roads. Both sides are also planning railways, pipelines and fibre optic networks. This is the largest deal in the history of two countries. If the implementation of the CPEC moves smoothly, China may double its investment.

Pakistan has been going through an unabated challenge with terrorism and chronic political instability. Yet, China still decided to undertake this mega-investment, which shows its deep stake in Pakistan. The changing geopolitical environment might shed a light on this audacious decision.

The gravity of world politics is shifting from the West to Asia, with China at its centre. This has increased competition between the US (the established superpower) and China (the rising power) who are both seeking to gain a strategic foothold, especially in the Asia Pacific region. The US's 'pivot to Asia' strategy, intensifying territorial disputes in the South China Sea and a resurging Japan under Prime Minister Shinzo Abe are all ringing Chinese alarm bells.

China is looking for allies in the region, and finds Pakistan is its most reliable partner. This relationship is grounded in geographical proximity, common security outlooks toward the region and 'trust' built over decades. China is also motivated by a desire to help Pakistan restore its 'glorious' past.

China and Pakistan's interests are converging in the changing geopolitical environment. Beijing wants to assert its sphere of influence in South Asia, the Middle East, get an access to the Indian Ocean and beyond. China also needs support against separatism in Xinjiang and is seeking to develop its Western region. To achieve some of those objectives, China has unveiled the One Belt, One Road project that will ultimately connect it with over 60 countries. Under this project, China will build a web of networks such as the Bangladesh–China–India–Myanmar Economic Corridor, the Silk Road in Central Asia, the 21st Century Maritime Silk Road and the CPEC.

The CPEC is the flagship of these projects. It acts as a bridge between land and sea, involves only one other country (Pakistan), and gives China the quickest route to the Indian Ocean and beyond. The CPEC will complement China's desire to modernise its Western region and deal with separatists in Xinjiang. For the terrorism-hit Pakistan, the CPEC could bring huge investment, infrastructural development, China's political and diplomatic support at international fronts.

China's economic assistance is also backed by strong defence ties. Within days of Xi's visit, China announced the supply of 50 JF-17 aircraft, jointly produced by China and Pakistan. The two sides have also finalised the largest defence deal for either side: six Chinese nuclear-capable submarines worth US$4–6 billion. China has already become Pakistan's largest arms suppliers and meets over 50 per cent Pakistan's weapons needs.

China's renewed engagement with Pakistan is not directed against India as is generally perceived. That might be Pakistan's wish, and the concern of some Indian and Western spectators, but it does not seem to be China's intention. Since the late 1980s, Beijing has separated its relationship with Pakistan from its relationship with India. China deals with each country independently. China looks at South Asia from a long-term perspective, and is not focused on the Indo–Pakistan rivalry. A stable South Asia and improved India–Pakistan relations will also serve China's interest more than any other big power.

Based on its geo-strategic location, Pakistan has acquired a new importance in Beijing's long-term strategy. This can be seen in China's bold investment in mega projects and burgeoning defence ties between the two nations. Given the high stakes, this will likely increase China's influence in Pakistan. Unlike in the past, Beijing may now take stand on issues affecting its interests.

At the same time Islamabad is cognisant that in the wake of a partial withdrawal from Afghanistan, relations with the US may enter into another phase of uncertainty. Islamabad has thus shown alacrity in intensifying ties with China, especially through a commitment to the early implementation of the CPEC. This deep congruence of mutual interests guarantees a durable Sino–Pakistani relationship into the future.

PAKISTAN REMAINS FAITHFUL PARTNER OF CHINA

In April when President Xi Jinping visited Pakistan, China and Pakistan elevated the bilateral relations to "all-weather strategic cooperation partners." China has established partnerships with a lot of countries in the world, but Pakistan is the only one that is called an "all-weather strategic cooperation partner."

For countries with different social systems and ideologies that want to collaborate with each other, the China-Pakistan relationship has become a model to follow. This type of relationship is not based on common values and systems, but on same or similar strategic and security interests. Today common security concerns still exist, and some new concerns like global terrorism and maritime security have arisen for both sides in recent years.

Since the beginning of the 21st century, the basis of China-Pakistan cooperation has expanded. The "One Belt, One Road" initiative and China-Pakistan Economic Corridor has enlarged bilateral strategic and cooperative partnership to a more comprehensive framework.

Before, the basis of the all-weather partnership mainly included political, strategic and security cooperation, now the closer economic ties have become a part of this basis, which makes two countries form a "community of shared destiny." The two sides not only have common economic interest and common security concerns, but also share the dream of national peace, stability, and prosperity. "Shared destiny" is the solid foundation for our cooperation in international affairs.

China-Pakistan international cooperation has some key features as follows: First, China and Pakistan respect principles, value friendship, and "share weal and woe." When dealing with international affairs, both sides take the Five Principles of Peaceful Coexistence as the basic principle; when facing international affairs, both sides advocate justice and fairness, protect the common interests of developing countries, and have the courage to speak up.

In addition, China-Pakistan cooperation is always based on close communication and coordination, deep understanding of the other side's situation and interest, and full consideration of the other side's feeling. Pakistan always gives China full support on the Taiwan, Tibet, Xinjiang, and South China Sea issues. China is also a strong supporter of the independence, sovereignty, territorial integrity, and national dignity of Pakistan.

In 1972, the People's Republic of China used its veto power for the first time to support Pakistan at the UN Security Council by refusing to admit Bangladesh, the former East Pakistan, to the UN. After 1989, every time when China was blamed by the US and other Western countries at the UN Commission on Human Rights, Pakistan was always the first one to stand up and speak for China.

China and Pakistan conform to trends of the times, expand scope of cooperation, and jointly resolve challenges. After the Cold War, especially in the 21st century, the world has seen a trend toward peace, development, and cooperation.

Apart from traditional security issues, more and more non-traditional challenges arise. As a result, China-Pakistan cooperation has expanded from political and security fields to economy and trade, climate change, food and energy security. China takes the interests of Pakistan and other developing countries into careful consideration when it negotiates with Western countries.

China and Pakistan support each other in regional cooperation. Pakistan actively supports China further deepening cooperation with the South Asian Association for Regional Cooperation. China supports Pakistan to become a full member of the Shanghai Cooperation Organization. Pakistan is one of the founding members of the China-initiated Asian Infrastructure Investment Bank, and shows solid support to the project. Pakistani scholars and diplomats actively support China's New Security Concept.

The China-Pakistan Economic Corridor will help Pakistan to advance its relationship with neighboring countries and become the hub of regional economic integration. On Afghan issues, China values Pakistan's unique role.

China and Pakistan can further strengthen bilateral policy coordination and strategic cooperation. They have a stake in each other's success. As a stronger peer, China should pay more attention to Pakistan's interest in international and regional affairs. As Pakistan makes progress in its economic development, China should support Pakistan becoming a member of APEC and RCEP.

However, people-to-people exchanges are the missing part in the foundation of China-Pakistan cooperation in international affairs. Our Pakistani friends enjoy a lot of advantages when contacting Islamic countries, so Pakistan could act as a bridge between China and Islamic countries for further cooperation and collaboration, especially in the process of building "One Belt, One Road" and realizing the Asian community of shared destiny.

CHINA-PAKISTAN RELATIONSHIP

For China, Pakistan is essentially a surrogate army. Owing to traditional military rivalry, India has for decades maintained a Pakistan centric strategic policy which keeps its military tied up and limits its options against China. According to Husain Haqqani, of Carnegie Endowment for International Peace, "For China, Pakistan is a low-cost secondary deterrent to India". "For Pakistan, China is a high-value guarantor of security against India." In this mutually beneficial friendship however, owing to Pakistan's limited strategic capability against India, China is essentially a needed ally, while China does not necessarily rely on Pakistan.

China-Pakistan relations are diverse, and the Chinese have a strong investment presence in Pakistan. According to Jing Huang, senior fellow in Asia Studies at the Brookings Institution, "Pakistan would welcome investments from China more than anywhere else because Chinese are our brothers and time-tested friends". The two countries have cooperated on a variety of large-scale infrastructure projects in Pakistan, including highways, gold and copper mines, major electricity complexes and power plants, and numerous nuclear power projects. Pakistan helps China on a range of issues, including "providing intelligence, fighting terrorism, and repairing relations with the Muslim world".

However, this strategic relationship has adopted a sinister dimension of proliferation of sensitive nuclear and missile technology to Pakistan. Commercially, as China began its economic reform and opening up in the early 1980s, defence industries and arms exporting companies were under tremendous pressure to tap into the lucrative international arms market. Pakistan became a valued customer for Chinese arms. Finally, given US concern about and emphasis on missile proliferation issues, Beijing has also found it useful to exploit them as bargaining leverage in dealing with Washington on issues important to China: US arms sales to Taiwan, TMD deployment in East Asia, among others. American intelligence reports have alleged that China has transferred complete M-11 missiles, missile related technology, and manufacturing assistance to Pakistan.

The M-11 is a single stage, solid fuelled missile with a reported range of 290 km and a payload of 800 kg. While technically the M-11 missile does not fall within the MTCR parameter, they have the inherent capability of being able to deliver a 500 kg payload over 300 km. The fact that China has resisted joining the MTCR as a formal member, coupled with its ambiguous interpretation and implementation of its bilateral commitments with the United States, raises questions as to the seriousness of Chinese commitment to arms control and nonproliferation.

Significantly, some news reports suggest Chinese security agencies knew about Pakistani transfers of nuclear technology to Iran, North Korea, and Libya. China also had longstanding ties with Abdul Qadeer Khan, known as the father of the Pakistani nuclear program, and head of an international black market nuclear network. "The Pakistani nuclear program is largely the result of Sino-Pakistani relations" says Huang.

China-Pakistan nuclear cooperation began in the early 1980s. The United States government and many Western analysts believe that China assisted Pakistan in developing nuclear explosives prior to its accession to the NPT in 1992. In 1983, US intelligence agencies reported that China had transferred a complete nuclear weapon design to Pakistan, along with enough weapons-grade uranium for two nuclear weapons. China also reportedly helped Pakistan operate its Kahuta uranium-enrichment plant. According to media reports the amount transferred was enough for making 10 nuclear weapons China also provided assistance and transferred dual-use materials that could be applied in the development of nuclear weapons. Beijing insists that China's assistance involved the provisions of peaceful technical information rather than weapons-related technologies or materials. According to Chinese Foreign Ministry spokesman Qin Gang, nuclear energy cooperation between China and Pakistan is "absolutely for peaceful purpose."

China allegedly involved Pakistani scientists in a nuclear test at its Lop Nur test site in 1989. On December 31, 1991, China signed a contract to build the Chashma 300-MW nuclear power reactor for Pakistan, and has agreed to build an additional three more reactors Chasma II (which is already under construction) and Chasma III and Chasma IV (III and IV are to be contractually agreed upon).

Beijing has adopted a number of measures to improve its proliferation image including publicly adopting responsible nuclear export policies after joining the International Atomic Energy Agency (IAEA) in 1984 and furthered its commitment by acceding to the Nonproliferation Treaty (NPT) in 1992. In addition, Beijing has formally enunciated three principles governing its nuclear exports: (1) acceptance of IAEA safeguards; (2) peaceful use only; and (3) no re-transfers to a third country without China's prior consent.

In 1993 China and the International Atomic Energy Agency (IAEA) signed an agreement to apply IAEA safeguards to a Chinese nuclear power station sold to Pakistan (INFCIRC/418). In 1994, China reportedly turned down a Pakistani request to "correct" Pakistan's nuclear weapons and to use the Chinese Lop Nur testing range.

In recent years, China has also promulgated domestic laws regulating nuclear and dual-use exports. It has also played a highly constructive role in the six party talks in restricting the North Korean nuclear weapons program and also international efforts in curbing the Iranian nuclear program. Beijing, while advocating a nuclear deal for Pakistan, has indicated that a more detailed study of the Pakistani request would be needed by the Chinese leadership.

However, significant concerns continue to emanate out of Chinese exports, particularly to Pakistan. In 1995, a major controversy erupted over suspected sales of 5,000 specially designed ring magnets from the China Nuclear Energy Industry Corporation (CNEIC) to a non-safeguarded Pakistani nuclear laboratory, which was allegedly involved in nuclear weapons work. China initially denied that the sale had taken place; a Chinese Foreign Ministry spokesman called the reports "groundless" and warned the United States not to impose sanctions based on "rumours."

Pakistan also denied that any transfer of sensitive nuclear technology had taken place. However, in talks with US officials, China eventually privately admitted that the sale had taken place, but argued that China should not be penalized for two reasons.

First, China insisted that CNEIC had arranged the sale without the knowledge or consent of the central government. Second, China argued that the ring magnets were not magnetized, and the Nuclear Suppliers Group (NSG) Trigger List only covers ring magnets magnetized at a specific tolerance. Suspicions of sensitive technological transfers resurfaced in August-September 1996, when reports indicated that China had agreed to sell a special industrial furnace and high-technology diagnostic equipment to a Pakistani nuclear facility, equipment which reportedly can be used in the construction of nuclear bombs. The reports were dismissed by the Chinese and investigators could not find sufficient evidence against China.

The May 1998 tests by Pakistan in response to similar tests by India, further fuelled suspicions over Pakistan's nuclear program. While scientists claimed it to be an indigenous test, many commentators allege that the tests could not have been possible without the explicit help of China. In response to Pakistan testing its nuclear weapons, China practically laid all blame on India. According to a statement from the foreign office "The present situation in South Asia has been caused solely by India. India conducted nuclear tests in disregard of strong opposition by the international community." In February 2001, the press reported that China's Seventh Research and Design Institute, which is overseen by the China National

Nuclear Corporation, supplied 50 ceramic capacitors to Pakistan's New Labs plutonium reprocessing plant. The Institute was reportedly paid through a bank account maintained by an official at the Pakistani embassy in Beijing. The Chinese-supplied Khushab reactor can generate enough plutonium for at least one nuclear weapon per year, and probably more. According to US think tank Institute for Science and International Security (ISIS), Pakistan is close to increasing several-fold its ability to make weapon-grade plutonium through developments at Khushab. The Khushab nuclear site in Punjab province originally consisted of one heavy-water reactor with a power of about 50 MW and a heavy water production facility. Details about the construction of the second and third reactors emerged in 2006 and 2007. "No electricity production equipment is seen in the (satellite) images. This is consistent with the purpose of the reactors being to produce plutonium for nuclear weapons," the report said. Chinese proliferation activities during the eight years of the Clinton administration resulted in Chinese entities subject to sanctions 17 times. In four years of the Bush administration, Chinese entities have been sanctioned a total of 50 times. In 2004 alone, 14 Chinese entities were sanctioned a total of 23 times.

Five companies—China Great Wall Industry Corporation, China Precision Machinery Import/Export Corporation, China North Industries Corporation (NORINCO), Wha Cheong Tai Company, Ltd., and Zibo Chemical Equipment Plant—and one Chinese national, Q.C. Chen, have all been sanctioned at least four times by the United States and are often referred to as "serial proliferators" by U.S. officials. For some entities, such as the China Great Wall Industry Corporation and China Precision Machinery Import/Export Corporation, the sanctions have been spread out over more than a decade. But for NORINCO and Zibo Chemical Equipment Plant, the sanctions have all occurred since 2003 and 2002, respectively.

Wider Proliferation Circle

Chinese proliferation to Pakistan has indirectly fuelled weapons activities across the world, especially owing to the role of disgraced Pakistan nuclear scientist Abdul Qadeer Khan. In 2004, as a result of on-site investigations into Libya's nuclear weapons program new details of the Pakistan-China collaboration were studied. As part of disarmament inspections, early Chinese nuclear weapons designs were handed over to IAEA inspectors by Libyan scientists, wrapped in plastic bags bearing an address in Islamabad.

Several recent developments have once again highlighted not only the central role that Beijing in developing Pakistan's nuclear arsenal, but also Dr. Khan's intimate links with China's nuclear establishment. According to Professor Mohan Malik of Security Studies at the Asia-Pacific Centre for Security Studies, Honolulu, "the Chinese seem to have been thoroughly beaten in the proliferation game by their own clients and allies-Pakistan and North Korea".

Reacting to reports about the Khan nuclear network, the Chinese Foreign Ministry spokesperson urged Islamabad to undertake the investigations "properly" and bring them to a conclusion "quickly." Professor Malik, draws attention to the Chinese preference for conducting investigations "properly" and ending them "quickly". This, he argues, reveals Beijing's apprehensions over exposing the Chinese nuclear establishment's long standing ties with Khan. Mallik argues that Khan's numerous visits to China's nuclear installations over the last three decades and gains accrued to China's weapons program from the Dutch centrifuge technology stolen by him in the mid-1970s are particularly sensitive issues for Beijing. A senior member of the Pakistan Muslim League (Quaid-e-Azam) told a Pakistani journalist that "Chinese officials had expressed a desire for the proliferation inquiry to end quickly as they feared that Dr. Khan would publicly detail his network's 'China connection,' thereby embarrassing a crucial ally that Pakistan considers a strategic counterweight to India."

Although the bomb designs sold to Libya were of a 1960s Chinese vintage, an analysis of Pakistan's May 1998 nuclear tests reveals that China may have supplied more advanced nuclear weapons designs of the late 1980s and early 1990s to

Pakistan, which may have been shared with other countries. The close cooperation between Chinese and Pakistani military agencies also leaves little doubt that the Chinese had greater knowledge about Khan's proliferation activities than is publicly reported.

SINO-INDIAN RELATIONS: IMPLICATIONS FOR PAKISTAN

Since the beginning of the twentieth century or more precisely the start of World War I, the world has been witnessing an intensive and extensive competition for balancing of power among states. The situation is no different now, although the dynamics of the New World Order have added more variables in the balancing equation. The variables were less natural and more man-made but their outreach and influence have made it beyond the capacity and capability of any State (read human being) to regulate or constrain the unfolding developments. The Cold War was an intense period of international politics and its demise culminated in the emergence of the culture of interdependence – *security and economic*. The Third World states have been the focus of this culture and, further, China and India are two of the six main actors and emerging powers. It is interesting to note that the advent of the unipolar world brought economic interdependence and only two decades later the states are finding themselves intertwined into deep security interdependence as well, making the future of economic prosperity and peace perilous. The China-Pakistan-India trilateral relations have an interesting economic and security interdependence equation. It not only reflects their bilateral misgivings but also how extra-regional states influence is keeping the regional multilateral mechanisms handicapped. China is self-reliant in its security capability but interdependent on the world economies for its economic development.

In 2009, the U.S., Japan and India were ranked as first, second and tenth, respectively, top trade partners of China. India, on the other hand, has both economic and security interdependence. For economy it is dependent on China and the U.S. China is India's largest trading partner and the U.S. second-largest. For its security or military capability, India is dependent mainly on Israel, Russia, France and the USA.

Pakistan, at the same time, is also locked into economic and security interdependence. It is mostly dependent on China for security and partially for economy. China is Pakistan's largest defence supplier, but in economic terms, it is the fourth largest trading partner after Europe, the UAE and the USA. Nevertheless, its tilt has always been towards the USA, owing to the superpower's military and diplomatic prowess.

Diplomatic Support

Pakistan has been a major source of diplomatic support for China in almost every hour of need whether it has been the support for Chinese rights over Tibet, Taiwan and the Xinjiang province or in the world's criticism of alleged Chinese human rights violations. Islamabad has been lending its supportive hand to Beijing at all platforms. Another very important aspect of Pakistan's diplomatic support to China is the facilitation of the American president's groundbreaking visit to Beijing in 1972. China largely owes Pakistan its opening to the world. Acknowledging this support of Pakistan, Prime Minister Wen Jiabao, while addressing Pakistan parliament, said: "At the crucial moments when China sought to break the external blockade, restore its lawful seat at the United Nations and achieve the normalization of relations with the United States, we received valuable help from Pakistan. On those major issues related to Taiwan, Tibet and Xinjiang, we have enjoyed Pakistan's consistent and full support."

Energy Corridor

Pakistan's strategic location, which links it to the West and Central Asian States, becomes even more significant for China in securing energy routes amid its growing economy: it is the energy corridor which Islamabad has offered to China to pay back its time-tested friend. In 2006, Pakistan developed the Gwadar port as a first step in an elaborate energy corridor proposal that is expected to ship Persian Gulf oil overland from

Gwadar to China. Pakistan will expectedly generate US$60 billion a year in transit fees in the next 20 years, and China will secure a cheaper energy route. The Gwadar Port, that has reinvented Pakistan as one of the region's largest energy players, is a highlight of a little-studied dimension of the global quest for depleting oil; the fact is being well gauged by Beijing. China is now the world's second-largest consumer of oil after the US. Its consumption is expected to double by 2025, with 70 per cent coming from the Middle East. Both India and China are competing for finite supplies. Gal Luft, executive director of the Institute for the Analysis of Global Security in Washington, once opined that Gwadar is the closest access point China has to the Persian Gulf. Pakistan is crucial to China's bid for regional influence. China is rapidly diversifying its sources (of oil transportation) by cutting billion-dollar deals from Sudan to Iran and scoping out alternative transport routes through Pakistan, Myanmar, Thailand, and Bangladesh.

Strategic Partnership

Their strategic partnership is a long-term, win-win commitment between the two nations with the objective to achieve specific goals by maximizing the effectiveness of either side's resources. This relationship is based on integrity, trust, dedication to common goals, and an understanding of each other's expectations and values. When President Pervez Musharraf when visited China in April 2006, Chinese President Hu Jintao proposed a "strategic partnership" with Pakistan to "consolidate and deepen bilateral relations." The proposal indicated the significance in which Pakistan is held by China as its strategic partner. Unfortunately, this partnership has been unable to avail its full potential. In this context, Prime Minister Wen Jiabao, during his December 2010 visit to Islamabad, pointed out, "the international and regional situations at present remain complicated. As all-weather strategic partners, China and Pakistan should communicate and cooperate closely and cope with challenges jointly ... China-Pakistan pragmatic cooperation is a key part of the bilateral strategic partnership and enjoys promising prospects. China expects to take concerted actions with Pakistan to bring more benefits to their people."

Military Cooperation: The Eye of the Tiger

Sino-Pak military ties can be described as the „eye of the tiger. They continue to flourish amid the Western criticism of Pakistan's nuclear weapons development; China has been Pakistan's largest defence supplier since 1965. Though China is investing heavily in a myriad of economic projects across Pakistan, including power and telecommunication projects in the troubled northern parts of the country, the bilateral military *and defence ties surpass every other sector. China's Sino-Indian* relations: implications for Pakistan 9 unabated military cooperation with Pakistan can be attributed to mutual rivalry with India and the latter's defence and nuclear cooperation with the US. In response to the Indo-US nuclear deal, China has "privately" agreed to follow a "step-by-step" approach to fulfilling Pakistan's aspiration for an expanded nuclear energy programme.

In the joint statement issued at the conclusion of Prime Minister Wen Jiabao's visit in December 2010, the two States "reiterated that they will continue to enhance mutual trust and cooperation in the military and security field in line with the principles and spirit of the Treaty of Friendship, Cooperation and Good-neighborly relations ... This is conducive to peace, security and stability of the two countries and the region. ... (They) agreed to step up personnel training, joint exercises, training and cooperation for national defence, science and technology, and collaboration in defence production ... (and) maritime security."

9

India's Muscular China-Pakistan Policy and Economic Corridor

Relations between Asian rivals India and China have come under considerable strain in the recent months as mutual misgivings are steadily mounting. A slew of issues has led to the current strain and is likely to continue, unless one or the other blinks. However, neither country appears to be in the mood to do so.

"Positions have hardened and India must be prepared for a period of strained relations with China and Pakistan," said former foreign secretary Lalit Mansingh.

Strategic moves

The strategic dynamic of the region is changing. China has been consistently backing Pakistan against India: Whether that be blocking India's entry to the Nuclear Suppliers Group, citing technical reasons for not supporting UN sanctions against Jaish-e-Mohammad leader Masood Azhar, or building massive infrastructure projects in PoK, which India claims as its own.

China is watching with some concern India's growing warmth with the US. Beijing believes that Washington is propping up New Delhi to balance China's increasing military might in the Asia-Pacific. India has also been vocal about the

South China Sea. During President Barack Obama's visit, India and US had issued a separate joint statement on the South China Sea calling for all parties to respect international laws.

The signing of the Logistics Agreement in Washington which allows India and US to use each other's facilities is being seen in Beijing as another step in that direction. The agreement had been in the works for years as the UPA government had refused to sign it as many in the Congress saw it moving into the US orbit. The UPA also did not want to annoy China as improving relations with its giant neighbour was a priority of the Manmohan Singh-led regime.

Prime Minister Narendra Modi met with President Xi Jinping in Hangzhou, where he was attending the G20 Summit hosted by China. In the bilateral talks, Modi spoke frankly. Unlike in the past when many things were left unsaid, Modi did not shy away from mentioning India's concerns about the China-Pakistan Economic Corridor. New Delhi has been publicly talking about its unhappiness about the $46 billion project, which was announced by Xi, during his visit to Pakistan. Not a word of this was mentioned to India, even though Xi flew to Islamabad after a successful visit to India, where he and the First Lady were entertained by Modi on the banks of the Sabarmati. "China should have at least informed India about it, considering India claims PoK. Courtesy demanded it," said Mansingh.

Unlike many other countries in the region, India has not been enthusiastic about Xi's One Belt One Road initiative. At the moment as China prepares to launch its ambitious project, India's protests are hardly likely to make an impact.

Uncertain times are ahead, unless China shows some concession, "As a matter of principle, both countries would have to be sensitive to each other's strategic interests. In order to promote positive convergences, we will also need to prevent negative perceptions. For this the specific actions by both countries would play the major role," MEA spokesperson Vikas Swarup paraphrased the prime minister as saying, at the briefing after the talks between the two leaders. Significantly, without naming Pakistan, China's all-weather friend, Modi said: "Our response to terrorism must not be motivated by political considerations." He also spoke of terrorism coming from the area. Although Pakistan was not named, the reference was obvious.

Significantly the CPEC is part of Xi's pet projects which he hopes will transform the entire Central Asian economy. The CPEC envisages rail, road and pipeline projects to ferry oil and gas from Gwadar Port (built earlier by China) in Balochistan to Kashghar in China's Xinjiang province through PoK. Pakistan is naturally enthusiastic about the CPEC. Political parties and more importantly, the army are fired up by the project, but people in Pakistan's restive Balochistan province are not.

India's open support for the Baloch cause announced by Modi in his Independence Day speech, has been hailed by the people there. Pakistan has long accused India of interfering in Balochistan and blamed Indian intelligence working out of Afghanistan of aiding Baloch "terror outfits". These charges will escalate in the days and months to come. Chinese interests will also be affected. This is why Shyam Saran, a former foreign secretary and astute diplomat believes that if India takes on China, as it is doing about the CPEC, it has to be ready to take the consequences. It is not just Pakistan now in PoK and Balochistan, but Chinese interests as well.

Mansingh however welcomed India's muscular stand on the South China Sea, Balochistan and Gilgit-Baltistan. "Chinese respond to strength and know the power game. Previously, India's foreign policy was about moral principles and not real politik. This is the way forward." The fact that India and the US are on the same page on China's aggressive stand in the South China Sea, is a plus. Japan, India, US, Vietnam are all ranged together and there is strength in numbers. Modi's visit to Hanoi ahead of the G-20 meet, was also a pointer that Delhi can also woo Beijing's neighbours.

Even though China will certainly not change its stand on the CPEC, India must continue to flag its concerns in every forum, said Mansingh. Uncertain times are ahead, unless China shows some concession. Allowing India smooth entry to the Nuclear Suppliers Group, when the issue comes up in the last quarter of the year, may change the equation.

CHINA PAKISTAN ECONOMIC CORRIDOR AND DEFENSE PACT

Pakistan China relationship started since early 1950's and started maturing in 1972 by formation of strategic alliance between the two countries. Maintaining close relationship with China is part of Pakistan's foreign policy as China is Pakistan's strategic partner in the East. It helps Pakistan maintain balance of power in the region, and with one of the leading nations like China by her side, Pakistan has gained significant importance in the region.

Sino-Pak relationship is an all-weather partnership and has been time tested, be it economic cooperation, military pacts or moral support in leading organizations, like the United Nations. The deep sea port of Gwadar plays an important role in further strengthening the ties of Pakistan and China. Recently Pakistan and China have been trying to revive the legendary Silk Road which is one of the oldest known trade route in the world.

Gwadar Sea Port Development

Gwadar Port is one of the most important deep sea ports in the world. It comes under the jurisdiction of the government-owned Gwadar Port Authority. It is strategically located near the straits of Hormuz and will give China direct access to Arabian Sea through which 40% of world's oil passes. Work on Gwadar Port was started in 1998 by a Chinese firm. It was divided into two phases with a total of 13 berths.

China Pakistan Economic Corridor has the potential of making Pakistan one of the most strategically important countries in the region.

Work on Phase I started in 1998 and was completed in December 2006, with a construction of a total number of four berths. It was inaugurated by former President Pervez Musharraf. After the completion of Phase I, Phase II development of the port was awarded to a Singaporean firm, PSA International, in February 2007. From 2007 till 2011, the progress made with regard to the development of the port, by the Singaporean firm, was very slow, due to which, Pakistan asked China to develop the port. In 2013, the Port development was awarded to a Chinese state-run company, called China Overseas Port Holding Company (COPHC). In almost two years, the Chinese firm was able to complete the construction, with a total of 9 berths, including two oil terminals. China's support has been critical in building the Gwadar sea port, which will benefit both countries.

China Pakistan Economic Corridor (CPEC) or Modern Silk Road

China Pakistan Economic Corridor has the potential of making Pakistan one of the most strategically important countries in the region. Recently, the Chinese President visited Pakistan for the inauguration of the Gwadar port, one of the key components of CPEC. The President of China announced a total of $45 billion investment in energy and infrastructure projects. This mammoth investment will provide job opportunities for locals, develop infrastructure, and provide power and energy to energy-starved Pakistan. This will also help contribute in the economic development of Pakistan.

China will also benefit from this economic corridor, which will greatly reduce China's trade route from 12000 kilometers via sea, to 2000 kilometers via land i.e. from Kashgar to Gwadar. It will also help revive the ancient trade route known as the Silk Road, which started nearly 2400 years ago. In future, China can also use Gwadar to build a naval base which will increase influence of China in the region. Furthermore, all the oil shipments from the GCC countries will be shipped via Pakistan to China. Also, non-oil goods could be imported to the world using Gwadar as a transit route, making Gwadar equally or more important than the Suez Canal of Egypt.

The CPEC project will include new infrastructures, like road links, 1800 km railway links from Gwadar to Kashgar, and a network of oil pipelines, connecting all the way from Gwadar oil terminals to Kashgar in Xinjiang, China.

A new airport, special tax-free economic zones, energy power plants and a dry port in Kashgar is also included in the project. The total cost of CPEC is USD 75 billion, out of which USD 45 billion has been provided by China to make it operable by 2020.

Defense Pacts and Maritime Interest

Military relationship between Pakistan and China are extremely strong, and are primarily based on geopolitical alliance, aimed at countering Indo-American influence in the region. Recent developments on Gwadar port and CPEC have made this relationship much stronger than before.

China is one of the main defense equipment suppliers to Pakistan Armed Forces. They have not only sold defense equipment but have also transferred the technologies to Pakistan.

The defense technologies that China has shared with Pakistan include, aircraft, such as multi-role fighter aircraft JF 17 and trainer aircraft Karakorum K8, cruise missile technology, space technology, Al Khalid tanks, ballistic missile systems, fast attack naval crafts, etc. China has provided Pakistan tailor-made advanced weapons, making Pakistan one of the strongest armed forces in the region.

Military relationship between Pakistan and China are extremely strong, and are primarily based on geopolitical alliance, aimed at countering Indo-American influence in the region.

China and Pakistan have found common ground in terms of maritime interest in the region. Gwadar port can be used for joint naval patrols in the Indian Ocean, further increasing the naval outreach of China and Pakistan in the region. Gwadar port will increase the countries' naval movements and further expand defense cooperation, especially in the naval field.

Fundamentals to make CPEC a success:

In order to make CPEC a success, there are some fundamental issues, which should be taken care of; these include terrorism, provision of special security, creation of new special economic zones, etc. Foreign rivals who want Gwadar port to fail, have already started highlighting issues on mainstream, as well as social media, through their Pakistani aides-de-camp, about missing persons. Campaigning under the banner of "Un-silencing Baluchistan", they are working to escalate the issue of Baluchistan liberation. On the other hand, terrorist organizations like the foreign-funded Baluchistan Liberation Army are also looking for an opportunity to target pipelines and trade routes of CPEC, once full-fledged construction begins.

Political rivals have started to downplay CPEC's success and have started creating issues regarding the route, stating alternative trade routes passing through Makran Coastal Highway, over to Lahore-Karachi motorway and all the way to Kashgar. Some political parties want the trade route to start from Baluchistan to Kashgar, via KPK only, and have started clamoring about not getting their fair share. In fact, the purpose of alternative route is to provide security for the corridor, and these routes are much more secure than the route passing through KPK at the moment. However, the government must address all these grievances, and make suitable amends, by taking all the provinces on board.

Pakistan should also tackle corruption to control the expenses of the project and ensure that projects don't get delayed due to corruption and unethical practices. Building new economic zones for CPEC will benefit Pakistan in the way of industrial development and create employment opportunities for local people. Awarding sub contracts to local companies rather than completely depending on Chinese contractors will also benefit Pakistan.

Chinese are shy investors; Pakistan should provide them guaranteed security, and take all possible measures to ensure the completion of the project on time, to build the investor's confidence. China may shelf the project if they see nonperformance from the government, and that will hurt Pakistan's image on the international level. Curbing terrorism, providing security for the trade corridor and ensuring the project is executed and completed on time, are the key fundamentals to make China Pakistan Economic Corridor a successful trade route in the region.

Renewable energy and Power shortfall

Since 2007, Pakistan has been hit by severe power outages due to mismanagement and improper planning for future power demands. China Pakistan Economic Corridor has brought with itself, attractive renewable energy projects, which in the long run could provide Pakistan to cope up with future power needs and reduce the power shortfalls in the country. Currently there is approximately 4600 MW shortfall in Pakistan out of 12000 MW actual requirement of electricity.

CPEC has also announced a solar power project which will generate 900MW electricity within a year's time. New hydro power projects will generate approximately 800 MW of energy, and wind power plant projects are also under consideration, with feasibility study under way. This means that alternative energy will generate approximately 2000 MW, along with new coal fired projects, which will be able to make up for the shortfall.

Gwadar port can be used for joint naval patrols in the Indian Ocean, further increasing the naval outreach of China and Pakistan in the region.

FUTURE PLANS OF GWADAR PORT

Future plans of Gwadar port includes building of bulk storage oil tanks, oil refinery, establishment of petrochemical industries, ship repair yard, shrimp farming, vessel building yards, cold storages and ice factories, and recreational water sports activities. These kinds of industries and activities will further increase employment opportunities in the country, which will improve the economy and place Pakistan amongst one of the leading economic countries in the region.

CPEC will play an important role in making Pakistan one of the most attractive transit trade routes in the world. This trade route, in future, can link central Asia via Afghanistan, and give the Central Asian countries an easier access of sea route to Far East and Australia. Hence, CPEC has a strong potential to revive the old Silk Road, with Pakistan being center stage in the entire revival process.

THE CHINA-PAKISTAN ECONOMIC CORRIDOR ONE YEAR ON

It has just been over a year since Chinese President Xi Jinping announced the China-Pakistan Economic Corridor (CPEC) during his inaugural state visit to Pakistan in April 2015. What has been the progress of the construction of the megaproject since then? Zhang Baozhong, the chairman of China Overseas Ports, the company that will run the Pakistani port of Gwadar, stated in late April 2016 that Gwadar will commence full operations by the end of 2016. Gwadar is essential to CPEC as it will connect CPEC with shipping on the Arabian Sea; and being close to the Straits of Hormuz, will serve as a strategic gateway for Middle Eastern oil shipments to be transported overland to China via CPEC's planned oil pipelines. Logistics will be transformed by CPEC, as container ships that today have to make the "the nearly 13,000 km sea voyage from Tianjin to the Persian Gulf through the Strait of Malacca and around India" can be replaced by cheaper container trucks that make "a mere 2,000 km road journey from Kashgar to Gwadar" (Lim, 2015; "Gwadar Port," 2016; "China-Pakistan," 2016).

Infrastructure that will connect Gwadar with the Chinese city of Kashgar in Xinjiang include highways and railways. Progress has been made this past year on the highway network. A 335 km section of the Karakoram Highway between the Sino-Pakistani border city of Khunjerab to Raikot has been upgraded, and a 59 km section of the Hazara Motorway between Burhan and Havelian is expected to be completed by the end of 2017 (Siddiqui, 2016). Pakistan's Prime Minister Nawaz Sharif is scheduled to visit Dera Ismael Khan on May 17, 2016 to inaugurate the CPEC Western Route. The initial phase of the Western Route — which when completed will connect Havelian with Gwadar — consists of a 285 km highway between Hakla and Yarik, including "eleven interchanges, nineteen flyovers, fifteen bridges, seventy-four underpasses, two hundred fifty-nine culverts, and three major bridges" ("PM to inaugurate," 2016; "PM to open," 2016). For the CPEC Eastern Route, construction work is expected to begin soon as China's State Council has just approved a 4.2 billion USD concessionary loan package for a 120 km section of the Karakoram Highway II between Thakot and Havelian, and a 392 km section of the Lahore-Karachi Motorway between Multan and Sukkur ("Pakistan, China," 2016). Apart from the construction of highways, CPEC's transportation infrastructure also includes the construction of rail lines, dry ports, as well as the Gwadar airport, the construction of which is scheduled to commence in the middle of 2016. Energy infrastructure — including hydropower dams — and industrial zones will also be constructed under the CPEC framework. By 2030, when projects under the third and final phase of CPEC are scheduled to be completed, the populations living in the currently underdeveloped communities in the CPEC region are expected to enjoy the economic benefits of industrial development provided by the new infrastructure (Yousafzai, 2016; "CPEC to Benefit," 2016).

In terms of regional economic integration, CPEC has attracted interest from Iran and the countries of Central Asia (Daud, 2016; "Central Asian states," 2015). The 2015 accessions of Afghanistan and Kazakhstan to the World Trade Organization, and regional trade agreements like the quadrilateral transit trade agreement between China, Kyrgyzstan, Kazakhstan, and Pakistan, have facilitated regional integration through trade, and CPEC is envisioned to accelerate this process of economic integration and transform Pakistan into a Central and South Asian economic hub. Indeed, despite reservations from India, which we shall shortly see, CPEC promises to serve as "a bridge between three engines of growth, China, South Asia and Central Asia, thus giving a stimulus to a deep regional economic integration and creating a trading bloc of 3 billion people, nearly half of the planet" ("Pakistan striving," 2015). Pakistan's Commerce Minister Khurram Dastagir notes that should the economic promise of CPEC come to fruition, this will offer significant progress for global development:

"Mind you these also include half of world's extreme poor. The deepening of economic integration will lower trade costs, essential for ending poverty. Trade is a critical enabler of growth, opening up opportunities of new and better work for the poor." ("Pakistan striving," 2015)

Security Concerns

Security threats to CPEC may have expanded over the past year. Pakistan's security apparatus has recently highlighted a threat from India's and Afghanistan's intelligence services "to encourage and assist Baloch violence against the CPEC" (Lee, 2016a). In March 2016, Pakistani security forces arrested an alleged Indian spy in Balochistan, a province with major CPEC projects, including the port of Gwadar (Johnson, 2016). The following month, General Raheel Sharif, Pakistan's Chief of Army Staff, identified India's intelligence agency RAW (Research and Analysis Wing) as being "blatantly involved in destabilizing" Pakistan and CPEC (Yousuf, 2016).

One reason for the alleged Indian interference is the section of CPEC which extends through Gilgit Baltistan to the Sino-Pakistani border. This is disputed territory which India identifies as Pakistan-occupied Kashmir (PoK). Indeed, India's Minister of State for External Affairs V. K. Singh recently stated that CPEC will extend "through a territory which belongs to India" ("Raised concerns," 2016). (Pakistan's Finance Minister Ishaq Dar has rebutted such claims, stating that CPEC will only extend through Pakistani territory (Kiani, 2015).) This has drawn the attention of anti-Chinese nationalists in India who see this as an attack by China on Indian interests (Lee, 2016b). Some, for example, see China as a "a reliable ally" of Pakistan's that "has always come to Pakistan's aid when India has seemed on the ascendant," and that its planned CPEC projects in Gilgit

Baltistan will legitimize what India has identified as "Pakistan's illegal occupation of these areas" (Pant, 2016). These are not fringe views. M. K. Narayanan, a former Indian National Security Adviser, states bluntly that CPEC poses a "major threat" to India, and that China's "One Belt One Road" global development strategy, of which CPEC is a showpiece megaproject, could have "the most degrading impact" on Sino-Indian relations ("Raised concerns," 2016).

To counter what they see as China's geostrategic advancements through its CPEC initiative, some Indian strategists recommend the military capture of Gilgit Baltistan and the rest of PoK, especially since this territorial seizure would "provide India a direct land link to Afghanistan and thence to the Central Asian Republics, both of which are increasingly falling into the Chinese sphere of economic and political influence" (Kalyanaraman, 2016). Of course, should a war between India and Pakistan over Kashmir break out, China would find itself dangerously entangled in a likely nuclear exchange between India and Pakistan. Worrisomely, India is not the only geostrategic threat to CPEC. As Peter Lee recounts:

"On the other hand, you have diehard separatists in Balochistan, PoK, Xinjiang, and Tibet eager to make it fail. You've got a pool of resentful Islamist extremists near the route of the CPEC in Pakistan, Xinjiang, Afghanistan, and Uzbekistan. You have China hawks in India and the United States who would be happy to see the CPEC turn into quagmire for the PRC." (Lee, 2016a)

As CPEC progresses past its first year of construction, its Pakistani and Chinese overseers will have to ensure that their security and intelligence apparatuses remain alert to these and all other possible threats to the megaproject.

CHINA'S CONTINUING SALIENCE IN PAKISTANI FOREIGN POLICY

With India's recent rise as an economic and political power of global significance, Sino-Indian ties are now at a critical juncture as India tries to find the right policy mix to deal with its most important neighbour. Meanwhile, Chinese strategists remain concerned about U.S. attempts to encircle China and the profound effect on Chinese security of an eventual integration of India into a U.S. alliance.

China, according to this view, needs to remain vigilant against the growing network running "from Japan to India" that would suffocate China. As India struggles to emerge as a global power with an ambitious foreign policy agenda, China can effectively scuttle Indian ambitions by continuing with its diplomatic and military support to Pakistan. Much to India's chagrin, China has given ample indications in the recent past that it wants to follow that path. With the civilian government of President Asif Ali Zardari under intense pressure from the United States to do more to fight terrorism emanating from Pakistani soil, there are calls in Pakistan to adopt a foreign policy that considers China and not the United States to be Pakistan's strongest ally and most significant stakeholder. China's emergence as the leading global economic power coupled with recent attempts by India and the United States to forge a closer relationship has helped this suggestion gain further credibility.

Washington has historically been accused of using Pakistan in times of need and then deserting it for a policy that favours stronger relations with India to serve the larger U.S. strategic agenda. Pakistan remains angry about U.S. indifference after the United States used it to funnel aid to Afghan mujahideen and then turned its back on Pakistan after the Soviet withdrawal. Whereas only around nine percent of Pakistanis view the United States as a partner, around 80 percent of the Pakistani population considers China a friend.

The Obama administration's July 2011 decision to suspend a portion of U.S. aid to the Pakistani military has led many in Islamabad to become even more forceful in underlining Beijing's importance for Pakistan. Reacting to the U.S. move, Islamabad's ambassador to Beijing, Masood Khan, was quick to suggest that "China will stand by us in difficult times as it has been doing for the past years." Though Beijing cannot replace Washington as an aid-provider to Pakistan, the tension in U.S.—Pakistan ties provides an opportunity for Beijing to deepen its relationship with Islamabad. As it is, China is considered a more reliable ally that has always come to Pakistan's aid when India has been on the rise, even to an extent that China has conveniently turned a blind eye to Pakistan's strategy of using terror as an instrument of policy against India. Not surprisingly, Pakistan has given China a "blank cheque" to intervene in India—Pakistan peace talks. Pakistan also seems to have allowed Chinese engineers to examine the remains of the stealth helicopter destroyed during the raid that killed Osama bin Laden despite a direct request from the United States that China not be allowed to do so.

Forecast for the "All-Weather" Relationship

With India's ascent in the global hierarchy and U.S. attempts to carve out a strong partnership with India, China's need for Pakistan is only likely to grow. As tensions rose between India and Pakistan after the November 2008 terror attacks in Mumbai, Pakistan's Chairman of the Joint Chiefs of Staff Committee went to China to seek that country's support, which was readily given. The visit resulted in the signing of a new agreement on military cooperation between the two nations, with Beijing agreeing to expedite the delivery of F-22 frigates to Pakistan's Navy.

Beijing has justified its arms sales to Pakistan on the grounds that India was buying similar weapon systems from the United States (it also is buying military hardware from the Russians). China has consistently defended Pakistan's desire for high capacity weapons systems as normal for an independent nation seeking to bolster its security. In the years preceding the attacks in Mumbai, China blocked UN sanctions against the dreaded Lashkar-e-Taiba (LeT) and Jamaat-ud-Dawa (JuD), the organizations that planned and executed the attacks, despite a broad global consensus favouring such a move. Only when tensions surfaced between Beijing and Islamabad on the issue of Chinese Uighur separatists receiving sanctuaries and training on Pakistani territory did China agree to a ban on JuD. More recently, China has refused to reconsider its objection in the United Nations to proscribing the Jaish-e-Mohammed's Maulana Masood Azhar and some prominent LeT operatives based in Pakistan, despite New Delhi's presenting detailed information on them to Beijing.

With the exception of China, other major global powers such as Britain, France, Germany, and Russia supported the U.S.—India nuclear deal as they were eager to sell nuclear fuel, reactors, and equipment to India. China, on its part, made its displeasure clear by asking India to sign the NPT and dismantle its nuclear weapons. The official Xinhua news agency of China commented that the U.S.—India nuclear agreement "will set a bad example for other countries."

Since the U.S.—India deal is in many ways a recognition of India's rising global profile, China was not very happy with the outcome and indicated that it would be willing to sell nuclear reactors to Pakistan. It was a not so subtle message to the United States that if Washington decides to play favourites, China retains the same right.

Not surprisingly, China's plans to supply two nuclear reactors to Pakistan in defiance of international rules have gathered momentum. Chinese authorities have confirmed that the China National Nuclear Cooperation has signed an agreement with Pakistan for two new nuclear reactors at the Chashma site Chashma III and Chashma IV in addition to the two that it is already working on in Pakistan.

This will be in clear violation of the Nuclear Suppliers Group (NSG) guidelines that forbid nuclear transfers to countries that are not signatories to the NPT or do not adhere to comprehensive international safeguards on their nuclear program. China has suggested that "there are compelling political reasons concerning the stability of South Asia to justify the exports," echoing Pakistan's oft-repeated compliant that the U.S.—India nuclear pact has upset stability in the region. The decision to supply reactors to Pakistan which has a record of dealing with North Korea, Iran, and Libya reflects China's growing diplomatic confidence and underscores its view of Pakistan as a prized South Asian strategic power. Recent suggestions emanating from Beijing that China is likely to set up military bases overseas to counter U.S. influence and exert pressure on India have been interpreted in certain sections in New Delhi as a veiled reference to China's interest in having a permanent military presence in Pakistan.

Even though it might not be politically possible for the Pakistani government to follow through on such threats and openly allow China to set up a military base, New Delhi fears that Islamabad might allow Beijing use of Pakistani military facilities without any public announcement. Indian concerns have also risen that China and Pakistan are coordinating their efforts in regard to border issues with India. The presence of the Chinese military in the Gilgit—Baltistan area of Pakistan Occupied Kashmir, purportedly to repair and upgrade the Karakoram Highway, has enormous implications for Indian security.

Overall, it has been rightly observed that China's policy toward Pakistan is "an object lesson in how to attain long-term national goals by calm calculation, forbearance, and diplomatic skill." Nevertheless, there are indeed limits to China—Pakistan ties.

The relationship remains fundamentally asymmetrical: Pakistan wants more out of its ties with China than China is willing to offer. Today, while Pakistan's domestic problems are gargantuan, China will be very cautious in involving itself even more. In September 2011, China Kingho Group, one of China's largest private coal mining companies, pulled out of what was to be Pakistan's largest foreign-investment pact, citing concerns for the security of its personnel. Moreover, the closer China gets to Pakistan, the faster India would move into the U.S. orbit.

Amid worries about the potential destabilizing influence of Pakistani militants on China's Muslim minority in Xinjiang, Beijing has also taken a harder line against Pakistan. The flow of arms and terrorists from across the border in Pakistan remains a major headache for Chinese authorities, and Islamabad's inability and/or failure to curb extremism makes it difficult for the Chinese to trust Pakistan completely. If Pakistan wants to keep receiving support from China, then it needs to demonstrate progress on this issue.

As tensions rose between China and Pakistan in the aftermath of violence in the border town of Kashgar in Xinjiang in August 2011, President Zardari went to talk directly with local leaders and businessmen in Xinjiang, recognizing that if he was not able to mend fences with local leadership, Sino-Pakistani ties might be in real jeopardy.

China, at least publicly, has continued to emphasize that its relationship with Pakistan is far more important than isolated incidents of violence. To be clear, Chinese involvement in Pakistan is unlikely to match the U.S. profile in the country in the short to medium term, and it is not readily evident if China even wants to match the United States.

But flirtation with Pakistan gives China crucial space for diplomatic maneuvering vis-a'-vis India and the United States, and it will continue to utilize the relationship in pursuit of its larger strategic objectives. Pakistan is not going to be a common interest that binds China with either India or the United States any time soon.

China was the only major power that openly voiced support for Pakistan after bin Laden's assassination, defending Islamabad and emphasizing that the Pakistani government may not have known about bin Laden's presence on its territory. During Prime Minister Gilani's visit, Chinese Premier Wen Jiabao affirmed that "Pakistan has made huge sacrifices and an important contribution to the international fight against terrorism, that its independence, sovereignty, and territorial integrity must be respected, and that the international community should understand and support Pakistan's efforts to maintain domestic stability and to realize economic and social development." Wen went on to state that China would like to be an "all-weather strategic partner," and would do its best to help the Pakistani government and people get through their difficulties. To underscore its commitment, China agreed to immediately provide Pakistan with 50 new JF-17 Thunder multi-role jets under a co-production agreement, even as negotiations continued for more fighter aircrafts including those with stealth technology.

Despite this generosity, Pakistan wanted even more from China underscored by its expressed desire to have China take over the operation of Gwadar port in the Arabian Sea west of Karachi, in which Beijing has invested heavily in recent years and which serves an important role in the projection of China's naval prowess in the region. Pakistan has suggested that the port could be upgraded to a naval base for Chinese use. China, however, immediately rejected this offer, not wanting to antagonize the United States and India with the formal establishment of a base in Pakistan.

Ever since Chinese and Pakistani leaders underscored their nations' commitments to each other's core security interests at the Bandung Conference in 1955, Pakistan has occupied a unique position in China's foreign policy calculus. Their relations have been described as "arguably the most stable and durable element of China's foreign relations." India has been the main factor that has influenced China's and Pakistan's policies vis-a'-vis each other. China, viewing India as a potential challenger in the strategic landscape of Asia, has tended to use Pakistan to counter Indian power in the region, while Islamabad has gained access to civilian and military resources to balance Indian might in the sub-continent. The China—Pakistan partnership serves the interests of both by presenting India with a potential two-front theatre in the event of war with either country. Each is using the other to balance India as India's disputes with Pakistan keep India preoccupied, distracting New Delhi from the task of reaching its potential as a major regional and global player.

Although some U.S. and Indian voices are asking the Obama and Singh administrations, respectively, to partner with China to restore stability in Pakistan, Pakistan's utility for China is only likely to increase, particularly as India continues its ascent in the global inter-state hierarchy and pursues a more ambitious foreign policy posture primarily to counter China, resulting in a further tightening of the Sino-Pakistan entente cordiale.

FIGHTING FOR BALOCHISTAN IS KEY TO MODI'S PAKISTAN POLICY

A significant part of the narrative of the nation is uncontested, if we don't give careful consideration to the neighbor's cases. Activists battling for a cause, particularly one that has a ton of mainstream feeling connected to it, are normally noisy and high pitched when holding forward at open fora. They have a tendency to be bellicose and turn unnecessarily forceful if their perspectives are repudiated.

One might say, uproarious discourse, contentiousness and hostility are important for successful activism. All things considered, if a dissident is a simple sucker, then his or her cause can't be worth battling for. In the meantime, unnecessarily pushy activism can put off individuals and make them unconcerned with causes that could be flawlessly real and meriting support.

History

Hence listening to professor Naela Quadri Baloch at a recent discussion on Balochistan organised by the Observer Research Foundation came as a pleasant surprise. She was soft-spoken yet firm, persuasive yet polite. She presented her case, or rather the case for free Balochistan, without taking recourse to either maudlin sentiments or theatrical hyperbole.

Much of the story of Balochistan is uncluttered and uncontested, provided we do not pay undue attention and attach unwarranted credibility to Pakistan's claims. In 1947, when British colonial rule came to an end in the Indian subcontinent, 535 princely states were given the option of either acceding to India or Pakistan through merger of territory, or remain free and independent. The Khan of Kalat, which comprised nearly all of Balochistan barring three minor principalities, was not too eager to accede to Pakistan. The Baloch were, and remain, a fiercely independent people with their own cultural and social identity, along with a land endowed with natural resources. That early impulse for freedom became the root cause of Balochistan's subsequent misery. Since its violent Caesarian birth, assisted by a scalpel-wielding Britain, on August 14, 1947, Pakistan has been as deceitful as its Quaid-e-Azam Mohammed Ali Jinnah was during his brief and bitter life as the ruler of a moth-eaten country, one half of which fell off the map in 1971.

Jinnah, the barrister helped the Khan of Kalat to prepare his brief for independence and a Standstill Agreement in the interim. Jinnah the smash-and-grab politician paved the path for Kalat's annexation by Pakistan on March 27, 1948. Thus was Balochistan forcibly converted into a province of Pakistan, against the wishes of the Baloch and their Khan.

Balochistan's struggle against Pakistani rule and Islamabad's "One Unit" policy has been relentless since the annexation of Kalat. Brutal repression by the Pakistani army has failed to break the spirit of resistance. Beginning with 1948-49, it has been horrific campaign to put down dissent and silence voice of freedom. There are several similarities between the Pakistani army committing hideous crimes in Bangladesh (then East Pakistan) and Balochistan. Mass killings, rape of women, laying human habitations to waste, targeted assassinations, Bangladesh saw it all during its Liberation War of 1971. Balochistan continues to witness these horrors.

Butcher

General Tikka Khan, nicknamed the "Butcher of Bangladesh", had the dubious distinction of also being called the "Butcher of Balochistan" for the bloody campaign he led from 1973-77. But for all the sorrow, grief and misery heaped on the people of Balochistan, they have risen again. The freedom movement, relaunched in 2004 continues unabated.

Divided by the Goldsmith Line of 1871, Balochistan is split between Pakistani and Iranian occupation, with some bits spilling into Afghanistan on account of the flawed Durand Line.

Britain understood the strategic importance of Balochistan and played its game accordingly to keep the Russians out.

Today, both Pakistan and Iran are leveraging that strategic importance to further their own economic and security interests. India's position on Balochistan has been, at best, ambivalent.

Notwithstanding the arrest of an Indian national (Pakistan claims he is a "RAW agent" and was arrested on its side of the Goldsmith Line; there are credible claims he was arrested by the Iranians and handed over to the ISI) it would be silly to imagine a grand Indian conspiracy in action. New Delhi has long been incapable of doing what Indira Gandhi did in 1970-71.

Option

Yet there is a case for an Indian policy on Balochistan. India did play a major role in propping up the Northern Alliance so as not to concede all ground to the Taliban and its mentor, Pakistan, in Afghanistan. A hands-off approach, therefore, is lacking in precedence, even if we were to discount India's proactive role in the liberation of Bangladesh from the tyranny of Pakistan. The issue is what should be that policy. Investing in Chabahar port that lies on the Iranian side of Balochistan cannot be a policy in entirety. At best, it will partially countervail China's captive port at Gwadar on the Pakistani side of Balochistan. That's one pawn moved. Next what?

One possible option is for India to declare moral and diplomatic support for the freedom movement in Balochistan, while calling for a peaceful resolution of the conflict. That would require gumption. Indeed, it would need the political courage of Mrs Gandhi coupled with popular support for a righteous cause that India believes in.

Great nations and rising powers have to be risk-takers. The inevitable backlash of supporting Balochistan's liberation war will no doubt be huge. But if Mrs Gandhi, prime minister of an impoverished nation, could turn up her nose at what the world thought, surely Narendra Modi, prime minister of the fastest growing economy, too can. A successful Balochistan policy premised on India's historical association with just causes would also lead to the forging of a successful Pakistan policy. Is the government game?

CHARGES INDIA OF INVOLVEMENT IN BALOCHISTAN

Pakistan alleges that the diplomats manning these Consulates are from Indian intelligence. Pakistan charges India of using the Jalalabad and Kandahar Consulates to fund, provide arms and training to Baloch nationalists who want independence from Pakistan. Islamabad had in the past charged that India and Afghanistan under Karzai had together helped to ferment trouble in Balochistan.

The Baloch problem began in the 1970's because of the lack of development in the province, despite being rich in gas and minerals. Zulfikar Ali Bhutto crushed the movement by calling in the army and air force. For a long time afterwards the movement remained dormant, though there was anger that the Gwadar port and other development work in the province created no jobs for the locals.

In 2004, the Baloch movement was resurrected by Akbar Bugti but he was killed in 2006 in a firefight with the Pakistan Army. India's Ministry of External Affairs issued a statement immediately afterwards: "The unfortunate killing of the veteran Baloch leader, Nawab Akbar Khan Bugti, is a tragic loss to the people of Balochistan and Pakistan. This military attack in which reportedly two of his grandsons were also killed and the heavy casualties in the continuing military operations in Balochistan underline the need for peaceful dialogue to address the grievances and aspirations of people of Balochistan. Military force can never solve political problems."

This did not go down well with General Pervez Musharraf and the army, who said it was inevitable that India which supported the Baloch movement would say this. Pakistan continues to make these allegations and had earlier complained to the US and Nato allies of India's role in Balochistan.

However, proof supplied by Islamabad has never been convincing. Former Prime Minister Manmohan Singh was torn apart by the opposition and his own Congress party, when Balochistan became a part of the joint statement released after his meeting with the then Pakistan prime minister Yusuf Raza Gilani, during a meeting in Sharm-el-Sheikh, the Egyptian resort town.

Manmohan Singh was accused of legitimising Pakistan's claims. The former PM had asked for proof, which Islamabad has not been able to substantiate with solid evidence. Whether India is actually involved in Balochistan is difficult to say as no government is ready to admit such covert operations. The important thing is that the Pakistan military believes this and want Indian presence in Afghanistan reduced to the embassy in Kabul. So an attack on the Consulate in Mazar-e-Sharif, is very much in line with the ISI policy in Afghanistan. In 2008, the Indian embassy in Kabul was attacked, where the defence attaché and a young diplomat were among those killed. Another attempt was made a few months later in 2009. In both cases the Haqqani network, a Afghan militant group close to Pakistan, was said to be behind the attack. The aim was to frighten India out of the country. In 2013, the Indian Consulate in Jalalabad was targeted, and several civilians were killed, though no Indian was affected.

After being isolated on Afghanistan during the latter part of the US and Nato campaign against the Taliban, Islamabad is back in the picture as the American's turn to Pakistan to get the Taliban to the negotiating table. The first round of Taliban talks with the Afghan government representatives, was also attended by Pakistan, US and China.

The disclosure of Mullah Omar's death and the infighting which followed led to a delay in holding the second round. It is now scheduled for sometime this month. In the meantime Taliban attack across Afghanistan has increased, with the hope of the Taliban negotiating from a position of strength. Pakistan is going all out to back the Taliban to ensure that its ally gets a major share in the new political set-up. Rawalpindi was to make sure that its enemies like India is cut to size in a new dispensation. But much will depend on what turn the talks take. India is watching from the sidelines.

BALOCHISTAN IN INDIA'S PAKISTAN POLICY: TIME TO UP THE ANTE

Prime Minister Narendra Modi's Independence Day speech from the ramparts of the Red Fort in New Delhi would have endeared him to the 'hawks' in the Indian foreign policy establishment as he came out openly in support of "freedom" for Pakistan's restive border province of Balochistan and Pakistan-occupied (administered) Kashmir (PoK). "I want to speak a bit about the people in Balochistan, Gilgit- Baltistan (GB), and Pakistan-occupied Kashmir," he had said. Earlier in the week at an all-party meeting on Kashmir, Modi had remarked that it was time for Islamabad to explain to the world "why it has been committing atrocities on people in PoK and Balochistan".

Some observers view the references to Balochistan, PoK and GB as indication of a significant aggressive change in India's Pakistan policy provoked by the recent Pakistani interference in the developments in the Kashmir valley; and as the proverbial last straw that has dented Modi's outreach to, and patience on Pakistan which he had persevered since his government came to power two years ago. It is also an indication of the government in New Delhi's conviction that external stimulus to the unrest in the Kashmir valley must end before any workable political solution can be found to the issues in Jammu and Kashmir within the framework of the Indian constitution.

This shift in India's outlook to Balochistan from the oblique reference at Sharm el-Sheikh (after a bilateral between the then India and Pakistani Prime Ministers at this Egyptian resort) some years back to this direct broadside from the Red Fort this month, has been under consideration before but India had not taken this path as it is fraught with geopolitical challenges and implications. The geopolitical challenges on the

Baloch issue are complex as Balochis reside not only in Pakistan but also in parts of Iran and Afghanistan. The plight and ethnic dispersion of the Baloch people mirrors that of the Kurds in the Middle East. India might face opposition from Iran and Afghanistan as it tenders its support for Baloch human rights and aspirations. Balochistan strife has a sectarian dimension which has been used by the US, Israeli and the Saudis in the past to build pressure on Iran.

Developments in Balochistan might also see Indian interest in Chabahar being targeted and may ultimately lead to the emergence of the Baloch region as a new theatre for superpower rivalries. Further, the absence of an organized national movement, the dominance of tribal leaders with shifting loyalties, the large presence of Afghan migrants (including the Taliban), active sectarian strife and heavy Pakistani repression, all hobble Baloch aspirations in the province.

But now that a turn in this direction has been taken, it is hoped that comes with an implementation plan, at least for the short term. To that end, India would be required to declare in clear terms its diplomatic and moral support in international fora for the Baloch cause for the policy to be effective. It would require more a more muscular and risk taking posture for its new foreign policy 'dare' to be effective. For starters it has its timing right.

Pakistan has never been more vulnerable as it is today - both geopolitically and economically - and if there was ever a time to get Pakistan to mend its ways, it is now. Pakistani backers in the Middle East are today alive to the perils of Islamist terror and its manifestations; Saudis are dealing with their Yemeni 'albatross' besides falling oil revenues and Turkey is distracted by its internal challenges. Iran has never been more aggressive to any external disruption and Afghanistan never so clear where its ills lie and what needs to be done for peace in the country. A world wracked by terrorism, migrants and an economic downturn has little appetite for Pakistani petty diplomacy and foolhardiness. The Pakistan Army, which always needs extra-national source of finances in addition to the revenue generated by its in-house sources, is also at a cross-over point. With the end of the US largesse, in consonance with its reduced reliance on Pakistan for its Afghanistan and Central Asia policy, followed by reduction in the flow of funds from the Middle East driven by their own crisis in the Syria, Iraq and Yemen and falling oil prices, the Pakistan army is gearing up to milk its next source of funds (for both near and mid-term) the China Pakistan Economic Corridor (CPEC). With its procedures set from bleeding the US/NATO logistics lines from Karachi to Afghanistan of just few years ago , Pakistan army after assuming full control of the security of the CPEC, will be well placed through army-owned logistics agencies to 'tax' the CPEC for its sustenance.

CPEC and the weight of the Chinese assurance behind it is a major source of the Pakistan's credit rating for inward foreign direct investment (FDI). It is projected that CPEC will directly create 700,000 jobs between 2015–2030 and boost annual growth by 2 to 2.5 percentage points. Besides improving physical infrastructure, the rolling out of CPEC is expected to build institutions, improve business environment and strengthen regulatory framework. CPEC is seen by rating agencies and foreign investors a one single major source of Pakistan's credit worthiness and its future economic fortunes.

Pakistan needs peace and security for CPEC to work. It needs people of GB, PoK and Balochistan as stakeholders in the CPEC and to that end meet their aspirations. India also must get the Chinese clear on certain aspects. One, GB and PoK are contested territories - the Chinese cannot just drive through - as they feel right now they can. Two, there will be no CPEC unless Pakistan mends its ways on Islamist terrorism. Terror-sponsorship has to end- India is not buying Pakistan's "we are also victims of terrorism" story. Three, in India's response to Pakistan's proxy war - targeting CPEC is game; presence of Chinese workers or troops does not change anything. At the same time, Chinese are welcome to invest and build infrastructure in India. Chinese would like to 'hyphenate' India and Pakistan; India does not.

India needs to revive the Research and Analysis Wing's (R&AW's) dirty tricks department - mirroring the activities of the ISI. For starters, re-export to Pakistan two of its main commodities to India – counterfeit currency and drugs. The counterfeit currency to strain the 'green shoots' of Pakistani economy and synthetic drugs to give its charitable organisations, such as the JuD of Hafeez Saeed, something better to be engaged with at home. Pakistan, therefore, before it 'sees' any vision 2020 or 2030 for itself and the rest of Central Asia, has to act as a responsible nation primarily by focussing inwards on its ill rather that getting the Saudi or the Chinese to prop it up. Sceptics do point out that Modi's call on the Balochistan, Gilgit-Baltistan and PoK is just an end to a means and may go little further than it has gone over the last few decades. But then a peaceful Jammu and Kashmir along with a more participative democracy in Balochistan, GB and PoK are the initial objectives of India's Pakistan policy.

PAKISTAN TO ACCOUNT FOR VIOLATIONS IN BALOCHISTAN: MODI

Accusing Pakistan of fomenting trouble in Indian-occupied Kashmir (IOK), Indian Prime Minister Narendra Modi on Friday said Pakistan would have to answer for its 'human rights' violation in Balochistan and the Pakistani side of the Kashmir.

Narendra Modi calls for end to Kashmir violence

"The root cause of unrest in Kashmir is cross-border terrorism which is being encouraged by our neighbouring country," the Indian premier was quoted by the AFP. Modi also he claimed that there was enough evidence to prove that Islamabad was fuelling unrest in the region. The IOK has been under a curfew since protests broke out over the killing last month of a popular freedom leader Burhan Wani. The unrest has resulted in the death of over sixty people.

Modi also promised to look into the grievances of those living there after meeting with national political parties to find ways of ending the ongoing violence in the troubled state.

Will engage with Pakistan for peace: Modi

"Since the time terrorism has started in Kashmir... so many sophisticated weapons have been seized by our security forces and so many foreign terrorists gunned down... Pakistan can speak a million lies but the world will not accept these," he said in a statement.

LEGITIMATE WERE MODI'S RECENT REFERENCES TO PAKISTAN'S TROUBLED REGIONS

On August 12, three days before Independence Day, when addressing an all-party meeting on the turmoil in the Kashmir Valley, Prime Minister Narendra Modi opened a new line of attack on Pakistan. He said India needs to talk of all parts of Jammu and Kashmir – Jammu, Ladakh, the Valley and Pakistan-occupied Kashmir (PoK). He did not elaborate then, though he returned to the subject in his Red Fort address to the nation on August 15. For India, he said, PoK was not merely the sliver of land along the Jhelum west of Jammu and Kashmir, as Pakistan perceived it, but the entire erstwhile portion of the Dogra kingdom to the north, now called Gilgit Baltistan. For far too long, India has been reluctant to voice this claim openly, perhaps hoping that Pakistan would take Indian acquiescence of their occupation as a trade-off for India retaining the Valley. In the same meeting, Modi lay the blame for the current turmoil, triggered by security forces killing a social media-hyped Hizbul Mujahideen commander Burhan Wani, on Pakistan's doorstep. He also announced a Rs 80,000 crore package for Jammu and Kashmir, besides steps like recruiting young people to the security forces, meant to suck the unemployed out of the resentful masses who became cannon fodder for puppeteers of the current imbroglio. The prime minister also instructed the Ministry of External Affairs to contact people from PoK living abroad to register their angst. Never before had such forthright instructions been made available to Indian diplomats abroad. The gloves were off.

Resplendent in his white kurta and pink shaded turban, Modi spent a bulk of his 100 minute speech on recounting his government's achievements in simplifying the delivery of services and boosting infrastructure. There was little about the main issues confronting the nation today – the Kashmir turmoil, 'cow protection' vigilantism and the anti-Dalit epidemic amongst Sangh right-wingers.

But surprisingly, even the foreign policy segment was scanty. One reference to Qatar, another to the border agreement with Bangladesh and then the rather interesting introduction of Pakistan's troubled regions. Significantly, the prime minister modified the reference to PoK by separately referring to the denizens of Gilgit. The clever introduction of the subject via people of those areas sending greetings to Modi unsheathed the weapon without flaunting it. There can be a number of possible outcomes

First, raising PoK/Gilgit is eminently justified as both are subjects of UN Security Council resolutions, bilateral agreements and an Indian parliamentary resolution. It is also an area seeing enhanced Chinese presence and is the route for the China Pakistan Economic Corridor (CPEC), thus assuming great strategic significance. As per Article 6 of 1963 Sino-Pakistan border agreement, it is accepted that the status of land ceded by Pakistan, including the Shaksgam Valley and its surrounding areas, will be finally determined "after the settlement of the Kashmir dispute between India and Pakistan" by negotiations between China and "the sovereign authority concerned." The exception is that if Pakistan gets sovereignty, the agreement stands as negotiated. Thus both countries accepted that India could well be the post-settlement "sovereign authority".

Thus India has been remiss for years when China has incrementally enhanced its presence in and through the entire region of Gilgit Baltistan, which is downstream from Leh, along the banks of the river Indus. Ethnically, the residents of those areas are akin to Ladakhis and are mostly Shia. Strategically, those areas have much greater significance today than the Kashmir Valley, although the Valley has become the touchstone for both India and Pakistan for defining their nationhood. Thus

Modi's broadside is a signal to both Pakistan and China that their actions will not go uncontested and India must have a voice in CPEC, linking it to the settlement of the Kashmir issue. The second issue raised by Modi was Balochistan. This issue is fraught with complications that need adumbration. To begin with, the question of the accession by the Khan of Kalat to Pakistan is not an international issue like Kashmir. India has never contested it nor is India a contiguous state. India could have had a horse in the race had it bought Gwadar from Oman when the possibility arose. It eventually got sold for $3 million to Pakistan in 1958. It was again the absence of strategic thinking at that stage, as India today would not be worrying about CPEC had it got a toe-hold on Pakistan's Makran coast.

The negative fall-out from raising a domestic Pakistani issue is already manifesting itself. I anticipated it on television when analysing the prime minister's speech minutes after its delivery. Pakistan has promptly said that Modi raising this merely confirms their allegation that India is abetting terror in Balochistan. We can expect Pakistan to start speaking more forthrightly on Maoist or other domestic Indian violence. On balance, perhaps it would have been best had the prime minister kept his focus on the trans-LoC parts of Kashmir controlled by Pakistan. Modi is attempting to break the Gordian knot of Pakistan keeping terror in play, despite international opprobrium, when dealing with India. Atal Bihari Vajpayee and Manmohan Singh tried to use conventional diplomatic tools to wean Pakistan off that strategy. They failed, as the Pakistani army is too deeply enmeshed in the terror game to abandon it altogether. Modi is now taking the battle to the ISI and the Pakistani generals. Whether it will work is uncertain. But it will certainly get messier in the short-run.

BEIJING'S RESPONSE TO INDIA-PAKISTAN TENSIONS AFTER 9/11

Since the late 1990s, China had become increasingly concerned over the gradual shift in the regional balance of power in South Asia, driven by the steady rise of India coupled with the growing US-India entente and the talk of "India as a counterweight to China" in Washington's policy circles, and by Pakistan's gradual descent into the ranks of failed states. Since the end of the Cold War, a politically dysfunctional and economically bankrupt Pakistan's flirtation with Islamic extremism and terrorism, coupled with its nuclear and missile programs, had alienated Washington.

However, the 11 September 2001 attacks changed all that. Pakistan saw an opportunity to revive its past close relations with the United States, shed its near pariah status, and enhance its economic and strategic position vis-à-vis India by instantaneously becoming a "frontline state" in the international coalition fighting global terrorism. In return, Washington lifted sanctions and agreed to provide Pakistan with billions of dollars in aid and debt rescheduling. From Washington's perspective, courting Musharraf made geopolitical sense because the Pakistani military not only knew a great deal about the Taliban, Osama bin Laden, and al Qaeda, but also because any US military operation against Afghanistan could not be successful without the bases, logistics, personnel, and airspace in neighbouring Pakistan. In Beijing, as a result, there were great expectations of a sharp downturn in US-India relations, because in many ways what happens on the Indian subcontinent is unavoidably a zero-sum game and Pakistan's new relationship with the United States did affect India negatively.

However, tensions between South Asia's nuclear-armed rivals rose sharply after the terrorist attacks at the Kashmir Assembly in October 2001 and the Indian Parliament on 13 December 2001. The attack on the Indian Parliament triggered a major deployment of Indian troops along the border with Pakistan, with Islamabad responding in kind. New Delhi warned of retaliatory, punitive military strikes against terrorist camps inside Pakistani-controlled Kashmir.

Although the Chinese Foreign Ministry spokesperson condemned these attacks, Chinese leaders and South Asia watchers were much more circumspect and ambivalent while lauding Pakistan's contribution to the war against terrorism.

A South Asia specialist from China's National Defence University, Wang Baofu, noted with satisfaction that under the new circumstances, "The United States, considering its own security interests, readjusted its policies toward South Asian countries and started paying more attention to the important role of Pakistan in the anti-terrorism war, therefore arousing the vigilance and jealousy of India."

Wang criticized India for "defin[ing] resistance activities in Kashmir as terrorism by taking advantage of the US anti-terrorism war in Afghanistan, thus putting more pressure on Pakistan through the United States," and praised General Musharraf for his "clear-cut attitude toward fighting against international terrorism)." Such a stance was not unexpected. For almost a decade, China had rejected India's proposal to issue a joint declaration against terrorism lest it be interpreted as a condemnation of Pakistan. Pakistan President General Musharraf made three trips to Beijing in less than a year (in December 2001, January 2002, and August 2002) for urgent security consultations with President Jiang Zemin and Premier Zhu Rongji and reportedly obtained "firm assurances of support in the event of a war" with India. At the time of heightened tensions in mid-January 2002, General Zhang Wannian, Vice-Chairman of China's Central Military Commission, met with General Muhammad Aziz Khan, Chairman of Pakistan's Joint Chiefs of the Staff Committee, and was quoted as telling Khan: "For many years the militaries of our two nations have maintained exchanges and cooperation at the highest and all levels and in every field.

This fully embodies the all-weather friendship our nations maintain." Zhang's reference to "cooperation... inevery field" (meaning the nuclear and missile fields) was a thinly veiled warning to India to back off. Later, Beijing matched words with deeds by rushing two dozen F-7 jet fighters, nuclear and missile components, and other weapon systems to shore up Pakistani defenses in the tense border face-off.Asecret "futuristic arms development cooperation" agreement was signed during General Musharraf's five-day visit to China in December 2001 to construct, among other weapons, an all-solid-fuel Shaheen III missile with a range of 3,500-4,000 kilometers to target all major Indian cities. The People's Liberation Army (PLA) troops from the Military Regions of Chengdu and Lanzhou and their respective subdivisions, the Xizang (Tibet) and Wulumuqi (Urumqi), along China's southern borders, were also put on alert in January to test their war preparedness should the conflict in the Indian subcontinent spill over onto Chinese soil.

The Chinese leaders had reportedly conveyed the following message to Musharraf: "China hopes Pakistan will not initiate any assault. Pakistan should not get involved in wars and instead focus on economic construction. However, if a war does break out between India and Pakistan, Beijing will firmly stand on the side of Islamabad." Soon thereafter, President Musharraf in a televised speech on 12 January 2002 announced a crackdown on extremist organizations waging jihad from Pakistani territory, and as a result, Indo-Pakistani tensions somewhat subsided. The Chinese media claimed some credit for "mediating" between the two sub-continental rivals despite the Indian government's aversion to the dreaded "m" word: "Mediated by the United States, China, Britain, and Russia, leaders of India and Pakistan recently expressed their desire to try to control the tense situation." 12 Interestingly, this stance contradicted then Indian Foreign Minister Jaswant Singh's statement during Premier Zhu's visit to New Delhi in January 2002 that "China has neither any intention, nor shall it play any mediatory role between India and Pakistan." Not only that, the Chinese Foreign Minister also succeeded in persuading his Russian counterpart to issue a "Joint Declaration on the India-Pakistan Situation," signaling to New Delhi that, for the first time, Beijing and Moscow had a unified stand on the dispute. In concrete policy terms, it meant that New Delhi could no longer count on the Russian veto in the UN Security Council in the event of a war.

Then came the 14 May 2002 terrorist attack on a military base in Jammu that killed 34 people, mostly women and children, once again escalating tensions along the border where more than one million troops backed by heavy armor, warplanes, and missiles were deployed. There was renewed tough talk of war, including nuclear war, on both sides of the border. Beijing called for restraint from both India and Pakistan and emphasized the need for peaceful dialogue to settle outstanding disputes. Chinese Defence Minister Chi Haotian also urged both countries to desist from a military conflict and not to threaten each other with nuclear weapons.

Describing the US diplomatic moves (i.e., the dispatch of Deputy Secretary of State Richard Armitage and Defence Secretary Donald Rumsfeld in early June 2002) to defuse the India-Pakistan military stand-off as "too little too late," the state-run media accused Washington of showing "no genuine desire to resolve the Kashmir issue." It noted that Washington had clearly not taken the tensions very seriously when it went on with a ten-day joint military maneuver with India on 16-26 May 2002, thereby implying that the Indo-US joint military exercise had emboldened India to up the ante against Pakistan. On 15 May, a Chinese official accompanying Foreign Minister Tang Jiaxuan during his visit to Islamabad told Pakistani journalists that China would back Pakistan in any conflict with India. Concerned over the "one-sided nature of public appeals" from Washington, Moscow, London, Paris, and Tokyo to General Musharraf to halt "cross-border terrorism" into Indian Kashmir, Chinese Foreign Minister Tang Jiaxuan told US Secretary of State Colin Powell on 27 May 2002 that "the international community should encourage direct dialogue between India and Pakistan in a more balanced and fair manner, which is the most effective way to lead South Asia towards peace and stability." Apparently, the growing threat of nuclear war and the prospect of Pakistani nuclear weapons falling into the hands of Islamic terrorists have made Washington lean heavily on Islamabad. In contrast, Beijing repeatedly asked New Delhi to do more to end the military stand-off while publicly calling for restraint by both sides and claiming to be even-handed. China continued to covertly side with its long-term ally, however, and is providing military wherewithal to Pakistan.

Meanwhile, in yet another television address on 27 May, Musharraf pledged that all militant infiltration across the Line of Control (LoC) would end, and he announced the banning of Lashkar-e-Toiba, the Jaish-e-Mohammad, and the Harkat-ul-Mujahideen—the three "*jihadi*" outfits at the forefront of terrorist activity in Indian Kashmir. From New Delhi's perspective, India's military deployment had succeeded in bringing the international focus on Pakistan as the home of pan-Islamic *jihadis* after the war in Afghanistan.

At the Conference on Interaction and Confidence Building Measures in Asia held in Kazakhstan in early June 2002, Chinese President Jiang Zemin pressed Indian Prime Minister Vajpayee to enter into direct talks with Pakistani President Musharraf to prevent the Kashmir conflict from exploding into a full-scale war. But the Indian government was so irked over Musharraf's playing of "the China card" that Vajpayee refused to budge. Later, in an interview with *The Washington Post*, the Indian Prime Minister complained that he saw "no basic change in China's policy. China continues to help Pakistan acquire weapons and equipment." In an article titled "Beijing as Guarantor of Pakistan's Security," a Russian weekly, *Nezavisimoye Voyennoye Obozreniye* (Independent Military Review), had reported that new security commitments have indeed been made to Pakistan by China since 9/11. New Delhi expressed its displeasure with Beijing by postponing scheduled visits by Indian Army Chief Padmanabhan and Prime Minister Vajpayee to China in October and November 2002.

The Nuclear Connection

There were other grounds for the cooling of relations between Beijing and New Delhi. In his testimony before the US Senate governmental affairs subcommittee in early June 2002, the Assistant Secretary of State for Nonproliferation, John S. Wolf, revealed that "China recently provided Islamabad with missile-related technologies, which include dual-use missile-related items, raw materials, and other accessories essential for missile manufacturing." In a sense, China's nuclear and missile assistance to a volatile Pakistan over the last two decades has now created the risk of a conventional conflict swiftly escalating into nuclear war. Beijing has not only provided Islamabad with nuclear bombs, uranium, and plants (all three Pakistani nuclear plants—Kahuta, Khushab, and Chasma— have been built with Chinese assistance) but also their delivery systems: readyto-launch M-9 (Ghaznavi/Hatf), M-11 (Shaheen), and a number of Dong Feng 21 (Ghauri) ballistic missiles. This cooperation has continued despite Beijing's growing concerns over the "Talibanization" of the Pakistani state and society. When Islamabad carried out a series of missile tests amidst heightened tensions apparently to warn New Delhi to back off, the Indian government drew the international community's attention to the Pakistani missiles' China connection. "We are not impressed by these missile antics, particularly when all that is demonstrated is borrowed or imported ability.... The technology used in the missiles is not their own but clandestinely acquired from other countries," said a spokesperson of the Indian External Affairs Ministry.

Pakistan's test of its nuclear-capable, medium-range, Shaheen ballistic missile in early October 2002, just days before the parliamentary elections, once again provoked India to level accusations of missile technology proliferation by China. India's outspoken Defence Minister, George Fernandes, long a critic of China, said that Pakistan's military had always depended on support from China ever since it was carved out as a homeland for South Asia's Muslims in 1947 following decolonization of British India. "Everyone knows what Pakistan will be without China. Its ego is boosted purely by the support it gets from China," Fernandes said at a party convention in Mumbai. Earlier, when India weaponized its nuclear capability through a series of tests in May 1998, Fernandes had described "China [as] the mother of Pakistan's nuclear bomb" and claimed that India's aim was to counter China's capability rather than Pakistan's, drawing protests from Beijing. When Pakistan came in the firing line following revelations in the US media about the missiles-for-nukes barter deal with North Korea, New Delhi argued that blame should also be put on China for making Pakistan a nuclear weapons state.

For New Delhi, Beijing's military alliance with Islamabad remains a sore point because the Sino-Pakistani nuclear nexus has introduced a new element of uncertainty and complexity in sub-continental strategic equations. While the attention of world leaders and the media has been focused on the nightmarish scenario of a nuclear Armageddon in South Asia and large-scale mutual assured destruction leading to the deaths of 12 to 30 million people, strategic circles in Islamabad and New Delhi have been discussing the pros and cons of a short, limited nuclear war in Kashmir. Media reports based on intelligence leaks have revealed the forward deployment by the Pakistani military of low-yield (five kilotons or less) tactical nuclear weapons (TNWs). Such small battlefield nuclear weapons have a one-mile destruction radius and could be used effectively against large troop concentrations and advancing tank formations along the LoC in Kashmir.

The Pakistanis seem to have taken a page out of China's book on tactical nuclear warfighting capability. Just as persistent Sino-Soviet disputes and the Soviet Union's conventional military superiority during the 1970s and 1980s gave China strong incentives to develop and deploy TNWs, the decade-long India-Pakistan border tensions and India's conventional superiority may have added momentum to Islamabad's efforts to deploy TNWs. Most of Pakistan's missiles acquired from China, such as the M-9, are short-range, solid-fueled, mobile, nuclear-capable missiles and can be used in a tactical mode. Asked to comment on reports that Pakistan has acquired TNWs, the Deputy Chief of the Indian Army, Lieutenant General Raj Kadyan, was quoted as saying that the "Indian Army has trained itself to cope with a tactical nuclear strike in the battlefield."

Tactical nukes can be launched over an unpopulated area from field artillery guns or aircraft to halt an enemy advance or in an effort to intimidate a numerically stronger enemy. Since the damage is localized or confined to a certain area, the danger of affecting the civilian population is greatly reduced as compared to a strategic nuclear weapon of the Hiroshima kind and therefore need not evoke massive retaliation by enemy forces. The mountainous terrain in Kashmir provides the perfect setting for their use.

In addition to the United States and Russia, only China is believed to have a large stockpile of about 120 TNWs or "baby nukes." Some of these were apparently delivered to Pakistan following the visit of PLA Deputy Chief and military intelligence boss General Xiong Guangkai (arguably China's most important military figure and the man who calls Pakistan "China's Israel") to Islamabad in early March 2002.27 If the reports of China's transfer of TNWs to Pakistan are indeed true, the question then is: Would India, which does not possess TNWs but has strategic nuclear weapons in abundance, keep a nuclear conflict limited or escalate it to the strategic level and respond with massive retaliation? Though New Delhi has long maintained that even a tactical nuclear strike on its forces would be treated as a nuclear first strike, and would invite massive retaliation, some Pakistani generals believe that a tactical strike would circumvent retaliation from India, since such an attack on an advancing tank regiment or infantry battalion (in contrast to a strategic strike killing millions of civilians), would not be provocation enough for all-out retaliation. They contend that the many layers of bureaucracy surrounding India's nuclear capability, the strength of world public opinion, and the fact that strategic command remains in civilian hands places severe doubts on India's willingness and ability to retaliate with a massive nuclear strike against an opponent, particularly in the face of only a limited tactical strike from Pakistan.

Some analysts attribute the recent lessening of tensions to the belated recognition in India's strategic circles that New Delhi cannot afford to dismiss Pakistan's repeated threats of using nuclear weapons as "mere posturing" or "bluffing" on Islamabad's part. They point to the Pakistani military's strong aversion to fighting a 1965-or 1971-type conventional war with India and offer this as the rationale behind Islamabad's decision to pull back from the brink on several occasions in recent history (in 1987, 1990, 1999, and 2002). Others believe that the tendency of Indian strategic planners to discount the threat of nuclear escalation may well be based on some fundamentally erroneous assumptions:

- That the United States cannot allow Pakistan to be the first Islamic country to use nuclear weapons to settle a territorial dispute, as it would mean the end of the global nonproliferation regime and encourage other countries to go nuclear to settle their territorial disputes as well.
- That the presence of US forces in Pakistan will be a constraining factor.
- That the international community (the United States, United Kingdom, China, or the United Nations) will intervene in time to prevent such a catastrophe.
- And that India can count on American and Israeli military support to seize or take out Pakistan's nuclear and missile infrastructure. These assumptions do not seem to be based on cold, clear-headed calculations of the strategic interests and influence of major powers (especially the United States and China) and may well be a sign of wishful thinking on India's part. It is worth noting that new strategic and geopolitical realities emerging in Asia since 9/11 have put a question mark over Beijing's older certainties, assumptions, and beliefs.

China's Concerns

Much to Jiang and his Politburo's chagrin, the US-led war on terrorism has developed in ways that could not have been foreseen, with potentially disastrous consequences for China's core strategic interests. A major unintended (and unsettling, from Beijing's standpoint) consequence has been not only to checkmate and roll back China's recent strategic expansion moves in Central, South, and Southeast Asia, thereby severely constricting the strategic latitude that China has enjoyed since the Cold War, but also to tilt the regional balance of power decisively in Washington's favour within a short period. The supposedly brief Unipolar moment in history seems to have turned into a long-lasting Imperial moment—a Pax Americana *par excellence*. More important, recent developments show how tenuous Chinese power remains when compared to that of the United States.

The fast-changing strategic scene not only undercuts Chinese ambitions to expand Beijing's power and influence in Asia, but also hems in the one country in the world with the most demonstrable capacity to act independently of the United States. Not surprisingly, the beginning of 2002 saw Chinese leaders and generals shedding their earlier inhibitions about publicly expressing concern over the growing "southern discomfort"—that is, ever-expanding US military power and presence in southern Asia after 9/11. China's Chief of the General Staff Fu Quanyou warned the United States against using the war on terrorism to dominate global affairs by saying "counter-terrorism should not be used to practice hegemony." On an official visit in April 2002 in Iran, Jiang Zemin openly repudiated the US stance against the Iranian and Iraqi regimes, saying, "Our opinion [on terrorism] is not the same as the United States." In Germany, he told the *Welt am Sonntag*: "We all want to fight terrorism. But the states involved in the fight against terror each have their own specific viewpoint."

China's initial optimism that new Sino-US-Pakistan triangular cooperation in the aftermath of 11 September 2001 would wean Washington away from New Delhi turned out to be wishful thinking as Bush Administration officials went out of their way to assure India that America's intensifying alliance with Pakistan would not come at India's expense. If anything, the current crisis has strengthened the American commitment to building stronger relations, including defence ties, with South Asia's preeminent power. However, China does not want to see India increasing its power, stature, and profile regionally or internationally. Beijing shares Islamabad's deep mistrust of India's strategic ambitions and seeks to prevent India's emergence as a peer competitor and a major strategic rival in

Asia. That is why Chinese strategists have long argued that China's pursuit of great power status is a historical right and perfectly legitimate but India's pursuit of great power status is illegitimate, wrong, dangerous, and a sign of hegemonic, imperial behaviour.

For its part, New Delhi has long accused Beijing of doing everything it can to undermine India's interests and using its ties with other states to contain India. Beijing is also alarmed over the growing talk in some con-servative policy circles in Washington and New Delhi of India emerging as a counterweight to China on the one hand and the fragile, radical Islamic states of West Asia on the other.

Earlier, when President Bush unveiled his missile defence plan, New Delhi responded far more positively than did most US allies. Some Indian strategic thinkers even see in the emerging US-India quasi-alliance an opportunity for "payback" to China. As G. Parthasarthy, former Indian Ambassador to Pakistan and Burma, put it: "Whether it was the Bangladesh conflict of 1971, or in the Clinton-Jiang Declaration in the aftermath of our nuclear tests, China has never hesitated to use its leverage with the Americans to undermine our security." Growing Chinese strategic pressure on the Malacca Straits has already led to maritime collaboration between India and the United States, with their navies jointly patrolling the straits.

More significantly, US-India strategic engagement has scaled new heights with the announcement of a series of measures usually reserved for close US allies and friends: joint military exercises in Alaska that would boost India's high-altitude warfare capabilities in the Himalayan glaciers of northern Kashmir where it faces Pakistan and China; sale of military hardware including radars, aircraft engines, and surveillance equipment to India; joint naval exercises and the training of India's special forces; and intelligence sharing as well as the joint naval patrols in the Straits of Malacca. Washington also reportedly gave the green light for Israel to proceed with selling the Phalcon airborne early warning and control system (AWACS) to India—something that was earlier denied to China for fear of enhancing Beijing's air surveillance and early warning capabilities in the Taiwan Strait.

All of these measures send an implicit signal to China of India's growing military prowess. In a cover story in the authoritative *Beijing Review*, one of China's noted South Asia specialists expressed concern over the US sale of arms to India which "enables it to become the first country to have close military relations with the world's two big powers—the United States and Russia." To make matters worse, in early May 2002 Prime Minister Koizumi of Japan, Beijing's other Asian rival, which sees China representing a clear and future threat to its security, called for a broadening of Japan's security cooperation with India.

Many Chinese strategists believe India is using the war on terrorism as a pretext to militarily subdue Pakistan or to destabilize and dismember the country. Pakistan is the only country that stands up to India and thereby prevents Indian hegemony over the region, thus fulfilling a key objective of China's South Asia policy. 39 As South Asia watcher Ehsan Ahrari points out: "India may end up intensifying its own rivalry with China by remaining steadfast in its insistence that Musharraf kowtow to its demands, especially if China calculates that US-India ties are harming its own regional interests. China, though still concerned about the continued activism of Islamist groups in Pakistan and contiguous areas, is not at all willing to see the regional balance of power significantly tilt in favour of India."

Though Beijing welcomes the new US commitment to prop up Beijing's "all-weather friend" after a decade of abandonment and estrangement, most Chinese strategists worry about the destabilizing consequences of a prolonged US military presence in Pakistan and increased influence on the future of Sino-Pakistan ties as well as on Pakistan's domestic stability. The Chinese are also believed to be "highly uncomfortable" with the four US military bases in Pakistan. Of special concern to Beijing is the US presence at Pasni in the Baluchistan region of Pakistan, where China is constructing a deep-water naval port at Gwadar, the inland Makran coastal highway linking it with Karachi, and several oil and gas pipeline projects.

Beijing has long been eyeing its construction of the naval base at Gwadar, at the mouth of the Strait of Hormuz in the Persian Gulf, as a bulwark against the US presence and India's growing naval power. Furthermore, the US military presence in Pakistan could sharpen the divide within the Pakistani military into pro-West and pro-Beijing factions, with China supporting the latter to regain ground lost since 9/11.44 The pro-Beijing lobby within the Pakistani military is reportedly getting restive and waiting to strike if and when General Musharraf falters. The pro-China faction within the Pakistani military could also join hands with the pro-Islamic fundamentalist faction opposing the US military presence on Pakistan's soil. Alternatively, it could throw its support behind those nationalist elements that find Pakistan's loss of its "strategic depth" in Afghanistan for elusive diplomatic gains very hard to digest. The US arms sales to India and joint US-Indian military exercises may further sour China's and Pakistan's willingness to assist Washington in its war on terrorism.

War Scenarios

It is said that each conflict simply prepares the ground for the next one or every war contains the seeds of another. The AfghanWar of the 1980s against the Soviet occupation culminated in the war on terrorism in 2001. Whether the war on terrorism will lead to another war or a clash of civilizations or a nuclear jihad in South Asia, only time will tell. Pakistan is, in the words of former Italian Foreign Minister Gianni De Michelis, "the fuse of the world." The provinces close to the Afghan border and home to the US military bases are now controlled by Islamic parties that created the Taliban and are openly sympathetic to the aims and ideals of al Qaeda. The rising anti-American sentiment in Pakistan as demonstrated in the recent elections has made the country increasingly unstable. Violence levels in Indian Kashmir also continue to rise. Many observers believe that Washington may have to rethink its strategy vis-à-vis Islamabad if the war on terrorism is to be won decisively. The complete dismantling of the al Qaeda terrorist infrastructure in Pakistan seems unlikely because of the apprehension within the Pakistani military that doing so would devalue Pakistan's importance in the US security strategy and once again make the United States turn its back on the country and make the country vulnerable to Western pressure and sanctions. It would also deprive Pakistan of invaluable Western aid and leverage vis-à-vis Washington and New Delhi.

One Chinese national security analyst argues that "what worries China more is the possibility that it could be drawn into a conflict, not between Pakistan and India per se, but between Pakistan and the United States, with the latter using India as a surrogate." With the top al Qaeda and Taliban leadership fleeing into Pakistan's Wild West and Pakistani-held Kashmir, Beijing knows full well that Pakistan is no longer the "frontline state" in the war on terrorism that it once was; it is, in fact, the battlefield in the war on terror.

Should the India-Pakistani conflict escalate into a nuclear one, neither the geopolitical nor the radioactive fallout will remain limited to South Asia. Indeed, the most worrisome scenario would be one where Pakistan is losing a conventional conflict and uses tactical nuclear weapons in a desperate effort to win or to salvage a face-saving defeat that would allow the regime to survive. (The risk-taking nature of the Pakistani military leadership suggests that such a scenario cannot be completely ruled out.)

Should India respond by launching strategic nuclear strikes resulting in the complete destruction of the Pakistani state, China would find it difficult to sit idly by. The next India-Pakistan war also could bring the United States and Pakistan on a collision course, with or without India acting as a US partner. Such a development would obviously present China with difficult choices. Open support for its closest ally would jeopardize China's relations with the United States and India.

But nonintervention on Pakistan's behalf could encourage India to solve "the Pakistan problem" once and for all, with or without a nuclear exchange, and thereby tilt the regional balance of power decisively in its favour. As Zhang Xiaodong put it: "There is the real possibility that a new Indian-Pakistani war will take place in the future. This war would be disastrous, as it would change the whole political balance in Central and South Asia," which is currently tilted in China's favour. Unrestrained Indian power could eventually threaten China's security along its soft underbelly—Tibet and Xinjiang.

Should post-Musharraf Pakistan disintegrate or be taken over by Islamic extremists, a new level of instability would rock the region and increase tensions among Pakistan, India, and China. Another dreadful scenario is one in which Chinese-made Pakistani nuclear weapons fall into the hands of the United States, Israel, or even India in the event of a civil war should al Qaeda or the Taliban declare jihad against Pakistan—the weakest ally in the US-led anti-terrorism coalition. 51 India would be tempted to militarily intervene in Pakistan if Islamists gain control over the nuclear weapons of its neighbour, either through a coup or civil war. Such a scenario could reveal information regarding China's own nuclear program and the extent of help provided by Beijing to Islamabad. The scenario of Pakistan in splinters, with one piece becoming a radical Muslim state in possession of nuclear weapons, can no longer be simply rejected as an alarmist fantasy.

Difficult Choices

These scenarios put Beijing on the horns of a dilemma. Some Chinese strategists see in the current South Asian crisis an opportunity to recover lost ground and thwart India's ambitions to challenge China's future economic and military primacy in Asia. Should another war between India and Pakistan break out, New Delhi's high hopes of an India-US alliance to counter China may never materialize, a welcome development from China's perspective. Some hawks in the PLAsee China even benefiting from an India-Pakistani nuclear war. Hideaki

Kase, a former special advisor to Japanese Premiers Takeo Fukuda and Yasuhiro Nakasone, believes that "China wants an Indo-Pakistan war, possibly a nuclear conflict, to weaken India." At the time of the 1999 Kargil War, one Chinese military official had reportedly told a Western diplomat that "should India and Pakistan destroy themselves in a nuclear war, there would be peace along China's southwestern frontiers for at least three decades, and Beijing needs 20 to 30 years to consolidate its hold over restive Tibet and Xinjiang provinces." However, this remains a minority viewpoint, as a nuclear war would have worldwide repercussions in terms of global economic depression, humanitarian crises, WMD proliferation, and China's developmental priorities.

Most Chinese analysts and policymakers believe that Beijing should have absolutely minimum involvement in a situation where there can be no clear winners. Some argue that Beijing should seize the opportunity to coordinate its South Asia policy with Washington as it is in the interests of both countries to avert the world's first nuclear exchange and to use India-Pakistan tensions to strengthen Sino-US ties.

While the Pakistanis are confident that if war comes with India, China will throw its weight behind Pakistan, diplomatically as well as militarily, the Indians remain adamant that the Chinese would not do so for fear of India playing "the Taiwan and Tibet cards." Interestingly, on 31 May 2002, the day Pakistan's new UN Ambassador, Munir Akram, issued an explicit nuclear warning to India, a Chinese Foreign Ministry spokesman denied a *Times of India* report that Chinese President Jiang Zemin had assured a US congressional delegation that China would not favour Pakistan in the existing tensions, and claimed that the report was "not based on facts." A Chinese South Asia analyst at Fudan University in Shanghai, Shen Dingli, told *The Wall Street Journal*: "China needs to send a message: For my own security I will intervene." Though Beijing may not overtly intervene in a limited war, China's geopolitical imperative requires it to come to Pakistan's defence if the latter's existence as a nation-state is threatened by India.

Clearly, there is a great deal more to the Chinese role in South Asia than meets the eye. In the final analysis, Beijing's response to the next India-Pakistan war will be shaped by its desire to protect Chinese national interests, no matter what the cost.

Geostrategic concerns require China to covertly side with Pakistan, while publicly calling for restraint by both sides and appearing to be even-handed. In the triangular power balance game, the South Asian military balance of power is neither pro-India nor pro-Pakistan, it has always been pro-China. And Beijing will take all means possible, including war, to ensure that the regional power balance does not tilt in India's favour. Even in the absence of a war, Pakistan hopes to continue to reap significant military and economic payoffs not only from the intensifying Sino-Indian geopolitical rivalry in southern Asia but also from what many believe is the coming showdown between China and the United States, which will further increase the significance of China's strategic ties with Pakistan. In the meantime, a major consolation for Beijing is that a stronger Pakistan aided by the United States, Western Europe, Japan, and international financial institutions would be better able to balance and contain rival India.

10

China-Pak's Balochistan Policy and Economic Corridor

Strategically Gwadar; Balochistan holds a dominant position in the Gulf Region as part of the „Great Game . It has enormous potentials to emerge as a regional hub and a future trans-shipment port. However the changed environments have a few concerns for the global key players to exploit its potentials to the fullest.

The China–Pakistan Economic Corridor (CPEC) is a development megaproject that aims to connect Gwadar Port in southwestern Pakistan to China's northwestern autonomous region of Xinjiang, via a network of highways, railways and pipelines to transport oil and gas. The economic corridor is considered central to China–Pakistan relations and will run about 3,000 km from Gwadar to Kashgar. Overall construction costs are estimated at $46 billion, with the entire project expected to be completed in several years. The Corridor is an extension of China's proposed 21st century Silk Road initiative. According to a Firstpost report, "this is the biggest overseas investment by China announced yet and the corridor is expected to be operational within three years and will be a strategic gamechanger in the region, which would go a long way in making Pakistan a richer and stronger entity than ever before."

Other than transport infrastructure, the economic corridor will provide Pakistan with telecommunications and energy infrastructure. The project also aims to improve intelligence sharing between the countries. China and Pakistan hope the massive investment plan will transform Pakistan into a regional economic hub as well as further boost the growing ties between Pakistan and China. The Pakistani media and government called the investments a "game and fate changer" for the region. According to *The Guardian*, "The Chinese are not just offering to build much-needed infrastructure but also make Pakistan a key partner in its grand economic and strategic ambitions." The project will also open trade routes for Western China and provide China direct access to the resource-rich Middle East region, bypassing longer logistical routes currently through the Strait of Malacca.

During the state visit of President of China Xi Jinping to Pakistan in April 2015, he wrote in an open editorial that "This will be my first trip to Pakistan, but I feel as if I am going to visit the home of my own brother." During his visit, Islamabad was dotted with slogans and signboards such as "Pakistan-China friendship is higher than the mountains, deeper than the oceans, sweeter than honey, and stronger than steel."

THE BALUCHISTAN ISSUE

So, what is going on in Baluchistan? Baluchistan is one of the 4 states/provinces of Pakistan. It constitutes roughly 40-43% of the land mass with only 5%-7% share in the population. It has the richest mineral and natural resources in the country, yet, is the most improvished area of Pakistan with the lowest literacy, health and infrastructre indices. Two days ago, "tribals" or "nationalists" or "foreign interests" launched an attack on the largest natural gas production facility in Sui, Baluchistan. This has halted the supply of natural gas to most of the country resulting in material and economic losses. The escalation comes after on-going sporadic violence in the region against the Pakistani military forces. The General unequivocally warned the tribal/nationalist/foreign elements that his retaliation will be swift and that "they will not even know what hit them".

This has set the stage for a show-down between Pakistan military and what the Pak media is terming "terrorist organizations" like the *Baluch Liberation Front* and *Baluch* Liberation Army. At least*Jang Daily* expressed severe doubt in their editorial about the mere existence of these organization (which is the usual hint that India is behind it all). If they, uh, google'd it, they would know that not only do these organizations exist and have a fairly comprehensive web presence but that their greivances are long standing and, at least to this Punjabi/ Kashmiri, fairly justified.

Let me start with a bit of history. The region was largely under Iranian kingly control and the autonomous principality of Kalat. The British wrested control away from the Khan of Kalat in the early 1840s and it became the staging ground for the various Afghan-British wars (the Great Game) in the later half of 19th century. The 1876 treaty between the Khan of Kalat and Robert Sandeman accepted the independence of the Kalat as an allied state with British military outposts in the region. After the 1878 Afghan War, the British established Baluchistan as a provinicial entity centered around the municipality of Quetta – Kalat, Makran, and Lasbella continuing to exist as princely realms.

The British interest in the region was largely to use it as a land-mass bulwark against Central Asian encroachments. Besides a train track, the development and settlement of British holdings excluded most of the tribal population. The administrative and legislative reforms of late 19th and early 20th century India overlooked Baluchistan. Around the 1930s, Baluchi nationalist parties emerged to contest for freedom from British rule. They took the princely state of Kalat as the focal point of a free and united Baluchistan. Iqbal's vision of autonomous federation of Muslim state included Baluchistan but the Khan of Kalat never brought into the Punjabi nationalist paradigm, arguing that the Kalat had special treaty powers. Baglar Begi Khan declared the independence of Kalat on August 15, 1947. He assured the neo-state of Pakistan that Kalat will participate in the defense and infrastructure but will be autonomous. That didn't go over well at all and the Pakistani army entered the region to occupy the area immediately. On

Mar 27, 1948, the Khan of Kalat gave in to the State of Pakistan and his old attorney M. A. Jinnah. His brother Abdul Karim Baloch refused to surrender and revolted until his arrest in 1950. Baluchistan was put under Governor General control and no elective body formed in Baluchistan until 1973.

After Partition, the threat of E. Pakistani – read Bengali – hegemony (55% of population at the time), forced the Punjabi military and civil elite (in 1947, Punjabis made up 77% of the army being only 25% of the population) to consitute W. Pakistan as One Unit in the 1956 Constitution. This was done presumably to guarantee equal representation for W. Pakistan but the measure was highly unpopular in Sindh, Baluchistan and NWFP because it meant rule of the Punjabi over their regional interests. Separatist, sub-national movements triumphing local languages and cultures and protesting Punjabi hegemony arose in all the three states. Especially in Baluchistan, the Khan of Kalat led a stringent opposition to the One Unit. But the wave of military dictatorships quashed all such designs. In 1970, Yayha Khan dissolved the One Unit to appease E. Pakistan but the horrific damage done by the army in soon-to-be-Bangladesh proved too much.

After 1971, the sub-nationalist movements in Sindh and Baluchistan demanded their fair share of the nationalist pie. With Bangladesh's independence, Punjab became the most populous and richest state in the country. It had 58% of the population while Baluchistan had 4%. Led by Bhutto's central populism, Baluchistan had its first elected body in 1972. The *National Awami Party* won the majority of the seats in Baluchistan and started making noises about state rights. In 1973, it was clear to the NAP that Baluchistan was the least developed province with the majority of civil and military bureaucracy coming from Punjab. They, quite correctly, saw this as a colonial exploitation. The discovery of natural gas reserves at Sui had made the area incredibly vital to Pakistan and Iran's developmental programs. The refusal by the Bhutto's central government to allow NAP internal autonomy escalated a tense situation into an outright revolt. Bhutto dismissed the

Baluchistan assembly and re-instituted Governor's rule. The Baluchi nationalists launched an all-out military resistance.

From 1973-1978, roughly 60,000 Baluchi tribesmen and militia have faced off against the Pakistani army. Iran, eager to quell any similar uprising in its bordering area, has contributed airforce and personnel to the Pakistani efforts. They bombarbed Baluchi villages into submission. Bhutto's ouster, via Zia's military coup, forced a calm onto the situation as Zia launched into his One Pakistan Through Islam program. The Afghanistan war, the Iranian revolution and the Zia's policies made Baluchistan into an island of outsider activity. US/UN aid for Afghani refugees poured into the metropolitan areas. During the 90s, the Benazir/Nawaz Sharif governments did little for Baluchistan as the Baluchi nationalist parties floundered in exile.

After The General landed into power (get it?), he tried to foster new relationship with Baluchistan. Over the last three years, the Kachhi Canal, Mirani Dam, Gwadar Port, Makran Coastal Highway, Saindak Copper Project and Quetta Water Supply Scheme were announced by Islamabad. Over 300 percent increase was made in the national budget for development programs in Baluchistan. Yet, allthese things have failed to materialize from paper into concrete.

These latest incidents emerge from the same calls for Baluchistan's equal share in the national programs and right to self-administer. The catalyst seems to be the assault on a female doctor, Dr. Shazia Khalid, by a gang of employees of the PPL at Sui. The company management, along with thelocal police, tried to quash the issue while the central authorities ignored all pleas to intervene. This caused the initial attack on *the Sui facility. Nawab Akbar Bugti, the leader of Democratic* National Party Baluchistan, clearly stated that the attack was borne out of frustration on the lack of action against the employees who did the assault and was NOT a nationalist struggle for freedom by the tribals. The General, on the other hand, is going to play this as another internal/extrenal threat to Pakistan and seems determined to carry out a military response. His pointed reference to the 1973 uprising is meant to warn the Baluchi tribals that he will not negotiate on his terms.

Today's actions by the tribals and the military response in Baluchistan can be understood within the context of the acrimonious central-regional relationship in Pakistan. The rights of states, the rights of minorities, the rights of individuals are all negotiated within the vaccum of Islamabad military power-brokers. Having no access to that, the aggrieved parties find no alternative except violent struggle. The history of MQM, of Sindh, of Waziristan and, of Baluchistan provide ample attestation to that reality. I hate to say it again but here it goes: there is no way out except a democratically elected and constituted assembly that will re-imagine Pakistan as a federation with a secular and civil Constitution at the helm.

ISLAMIC CONQUEST OF BALOCHISTAN

Arab forces invaded Balochistan in the 7th century, converting the Baloch people to Islam. Arab rule in Baluchistan helped the Baloch people to develop their own semi-independent tribal systems, which stronger forces frequently threatened. In the 17th century, Baluchistan was dominated by Ahmedzai Baloch tribe of Kalat region, which ruled Balochistan from 1666-1948).

In the 14th year of the Hijra, 636-6CE, Rai Chach marched from Sindh and conquered Makran. However, in 643 the Arabs reached Makran. In early 644 CE, Caliph Umar sent Suhail ibn Adi from Bosra to conquer the Karman region of Iran. He was made governor of Karman. From Karman he entered western Baluchistan and conquered the region near Persianfrontiers. Southwestern Balochistan was conquered during the campaign in Sistan that same year.

During Caliph Uthman's reign in 652, Balochistan was reconquered during the campaign against the revolt in Karman under the command of Majasha ibn Masood. It was first time western Baluchistan came directly under the laws of the

Caliphate and paid grain tributes. Western Baluchistan was included in the dominion of Karman.

In 654, Abdulrehman ibn Samrah was made governor of Sistan. He led an Islamic army to crush the revolt in Zarang, now in southern Afghanistan. Conquering Zarang, a column moved northward to conquer areas up to Kabul and Ghazni in the Hindu Kush mountains while another column moved towards northwestern Baluchistan and conquered the area up to the ancient cities of Dawar and Qandabil (Bolan). By 654 the whole of what is now Pakistan's Baluchistan province was under the rule of the Rashidun Caliphateexcept for the well-defended mountain town of QaiQan, which was conquered during Caliph Ali's reign.

Abdulrehman ibn Samrah made Zaranj his provincial capital and remained governor of these conquered areas from 654 to 656, until Uthman was murdered.

During the Caliphate of Ali, the areas of Balochistan, Makran again broke into revolt. Due to civil war in the Islamic empire Ali was unable to take notice of these areas, at last in the year 660 he sent a large force under the command of Haris ibn Marah Abdi towards Makran, Baluchistan and Sindh. Haris ibn Marah Abdi arrived in Makran and conquered it by force then moved north ward to northeastern Balochistan and re-conquered *Qandabil* (Bolan), then again moving south finally conquered Kalat after a fierce battle. In 663 CE, during the reign of Umayyad Caliph Muawiyah I, Muslims lost control of northeastern Balochistan and Kalat when Haris ibn Marah and large part of his army died on the battle field suppressing a revolt in Kalat. Muslim forces latter re-gained the control of the area during Umayyads' reign. It also remained part of Abbasid Caliphate's empire.

Arab rule in Balochistan lasted until the end of the 10th century. The parts of Balochistan best known to them were Turan (the Jhalawan country) with its capital at Khuzdar,and Nudha or Budha (Kachhi). Around 976, Ibn Haukal found an Arab governor residing in Kaikanan (probably the modern Nal) and governing Khuzdar during his second visit to India.

Medieval era

Shortly afterwards, western Balochistan fell to Nasir-ud-din Sabuktagin. His son, Mahmud of Ghazni, conquered the whole of Balochistan. After the Ghaznavids, the area passed to the Ghurids. A little later, western Balochistan, Iranian Balochistan, became part of the dominion of Sultan Muhammad Khan of Khwarazmian (Khiva) in 1219. However, in around 1223 a Mongol expedition under Chagatai, the son of Genghis Khan, penetrated as far as Makran. A few years later, southeastern Baluchistan briefly came under the rule of Sultan Altamsh of Delhi but soon came back under Mongol rule. The raids organised by the Mongols have left a lasting mark on history of Baluchistan, from Makran to Gomal the Mongol (known to the people as Mughal) and the atrocities they caused are still well known.

Afterwards part of the history of Balochistan centres around Kandahar and it was in this area in 1398 that Pir Muhammad, the grandson of Timur, fought the Afghans in the Sulaiman mountains. According to local tradition Timur himself passed through Marri country during one of his Indian expeditions.

The succeeding century is one of great historical interest. The Pakistani Baloch extended their power to Kalat, Kachhi, and the Punjab, and the wars took place between Mir Chakar Khan Rind and Mir Gwahram Khan Lashari which are so celebrated in Baloch verse. In these wars a prominent part was played by Amir Zunnun Beg, Arghun, who was governor of Kandahar under Sultan Husain Mirza of Herat about 1470. At the same time the Brahuis had been gradually gaining strength, and their little principality at this time extended through the Jhalawan country to Wadh.

The Arghuns gave way to Babur shortly afterwards. From 1556 to 1595 the region was under the Safavid dynasty. The army of Akbar the Great then brought what is now Pakistani Balochistan under control of the Mughals of Delhi until 1638, when it was again transferred to Persia. According to the Ain-i-Akbari, in 1590 the upper highlands were included in the sardar of Kandahar while Kachhi was part of the Bhakkar sardar of the Multan Subah. Makran alone remained independent under the Maliks, Buledais, and Gichkis, until Nasir Khan I of Kalat brought it within his power during the 17th century.

From the middle of the 17th century large parts of Baluchistan remained under the Safavids until the rise of the Ghilzai in 1708. Nadir Shah defeated Ghilzai and in the first part of the 18th century, he made several expeditions to, or through, Baluchistan. Ahmad Shah Durrani followed. The northeastern part of the country, including almost all of the areas now under direct administration, remained under the more or less nominal suzerainty of the Sadozais and Barakzais until 1879, when Pishin, Duki, and Sibi passed into British hands by the Treaty of Gandamak. The whole of Western Baluchistan had been consolidated into an organized state under the Ahmadzai Khans.

As Muslim dynasties held Baluchistan from about the 7th century, we must look to an earlier period for the date of the Sewas; and it is not improbable that they were connected with the Rai dynasty of Sind, whose genealogical table includes two rulers named Sihras. The Mirwaris, from whom the Ahmadzais are descended. In their earlier legends we find them living at Surab near Kalat, and extending their power thence in wars with the Jats or Jadgals. They then fell under the power of the Mongols; but one of their chiefs, Mir Hasan, regained the capital from the Mongol governor, and he and his successors held Kalat for twelve generations till the rise of Mir Ahmad in 1666-7. It is from Mir Ahmad that the eponym Ahmadzai is derived.

Britain and Iran divided Baluchistan into many parts. In the 19th century, nationalists in western Baluchistan revolted against the Persian occupation. At the end of 19th century, when Sardar Hussein Narui Baloch started an uprising against Persiawhich was crushed by joint Anglo-Persian mission forces. The struggle between the Persian Qajar dynasty, and the British in eastern Baluchistan, gave western Baluchis a chance to gain control of their territory in Western Baluchistan. At the beginning of the 20th century, Bahram Khan succeeded in gaining control of Baluch- lands. In 1916, the British empirerecognized him king of Baluchistan.

Mir Dost Muhammad Khan Baluch, Bahram Khan's nephew, succeeded to the throne, and in 1920, he proclaimed himself *Shah-e-Baluchistan* (Persian for King of Baluchistan) but in 1928, Reza Shah came into power and Persian forces started operations against Baluchi forces with the help of British. The Baluch were defeated and Mir Dost Muhammad Khan Baluch captured. In the same year, Mir Dost Muhammad Khan Baluch was executed in a Tehranprison. Baluchis were not content with the British, and raised their voices against the occupation of Western Baluchistan byPersia at Baluch Conference of Jacobabad.

UNDERSTANDING PAKISTAN'S MILITARY

A guided tour of Pakistan's Army, from its role within Pakistani nationalism, prospects of mutiny, and the relationship of the ISI to the Jihadi world, to hostilities with India, suggests that some key ways of defusing the situation may be being neglected Voltaire remarked of Frederick the Great's Prussia that "Where some states have an army, the Prussian Army has a state." In view of the sheer size, effectiveness and wealth of the Pakistan military and associated institutions compared to the rest of the state, much the same could be said of Pakistan.

The Pakistani military is the only Pakistani state institution which works as it is officially meant to – which means that it repeatedly does something that it is not meant to, which is to overthrow what in Pakistan is called "democracy" and seize control of the state from other institutions. The military has therefore been seen as extremely bad for Pakistan's progress, at least if that progress is to be defined in standard western terms.

On the other hand, it has also always been true that without a strong military, Pakistan would most probably long since have disintegrated. That is more than ever true today, as the country faces the powerful insurgency of the Pakistani Taliban and their allies. The Taliban threat makes the unity and discipline of the Army of paramount importance to Pakistan and the world – all the more so because the deep unpopularity of US strategy among the vast majority of Pakistanis has made even the limited alliance between the Pakistani military and the US extremely unpopular in Pakistani society, and among many soldiers.

The Pakistani military owes its success as a modern institution to the fact that it has to a considerable extent separated itself from the political culture of the rest of the country, which revolves around kinship, factions, and patronage – which alas all too often shades over into corruption and even kleptocracy. Of course, corruption does exist within the military, but to nothing like the same extent as in the rest of society.

The military has been able to achieve this separation because of two deeply intertwined and mutually dependent factors: a collective ethos which promotes honest service to the military as an institution; and a *great deal of money*.Without the resources to reward the soldiers adequately and provide them with decent services, the collective ethos of service, honesty and discipline could not be maintained. On the other hand, without this collective ethos, many of the resources given to the military would simply be stolen, as they are in the rest of the state.

To put it another way, the military's success as an institution and its power over the state comes from its immunity to kinship interests and the corruption they bring with them; but it has only been able to achieve this immunity by turning itself into a sort of giant kinship group, extracting patronage from the state and distributing it to its members.

The scale of military spending has severely limited funds available for education, development, medical services and infrastructure. If continued, this imbalance risks eventually crippling the country and sending Pakistan the way of the Soviet Union – another country which got itself into a ruinous military race with a vastly richer power. On the other hand, the rewards of loyal military service have also helped to prevent military mutinies and coups by junior officers – something that would plunge Pakistan overnight into African chaos, and usher in civil war and Islamist revolt.

Our mad dog

As a Lt Colonel fighting the Pakistani Taliban told me in July 2009:

"The soldiers, like Pakistanis in general, see no difference between the American and the Russian presences in Afghanistan. They see both as illegal military occupations by aliens, and that the Afghan government are just pathetic puppets. Today also, they still see the Afghan Taliban as freedom-fighters who are fighting these occupiers just like the Mujahedin against the Russians. And the invasion of Iraq, and all the lies that Bush told, had a very bad effect – soldiers think that the US is trying to conquer or dominate the whole Muslim world. But as far as our own Taliban are concerned, things are changing.

Before, I must tell you frankly, there was a very widespread feeling in the Army that everything Pakistan was doing was in the interests of the West and that we were being forced to do it by America. But now, the militants have launched so many attacks on Pakistan and killed so many soldiers that this feeling is changing... But to be very honest with you, we are brought up from our cradle to be ready to fight India and once we join the Army this feeling is multiplied. So we are always happy when we are sent to the LOC [the Line of Control dividing Pakistani and Indian Kashmir] or even to freeze on the Siachen.

But we are not very happy to be sent here to fight other Pakistanis, though we obey as a matter of duty. No soldier likes to kill his own people. I talked to my wife on the phone yesterday. She said that you must be happy to have killed so many miscreants. I said to her, if our dog goes mad we would have to shoot it, but we would not be happy about having to do this."

Between 2004 and 2007 there were a number of instances of mass desertion and refusal to fight in units deployed to fight militants, though mostly in the Pathan-recruited Frontier Corps rather than in the regular Army. In these morally and psychologically testing circumstances, anything that helps maintain Pakistani military discipline cannot be altogether bad – given the immense scale of the stakes concerned, and the consequences if that discipline were to crack.

Fortunately, commitment to the Army, and to the unity and discipline of the Army, is drilled into every officer and soldier from the first hour of their joining the military. Together with the material rewards of loyal service, it constitutes a very powerful obstacle to any thought of a coup from below, which would by definition split the Army and would indeed very likely destroy it and the army altogether. Every military coup in Pakistan has therefore been carried out by the Chief of Army Staff of the time, backed by a consensus of the Corps Commanders and the rest of the High Command. Islamist conspiracies by junior officers against their superiors (of which there have been two over the past generation) have been penetrated and smashed by Military Intelligence.

Morally Superior

The Pakistani military therefore, more even than most militaries, sees itself as a breed apart, and devotes great effort to inculcating in new recruits the feeling that they belong to a military family different from (and vastly superior to) Pakistani civilian society. The mainly middle-class composition of the officer corps increases contempt for the "feudal" political class. The Army sees itself as both morally superior to this class, and far more modern, progressive and better-educated.

This belief is also widely present in Pakistani society as a whole, and has become dominant at regular intervals. It is sadly true that whatever the feelings of the population later, every military coup in Pakistan when it happened was popular with most Pakistanis, including the Pakistani media, and was subsequently legitimized by the Pakistani judiciary. As Hasan-

Askari Rizviwrites, "the imposition of martial law was not contested by any civilian group and the military had no problem assuming and consolidating power."

It is possible that developments since 2001 have changed this pattern, above all because of the new importance of the independent judiciary and media, and the way that the military's role both in government and in the unpopular war with the Pakistani Taliban has tarnished their image with many Pakistanis.

However, this change is not proven yet, and depends critically on how Pakistani civilian governments perform in future. On that score, by the summer of 2009, only a year after Musharraf's resignation, many Pakistanis of my acquaintance, especially in the business classes, were once again calling for the military to step in to oust the civilian administration of President Zardari – not necessarily to take over themselves, but to purge the most corrupt politicians and create a government of national unity or a caretaker government of technocrats.

Military loathing for the politicians is strengthened by the fact that Pakistani politics is dominated by wealth and inherited status, whereas the officer corps has become increasingly socially egalitarian, and provides opportunities for social mobility which the Pakistani economy cannot, and a position in the officer corps is immensely prized by the sons of shopkeepers and big farmers across Punjab and the NWFP.

This allows the military to pick the very best recruits, and increases their sense of belonging to an elite. In the last years of British rule and the first years of Pakistan, most officers were recruited from the landed gentry and upper middle classes. These are still represented by figures like former Chief of Army Staff General Jehangir Karamat, but a much more typical figure is the present COAS (as of 2010), General Ashfaq Kayani, son of an NCO. This social change reflects partly the withdrawal of the upper middle classes to more comfortable professions, but also the immense increase in the numbers of officers required.

Meanwhile, the political parties continue to be dominated by "feudal" landowners and wealthy urban bosses, many of them not just corrupt but barely educated. This increases the sense of superiority to the politicians in the officer corps – something that I have heard from many officers and which was very marked in General Musharraf's personal contempt for Benazir Bhutto and her husband.

I have also been told by a number of officers and members of military families that "the officers' mess is the most democratic institution in Pakistan, because its members are superior and junior during the day, but in the evening are comrades. That is something we have inherited from the British".

This may seem like a ludicrous statement, until one remembers that in Pakistan, saying that something is the most spiritually democratic institution isn't saying very much. Pakistani society is permeated by a culture of deference to superiors, starting with elders within the family and kinship group. Pakistan's dynastically-ruled "democratic" political parties exemplify this deference to inheritance and wealth; while in the Army, as an officer told me:

"You rise on merit – well, mostly - not by inheritance, and you salute the military rank and not the sardar or pir who has inherited his position from his father, or the businessman's money. These days, many of the generals are the sons of clerks and shopkeepers, or if they are from military families, they are the sons of havildars [NCOs]. It doesn't matter. The point is that they are generals."

Pakistani Nationalism

The social change in the officer corps over the decades has led to longstanding Western fears that it is becoming "Islamized", leading to the danger that either the Army as a whole might support Islamist revolution, or that there might be a mutiny by Islamist junior officers against the high command. These dangers do exist, but in my view only a direct and massive attack on Pakistan by the US could bring them to fruition. It is obviously true that as the officer corps becomes lower middle class, so its members become less westernized and more religious – after all, the vast majority of Pakistan's population are conservative Muslims. They are many different kinds of conservative Muslim, and this is also true of the officer corps.

On the whole, by far the most important aspect of a Pakistani officer's identity is that he (or sometimes she) is an officer. The Pakistani military is a profoundly shaping influence as far as its members are concerned. This can be seen amongst other things from the social origins and personal cultures of its chiefs of staff and military rulers over the years. It would be hard to find a more different set of men than Generals Ayub, Yahya, Zia, Musharraf, Beg, Karamat and Kayani in terms of their social origins, personal characters and attitudes to religion. Yet all have been first and foremost military men.

This means in turn that their ideology was first and foremost Pakistani nationalist. The military is tied to Pakistan, not the universal Muslim ummah of the radical Islamists' dreams; tied not only by sentiment and ideology, but also by the reality of what supports the Army. If it is true, as so many officers have told me, that "No Army, no Pakistan", it is equally true that "No Pakistan, no Army".

In the 1980s General Zia did undertake measures to make the army more Islamic, and a good many officers who wanted promotion adopted an Islamic façade in the hope of furthering this. Zia also encouraged Islamic preaching within the army, notably by the Tabligh-e-Jamaat.

However, as the careers of the generals Karamat and Musharraf indicate, this did not lead to known secular generals being blocked from promotion; and in the 1990s, and especially under Musharraf, most of Zia's measures were rolled back. In recent years, preaching by the Tabligh has been strongly discouraged, not so much because of political fears (the Tabligh is determinedly apolitical) as because of instinctive opposition to any groups that might encourage factions among officers, and loyalties to anything other than the Army itself. Of course, *the Army has always gone into battle with the cry of Allahu* Akbar(God is Great) – just as the old German army carried

Gott mit Uns (God with Us) on its helmets and standards; but according to a moderate Islamist officer, Colonel (retd) Abdul Qayyum:

"You shouldn't use bits of Islam to raise military discipline, morale and so on. I'm sorry to say that this is the way it has always been used in the Pakistani army. It is our equivalent of rum – the generals use it to get their men to launch suicidal attacks. But there is no such thing as a powerful jihadi group within the army. Of course, there are many devoutly Muslim officers and jawans, but at heart the vast majority of the army are nationalists, and take whatever is useful from Islam to serve what they see as Pakistan's interests.

The Pakistani army has been a nationalist army with an Islamic look." However, if the Army is not Islamist, its members can hardly avoid sharing in the bitter hostility to US policy of the overwhelming majority of the Pakistani population. To judge by retired and serving officers of my acquaintance, this includes the genuine conviction that either the Bush administration or Israel were responsible for 9/11. Inevitably therefore, there was deep opposition throughout the Army after 2001 to US pressure to crack down on the Afghan Taliban and their Pakistani sympathizers. "We are being ordered to launch a Pakistani civil war for the sake of America", an officer told me in 2002. "Why on earth should we? Why should we commit suicide for you?"

Mutineer Scenarios

In 2007-2008, this was beginning to cause serious problems of morale. The most dangerous single thing I heard during my visits to Pakistan in those years was that soldiers' families in villages in the NWFP and the Potwar region were finding it increasingly difficult to find high-status brides for their sons serving in the military, because of the growing popular feeling that "the Army are slaves of the Americans", and "the soldiers are killing fellow Muslims on America's orders."

By late 2009 the sheer number of soldiers killed by the Pakistani Taliban and their allies, and still more importantly the increasingly murderous and indiscriminate Pakistani Taliban attacks on civilians, seems to have produced a change of mood in the areas of military recruitment. Nonetheless, if the Pakistani Taliban are increasingly unpopular, that does not make the US any more popular; and if the US ever put Pakistani soldiers in a position where they felt that honour and patriotism required them to fight America, many would be willing to do so. The most dangerous moment in my visits to Pakistan since 9/11 came in August-September 2008, when on two occasions US forces entered Pakistan's Tribal Areas on the ground in order to raid suspected Taliban and Al Qaeda bases. On the second occasion, Pakistani soldiers fired in the air to turn the Americans back. On September 19th 2008 the Chief of the Army Staff, General Kayani, flew to meet the US Chief of the Joint Staffs, Admiral Mike Mullen, on the US Aircraft Carrier USS Abraham Lincoln, and in the words of a senior Pakistani general "gave him the toughest possible warning about what would happen if this were repeated".

Pakistani officers from Captain to Lt General have told me that the entry of US ground forces into Pakistan in pursuit of the Taliban and Al Qaeda is by far the most dangerous scenario as far as both Pakistani-US relations and the unity of the Army is concerned. As one retired general explained, drone attacks on Pakistani territory, though the ordinary officers and soldiers find them humiliating, are not a critical issue because they cannot do anything about them: "US ground forces inside Pakistan are a different matter, because the soldiers can do something about them. They can fight. And if they don't fight, they will feel utterly humiliated, before their wives, mothers, children. It would be a matter of honour, which as you know is a tremendous thing in our society. These men have sworn an oath to defend Pakistani soil. So they would fight. And if the generals told them not to fight, many of them would mutiny, starting with the Frontier Corps."

At this point, not just Islamist radicals but every malcontent in the country would join the mutineers, and the disintegration of Pakistan would come a giant leap closer.

BALOCH NATIONALISM

It is this centralized, thoroughly alien character of the State's writ in Balochistan, then, that has inspired the conflict between the Baloch and the center. In an interview with Tariq Ali in 1981, Ataullah Mengal, a prominent nationalist politician, summarized these grievances in compelling fashion:

"When I was in Mach gaol in Balochistan, the situation was brought home to me very vividly. A prison warder is the lowest-paid government employee. There were 120 warders in the gaol, but only eleven of them were Baloch. If anyone had stated this, he would have been denounced as a traitor. When we took office in 1972, there were a total of 12,000 government employees in twenty-two grades. Only 3,000 were Baloch... There are only a few hundred Baloch in the entire Pakistan army. The famous Baloch regiment has no Baloch in it! ... The officers were from the Punjab and the soldiers from the Frontier. If you land at Quetta airport today and visit the city, you will soon realize that 95 per cent of the police constables have been brought from outside." (Ali 1983, 117)

In the six decades since Pakistan was founded, there have been five uprisings — three minor ones in 1948, 1958-1960, the mid-1960s, a major insurgency between 1973-1977, and a low-level conflict beginning in the early 2000s that festers to this day.

The character of these clashes has evolved as the province has developed. None of the early skirmishes had widespread military or political support. (Harrison, 25-29) Nonetheless, the Pakistani Army's treacherous conduct in the deals that concluded both the 1948 and 1958-1960 conflicts was fodder for future nationalists. In each, the Army promised amnesty to insurgents in exchange for laying down arms, but retreated from their commitments once a deal was made.

In the 1960s, under the leadership of Sher Mohammad Marri, a self-described "Marxist-Leninist," a network of base camps was constructed with the aim of organizing a guerrilla movement. Sporadic clashes continued through the end of the decade, until the fall of Ayub Khan's government in 1969 led to the withdrawal of One Unit. Though, once again, the movement could hardly be said to have had broad support, its infrastructure would prove important to the popular insurgency that erupted in the 1970s. (Harrison 29-30, 33)

This war (1973-1977), and the events immediately preceding it, marked a decisive turning point in the nature of Baloch nationalism, as its chief organizations began to acquire a clear mass character. A left-wing coalition of nationalists and communists from all corners of Pakistan, the National Awami Party (NAP), had been founded in 1957 to protest Ayub's imposition of One Unit. The organization channeled the "triune influence of provincial Autonomists, populism, and mass hostility to the pro-American foreign policy of successive governments" in a radical, left-leaning program. (Ali, 59)

Within the NAP worked the most prominent opposition figures in Balochistan, at the time: Khair Baxsh Marri, Ghaus Bux Bizenjo, and Attaullah Mengal. The three were significant tribal figures, but the party they headed had succeeded in building, as Balochistan developed, a non-tribal political base. In the 1970 elections after the fall of the military government, the NAP had won an overwhelming majority of Baloch votes.

As a consequence of the murderous war waged by the military establishment and Zulfikar Ali Bhutto in East Pakistan in 1971 [resulting in the independence of Bangladesh, formerly East Pakistan — ed.], the NAP government didn't take office until May 1972. Bizenjo became governor, and Mengal chief minister. Their government, though, proved terribly precarious.

By 1972, Bhutto found himself in a weak political position due to his betrayal of the constituencies that had thrust him into power. In this context, an independent opposition (the NAP governed, in coalition, in two of the four provinces) represented an additional threat, made worse by the NAP's unsettling designs to abolish the sardari system in Balochistan, and to assert provincial prerogatives against a Punjab-dominated bureaucracy. (Ali, 113)

International pressures were severe, as well, and Bhutto is alleged to have taken the decision to dismiss the NAP government in February 1973 on the urging of the Shah of Iran, who thought "letting the Baluch have provincial self-government...would give his Baluch dangerous ideas." By April 1973, Baloch guerrillas had begun to ambush army convoys, in response to which Bhutto dispatched four divisions to the province. (Harrison, 34, 36)

The ensuing war pitted as many as 55,000 guerrillas, disparately organized under "seven separate sets of leaders," against some 80,000 Pakistani troops. (Harrison, 71) After some initial success in the first year of the war, the superior organization and weaponry of the Army told. By September 1974, after a battle in which the Army lured several thousand Marri guerrillas into the open by attacking their families, the war had turned in the State's favor. (Harrison, 38)

Pitched hostilities continued until late 1975, but it wasn't until after Bhutto's ouster by Zia ul-Haq, in July 1977, that a truce was reached with the then-imprisoned triumvirate of Bizenjo, Mengal and Marri. As many as 6,000 Baloch had died in the fighting, and the use of torture by the Pakistani Army was commonplace. (Akbar 2011, 112; Jahnmahmad 1988, 312-313)

The peace deal ended the insurgency, and Zia released several thousand Baloch political prisoners, but none of the province's substantive grievances were addressed. The failure of the insurgency, in turn, had the effect of exacerbating the divisions between Baloch nationalists, the more militant of whom regarded the deal with Zia as a betrayal. (Jahnmahmad, 223) It marked, also, the beginning of the end of political alliances between nationalists, across provinces.

The 1980s and 1990s were characterized by a few significant developments, though not overt conflict. Those in alliance with Mengal and Bizenjo turned to political contestation, moderate and middle-class-based wings of the national movement emerged, and the central student organization (the Baloch Students Organization) also continued to grow.

Khair Baxsh Marri, who remained committed to military struggle, stayed in exile in Afghanistan until the fall of the Najibullah government in 1992; his son, Balaach Marri, was important to relaunching the guerrilla struggle in the early 2000s.

Unfortunately, none of these efforts proved particularly successful at winning concessions from the central establishment, either under Zia or during the democratic governments of the 1990s. For this reason, a renewal of hostilities was inevitable.

The sparks were a series of incidents in the early-mid 2000s, under the Musharraf dictatorship, that exemplified the State's deep disregard for Baloch rights and aspirations. Musharraf commenced plans to develop a deep-sea port at Gwadar, which was controversial because it both grabbed land from locals and employed a disproportionate number of non-locals. He also expanded the State's network of military cantonments, building on land acquired from pliable sardars.

In 2000, he imprisoned Khair Bux Marri, then in his 80s, on the concocted charge of being complicit in the assassination of a Balochistan High Court judge. In 2002, he deployed troops to blockade the town of Dera Bugti, alleging that Akbar Bugti, head of the Bugti tribe and historic figure in the province, was protecting rebels who were sabotaging the infrastructure for the extraction of natural gas. Three years later, the rape of a female doctor by Army members in a nearby hospital led to continuous clashes between the Bugti tribe and the Frontier Corps (a federal paramilitary force).

In August 2006, Musharraf escalated the conflict dramatically, outrageously ordering the murder of Akbar Bugti by helicopter attack on his hideout in the hills. By August 2009, ensuing clashes between the Army and various Baloch rebel groups had displaced as many as 200,000 people. (Akbar, 171)

The Present

Despite the transition to democracy in 2008, the Pakistan Peoples Party government has proved at best unable and at worst unwilling to take the necessary steps to resolve the situation in the province, where assassinations, abductions, and the military's general presence remain part and parcel of daily life.

The conflict today resembles the dynamics characteristic of any protracted clash with an occupying authority. Rebels target the infrastructure and personnel of the Pakistani State (from government buildings to gas pipelines), and occasionally even target the non-Baloch population of the province ("settlers").

The State, having greatly expanded its network of check posts and patrols inside the province, tramples unhesitatingly on the civil liberties of the Baloch population.

Assassinations of prominent political figures are routine, and nationalists estimate that a few thousand Baloch have disappeared into the dungeons of the Pakistani State (the infamous "missing persons"). (Akbar, 171. The figure given here is 5,000, though estimates vary widely.) An Amnesty International report covering October 2010 to February 2011 documented an average of 15-20 extrajudicial assassinations a month. Schematically, one can think of the nationalists as divided into three broad wings. First, there are the armed groups committed to attacking the infrastructure and personnel of the Pakistani State. The most prominent of these groups are the Baloch Liberation Army (Balaach Marri, its alleged leader, was murdered in November 2007), and the Baloch Republican Army.

Second, there are several mass, urban-based organizations who have rejected the strategy of parliamentary politics and are resolutely committed to the same goals as the armed resistance. This wing formed the Baloch National Front in February 2009. Only two months after its founding, three of its leaders were abducted, in broad daylight, from the office of the lawyer they shared. They were reportedly killed the same night, and their bodies recovered four days later. (Akbar, 135 and 147-9)

Third, there are the more traditional political parties, who have yet to fully forfeit the strategy of relying on conventional forms of politicking — these include the Balochistan National Party (led by Attaullah and his son, Akhtar Mengal), the National Party (founded by Mir Hasil Khan Bizenjo, Ghaus Bakhsh's son), and the Jamhoori Watan Party (led by Talal Akbar Bugti, one of Bugti's sons). As the situation in the province has deteriorated, these parties' commitment to the political process has been tested.

But even after Bugti's assassination, only the BNP decided to immediately resign from office, significantly also ditching its program of provincial autonomy in favor of demanding self-determination. (Akbar, 178) The tragedy remains that, across the board, the nationalists' goals are not matched by the requisite military or political clout. Despite the development of some industrial clusters in the areas bordering Karachi, Balochistan has not developed into a significant site of capital accumulation.

Neither the odd mega-development nor the resource extraction infrastructure employ considerable numbers of locals, which means that the nationalists' capacity to impose crippling costs on Pakistan's ruling class is limited to attacks on this infrastructure from without. These are significant in frustrating the State's further designs for the province, certainly, but it's unclear that they will succeed in bringing the Pakistani elite to its knees. Similarly, the agitation of students and the middle classes remains a formidable index of the illegitimacy of the Pakistani project, but the State currently seems content to meet the challenge through its repressive arms. Whether this route, too, will win the concessions Baloch nationalists seek remains indeterminate, at best.

The Left's Job

For the Left, the principal obligations are fairly clear. None of the leading organizations in Pakistan have significant membership in Balochistan, which is thoroughly dominated, politically, by the nationalists. Their growing sense of alienation from Pakistan has eroded, it seems, the sorts of links to other nationalists and the Left that the NAP represented in its heyday.

Given this, the Left's task is to fight where it stands — to protest the brutality of the State's response to Baloch aspirations in Sindh, Punjab, and Khyber-Pakhtunkhwa. Successful, large-scale protests in these provinces could have considerable effects on State policy. They would also go some way to restoring political relations with Baloch nationalists.

The trouble, of course, is that this remains aspirational — not because the legitimacy of the Baloch struggle is unrecognized, but rather because of the persistent weakness of Left organization. Mobilizing the infrastructure that does exist for the defense of constituencies' self-interest is difficult enough; but organizing textile workers in Punjab, for example, to strike in solidarity with the Baloch demands a level of organization that just doesn't exist.

It is further incumbent upon the Left to publicly reject the narratives employed to undermine the legitimacy of the Baloch rebellion. It's often argued that the rebellion is backward-looking, insofar as it has been prominently led by sardars (the triumvirate of the 1970s, most famously) who fight because they're opposed to the modernization. Occasionally this finds echoes in progressive assessments of the movement.

The reality, though, is quite different. Not only have the vast majority of sardars always been more pro-government than their population, the legitimate political outlets of the Baloch (be they sardar-led, or not) have consistently made the abolition of sardari and the modernization of the province one of their principal demands. (Jahnmahmad, 216, 254) The State's claim that it has been frustrated by a handful of recalcitrant sardars in its genuine intentions to develop Balochistan is belied by the conditions of the territories governed by pro-government sardars.

As Attaullah Mengal noted in a 2006 interview, "There are 72 sardars sitting in Musharraf's lap... But the state of those sardars' areas is as deplorable as that of any other area in the province." (Akbar, 242)

Second, rebels' targeting of civilian settlers is frequently cited to dismiss them as "terrorists." At best, it's claimed that both parties to the conflict — the State, and the insurgents — are guilty of violating the civil liberties of bystanders. The Left has an obligation to clarify that this perspective is unforgivably apolitical. The structuring asymmetries of the conflict — decades of oppression, exclusion and repression — are the soil in which the "excesses" of the Baloch rebellion have germinated.

There is, certainly, a comradely brand of accountability that might be brought to bear; assassinations of civilian "settlers" are, after all, almost certainly politically counterproductive. But there is little utility to making strategic proclamations from positions of irrelevance, for the purposes of moral purity. Critics, unsurprisingly, will have to earn the right to be heard.

As Pakistan marks the 65th anniversary of its independence, the ongoing rebellion of the Baloch is a damning verdict on the country's ruling-class. The fact that the national question remains arguably the most salient fault line in the country's politics — not just in Balochistan, but in Sindh, Khyber-Pakhtunkhwa, Gilgit-Baltistan, and even inside Punjab itself — illustrates the colossal failure of the State's attempts to chloroform popular aspirations in the hollow language of "national unity." The different movements vary widely in the extent to which they deserve the Left's allegiance. But as a rule, for a weak Left that has its most significant constituencies in the core of the country, the (re)construction of a pan-Pakistan popular movement will be impossible if progressives are dismissive of provincial nationalism. To the credit of the existing Left, this is widely understood, even if much work remains to be done.

CHINESE INTERESTS

Chinese naval presence at this critical choke point of Gulf can not only check the INDO-US domination of Indian Oceanbut can also strive to achieve its aim of being a naval power . Apart from the utilisation of port an existing land link can be of help to China in improving its ever expanding trade to Central Asia, Middle East and Africa, as it will reduce the sea distance to 2500 km instead of 10000 . Gwadar offers China, a tactical position in the energy rich Caspian Region thus, affording a substitute trade route for the western Xinjiang province, thus utilising it as a trade route through Gwadar Deep Sea Port. Chinese s economy is expanding at the rate of about 9% every year with trade volume of U.S $1.76 trillion and GNP ranging up to 7.3%. China has foreign exchange reserves of U.S $ 600 billion. Having such a strong and a potent economic growth rate China is expected to be the world leading economy in year 2025.

China has provided an all-out assistance for the development of Gwadar Deep Sea Port to Pakistan thus, strengthening the vital geo-strategic ties with each other in an expanding global village. Numerous strategic and economic aspects of Chinese interest in this project are explained below:

The Gwadar port is very prudent for the Chinese economy especially for the economic development of its south western Xinjiang Province; providing an economic opportunity for Uighurs, which can improve the relations of neighbouring Muslims from two countries.

The Gwadar Port can provide the Chinese with a listening post to observe the naval activities of USA in the Persian Gulf 460 km further west of Karachi and away from Indian Naval Bases of Gujrat and Mumbai.

In military and strategic terms, Gwadar Port can help China to monitor the SLOCs from the Persian Gulf as about 60% of Chinese energy requirements come from the Persian Gulf and transit along this approach. Recently on 30 Jan Pakistan Government has allowed of concession accord about Gwadar Port to China from Port of Singapore Authority; which has caused serious and immediate concerns for India .

The Indian activities in the Persian Gulf and Gulf of Aden have always been an eye sour for the Chinese s. Zhao Nanqi, director of the General Staff Logistics Department of the Chinese Navy issued a top-secret memorandum explaining the People Liberation Army s strategic plans to enhance control over Pacific and the Indian Ocean in accordance with the "high-sea defence" policy by pursuing its „string of pearl strategy . Zhao stated that "We can no longer accept the Indian Ocean as only an ocean of the Indians". A naval base; at the gate way to will help China in checking the Indian hegemonic designs in the region. Presence at Gwadar would help China to keep track of oil transportation in Persian Gulf. Gwadar Port is an alternate for China if the route through Malacca strait is denied to her for access to Asia, Europe and Africa.

Interests of CARs

Central Asia and South Asia, encompassing Caspian Region, Central Asian Republics, Afghanistan, Iran and the energy-rich „lake called the Caspian Sea; which has formed the region as a centre piece in the international arena. The CARs, besides their utter unwillingness are still dependant on Russia .

In order to shun away the effect of Russian influence; there are two routes available to reach warm waters, one passing through Iran (Chahbahar) neighbouring Balochistan and the other leading through Balochistan (Gwadar). Due to prevalent international environment, western countries are not in favour of the trade route through Iran; hence Gwadar emerges as a more viable alternate port for reasons mentioned below:

The Caspian Region is in need of a suitable route for pipeline and Gwadar as a gateway to Strait of Hurmoz is the most suitably option. In order to bridge the geographical gap Turkey proposed to establish a railway link between Central and South Asia (India), the proposal failed because of the terrestrial limitations. In the present global circumstances and availability of Silk Route Pakistan appears to be the best option.

With the development of Gwadar port, all trade to and from CARs is definite to adopt the shortest available route via Gwadar and the trade benefits of Pakistan are expected to multiply. The proven CARS reserves and production will have following implications on Gwadar Port: Estimated production of dry cargo is more than liquid cargo, which entails requirement of larger ships and thus Gwadar Deep Sea Port will prove better. Kazakhstan and Kyrgyzstan will produce more dry cargo than other CARs and Gwadar will prove to be the shortest access to warm waters.

Kazakhstan, Turkmenistan and Uzbekistan having more liquid cargo can export it through pipelines and can have an alternate routes to Mediterranean Sea through Caspian Region which is about 1800 km long route whereas through Balochistan will be only 1400 km long. The investment for liquid cargo passage through pipeline via Gwadar, Caspian Region and China will be 2 to 2.5 billion U.S $, 3.3 billion U.S $ and 35 billion U.S $ respectively.

Interests of Afghanistan

Afghanistan has been gifted with a number of natural resources. These resources are not fully exploited and the process is unlikely in the near future too. On the other hand Afghanistan currently has few exports i.e. steel, agriculture, textiles, etc. It is most likely that the country will be dependent on the imports and the aid from the donor nations, for which it had to depend on a transit agreement with Pakistan . Whatever the likely imports or the exports, Pakistan can benefit from them by providing a safe transit route through Gwadar. A few facets which will influence the significance of the Gwadar port for Afghanistan are as follows:

- Gwadar provides the shortest possible access for Afghanistan to the Indian Ocean and is most cost effective.
- The local Pushtuns have religious, cultural and economic linkages with Pakistan.
- For a developing and a landlocked country like Afghanistan, which is in need of immediate access to warm waters Gwadar appears to be a most suitable opportunity.
- The U.S would like that the Afghan trade should be routed through Pakistan and not through Iran.
- Afghanistan will get all the port related amenities, warehousing services, transit conveniences and import opportunities.

U.S and Indian Interests

Since the end of World War-II U.S occupied a place of importance in the Afghanistan s economic and social development. Afghanistan believed that good and active relations with U.S were not only important for the economic and social development but also for the maintenance of their policy balance .

Presently due to U.S war against terror in the Afghanistan – Pakistan neighbouring areas; the U.S access to CARs is being delayed and CARs are also finding it difficult to access the warm waters of Indian Ocean.

The emerging power; China is an eye sour for U.S objectives in the energy transporting Indian Ocean. Chinese„ sting of pearls strategy is further compounding the problems of Indian Ocean domination; for which is now mostly relying on India and thus allowing it to keep pricking Pakistan in Balochistan with help of Karzai Government in Afghanistan. India is constructing Chahbahar Port for Iran; 72km west to offset the Gwadar Port and is causing disturbance in Balochistan to hide the Kashmir Issue. U.S is poised to allow India to fill in the power vacuum in Afghanistan once it pulls out partially from Afghanistan.

European Interests

Although the Western nations are not part of the region, but this port in Balochistan is strategically important for due to the following reasons:-

- The European monetary alliance also points at the Arabian Sea, passing through Afghanistan, on the coast of Balochistan.
- Afghanistan has the option of using the trade route through Iran, which is contrary to the U.S interest; hence route through Gwadar would be a more viable option.
- To counterbalance the Russian concerns on energy transportation through Caspian Region.

Conclusions

The diminishing sardars and sham politicians are exploiting the innocent Balochies by inspiring a sense of deprivations which has been caused by them so as to put the blames on others. Few are indirectly cooperating with India and present Karzai Government of Afghanistan.

India is taking part in covert activities against Pakistan to divert the global attention from the core issue of Kashmir between India and Pakistan and also to support the Iranian Chahbahar Port to counter balance the Gwadar Port.

With the development of Chahbahar Port India is not only gaining the economic advantages but is also damaging Pakistan foreign policy versus Iran. The urgency on India s part was visible in foreign secretary Nirupama Rao s speech ahead of meeting.

As per International Media India is in endeavouring to create a freedom movement in Balochistan and is trying to highlight the same. India is projecting the Balochi aspirations of independence from Pakistan through a few of overseas Balochies, that too mostly non Muslims. The insurgency has no Islamic form; rather efforts are being made to lead it towards an ethnic divide. It is supporting various militant groups like Balochistan Liberation Army, Baloch Liberation Front and Baloch People s Liberation Front. "There is a need for accelerating our joint efforts to fully realize the potential of the Chahbahar port. This is a project that is in the common interest of not only India, Iran and Afghanistan, but also Central Asia23".

Some disgruntled politicians like Shazan Bughti grandson Nawab Akbar Bughti are now in Kabul and are being patronized by Afghan Government. Such politicians who have lost their strength in ancestral areas are still being projected as truly influential leaders by the media.

Only a small group of Balochi people are taking part into the anti development activities for their vested interests, so it will not be justified to blame all the Balochies, who have always sided by the Pakistan.

Incidents of unrest in parts of Quetta and Khuzdar should not be pronounced or projected as source of unrest in complete Balochistan, which covers almost 44% of the Pakistan s area. There is quite unrest in Kashmir and North East of India too.

Pakistani Media is highlight this facet merely what they listen from a few individuals at Islamabad, who talk for their vested interests. Baloch sardars with diminishing authority are being projected as god father and their views are being valued beyond limits. There is a definite loud whispering in the educated population against the Sardari system.

Sincere and a dedicated motivation may it be political one coupled with better health and education standards will overcome many issues. The relations between Balochistan and the Centre will depend upon the sincerity of the Central Government. Respect of a Baloch is a centre piece and must always be truly valued and exercised.

Pakistan can t close eyes to Indian Supported BLA s target killing, albeit small in quantity and quality. There is a need to launch a prudent and a pragmatic media campaign highlighting the Indian involvement in Balochistan. Awareness and education is need of the hour for the development of Balochistan. Pakistan Army is running various pragmatic education programmers. It is also settling the tribal disputes to start the mining of energy and other natural resources.

Social and development activities like health care, provision of water, education, resolution of tribal conflicts and mining opportunities being provided by the Pakistan Army are now being welcomed by the Balochi Masses but such activities are not liked by the sardars and politicians; as they consider it a cause of their diminishing authority and in order to refrain from the army s involvement they wrongly project that Balochies do not like army.

PAKISTAN VS. BALOCHISTAN

Pakistan has further accelerated violence against its ethnic Baloch minority following an unprecedented hearing of the

U.S. House Committee on Foreign Affairs which voiced deep concern over the appalling human rights violations allegedly committed by the army in the country's largest province of Balochistan. While Pakistan's foreign office, the embassy in Washington, D.C. and the National Assembly passed a unanimous resolution which "strongly condemned" the hearing by terming it "blatant interference" of the United States into its 'internal matters,' rogue intelligence agencies linked to the godlike military have chosen a ruthless path to vent retribution.

On Feb. 13, the bullet-riddled dead body of Sangat Sana Baloch, 27, a prominent leader of the secular Baloch Republican Party (BRP), was dumped in a desolate southern district of Balochistan. The young leader had 'disappeared' on Dec. 7, 2009, from a town 50 kilometers away from Quetta, the capital of the gas and gold-rich Balochistan. Considering the pattern of the young leader's mysterious disappearance which matched with hundreds of previously documented similar cases, Sana's partypointed fingers at Pakistan's infamous Inter-Services Intelligence (ISI), the secret wing of the army, and its affiliates, for killing the opposition leader.

Sana had been shot 30 times to the head and chest by his captors, family members said. "This is Islamabad's reaction to the congressional hearing in Washington which highlighted Pakistan's crimes against the Baloch," says Abdul Qadir Baloch, vice chairman of the Voice for the Missing Baloch Persons, a community-based organization comprising of the family members of hundreds of missing activists. The 60-year old-former bank employee joined the campaign after his own 35-year-old son Jalil Reki, BRP's central information secretary, was whisked away by, he alleges, the spymasters on Feb. 13, 2009. The BRP demands a separate homeland for the Baloch people. After two year's disappearance, Reki's tortured dead body was eventually thrown on the roadside after Mr. Baloch snubbed official threats to give up the movement seeking the release of the missing persons.

There were no official charges against Mr. Baloch's son, nor was the latter ever produced before a court of law in these two years to legally defend himself. Pakistan's judiciary lacks the teeth to bite army agents who abuse their official powers. In a June 2011 report, the Human Rights Commission of Pakistan (HRCP), an independent nonpartisan rights watchdog, said the enforced disappearances had created an "acute climate of fear" amongst the civilians and had contributed to the growing alienation of the people from the state and hatred towards the security forces and intelligence agencies under the control of the Pakistan military.

"Young men between 16 to 25 years of age were being particularly targeted. Many of them were either students or unemployed youth. Some of the incidents indicated random picking up of young men, for example, from picnic spots and markets," reported the HRCP after conducting extensive field research in the conflict-stricken province.

Pakistani authorities have remained engaged since 2004 in brutally suppressing an indigenous uprising, led by the native Balochs, which calls for an end to exploitation and manipulation of their mineral wealth by the dominant Punjabis. What began as a mere demand for maximum internal autonomy until recently, brutal state violence has taken the movement to a point of no-return where the irreconcilable young Balochs seek absolute independence.

The Congressional sub-committee hearing flabbergasted Pakistan by fully backing the Baloch right to self-determination arguing that people had a right to liberate themselves from abusive governments such as Pakistan's vis-a-vis the Baloch.

"Balochistan deserves our attention because it is a turbulent land marked by human rights violations committed by regimes that are hostile to America's interests and values," said GOP Congressman Dana Rohrabacher, who chaired the hearing which was attended by another four Congressmen.

In the aftermath of the hearing, which spotted the loopholes in Pakistan's justice and governance system, Islamabad — Washington's inconsistent ally in the war on terror — has not made any promises to work with the international community to steadily halt arbitrary disappearances, torture and targeted killings of political opponents. Instead, diplomats, politicians and even the media in Pakistan have joined hands in calling brutalities against the Baloch as "Pakistan's internal matter." Ironically, Chaudhry Nisar Ali Khan, Pakistan's leader of the opposition, moved a resolution in the parliament on Feb. 13 against the hearing where Human Rights Watch and the Amnesty International representatives also testified and confirmed the misuse of state power against innocent civilians.

Describing the congressional hearing as "totally unacceptable" and "ill-informed," the Pakistani parliament urged the U.S. Administration to play "a more proactive role" to discourage such events in the future.

"This House strongly condemns the blatant interference in Pakistan's internal affairs evidenced by U.S. Congressional Foreign Relations Sub-Committee hearing on Balochistan on 8th February, 2012... the holding of such a hearing... cannot but jeopardize the healing process and further inflame public opinion against the U.S. by adding to the prevailing sense of mistrust and suspicion regarding U.S. intentions towards Pakistan," the resolution warned.

Despite Pakistan's condemnation of the congressional hearing, U.S. ambassador to Pakistan, Cameron Munter, has repeatedly expressed concern over human rights issues in Balochistan.

"There is no doubt that people in Balochistan are facing human rights abuses," he said in a fresh interview with a Pakistani newspaper. "U.S. administration should take up the 'alarming issue' [of Balochistan] with Pakistani leaders. This is an important issue for us to be discussing with the Pakistani government."

Ali Dayan Hasan, Pakistan Director at the Asia Division of the Human Rights Watch, who also testified on Feb. 8, takes a blunt position against Pakistan's objections. He says certain human rights violations, such as torture, do not fall in the category of nations' "internal matter." According to him, Pakistan, in spite of being a signatory of the International Convention on Civil and Political Rights (ICCPR) and

Convention Against Torture, is not fulfilling its obligations in Balochistan.

"We do not subscribe to the argument that criticizing human rights abusers is interference in internal affairs," he says, "Torture is a very serious crime which falls under universal jurisdiction ... any act of torture or torturer can be held accountable anywhere in the world." Mr. Hasan warns Islamabad, "You can't kill your own people and then call it an internal affair. As long as there is no reaction on the part of the Pakistani government to our reports and recommendations, we will continue to highlight human rights abuses because this is our job and mandate."

While the Congressional hearing has helped to bring the Balochistan conflict in spotlight, it has also increased the risk of more state-sponsored violence and torture against the Balochs. Seen in the backdrop of the post-hearing killings, the future in Balochistan looks bloody and murky. The congressional event and official expression of deep concern have, unfortunately, generated false but extremely unrealistic expectations among the Baloch youth who have hastily concluded that the U.S. has probably made up its mind to support their "freedom struggle" against Pakistan.

Given the complicated and unmanageable relationship the United States has had with Pakistan, it is clear that Washington enjoys very limited influence on Pakistan. For instance, it has failed to press Pakistan to act like a responsible partner in the War on Terror by cutting links with Islamic terrorist groups. Therefore, it is too naive to hope that the U.S. can truly play a crucial role in ending human rights violations in Balochistan.

Bibliography

Alam, Aftab : *US Policy Towards South Asia: Special Reference to* China-Pak Relations, Raj, Delhi, 1998.

Alperovitz, Gar. *The Decision to Use the Atomic Bomb.* New York: Vintage Books, 1996.

Anil, K.C.: Military and Democracy in South Asia : Challenges, Politics and Power, Sumit Enterprises, Delhi, 2009.

Arend, A.: *International Law and the Use of Force,* London, Routledge, 1993.

Barber B.R.: *Strong Democracy. Participatory Politics for a New Age.* Berkeley, University of California Press, 1984.

Bhat, T.P. : India and China : Trade Complementarities and Competitiveness, Bookwell, Delhi, 2008.

Buzan, Barry : *Security: A New Framework for Analysis.* Boulder: Lynne-Rienner Publishers, 1998.

Dashti, Naseer: The Baloch and Balochistan: A Historical Account from the Beginning to the Fall of the Baloch State, Trafford Publishing, 2012.

Digumarti Bhaskara Rao: Military Conversion : Impact on Science and Technology, Discovery, Delhi, 2003.

Donnan, H. and Wilson, T. M.: Borders: Frontiers of Identity, Nation and State, Oxford: Berg, 1999.

Gao, Mobo: The Battle for China's Past: Mao and the Cultural Revolution, London, Pluto Press, 2008.

Gilbertson, George W.: The Balochi language. A grammar and manual. Hertford: Stephen Austin & Sons, 1923.

Gottlieb, Thomas M.: Chinese Foreign Policy Factionalism and the Origins of the Strategic Triangle. Santa Monica, CA: RAND Corporation, 1977.

Hoffman, Bruce, *Inside Terrorism,* New York: Columbia University Press, 1998.

Hussain Mushahid: *Pakistan: Problems of Governance,* Vanguard 1993.

Imtiaz, A.: *State and Foreign Policy: India's Role in South Asia,* New Delhi, Vikas, 1993.

Jha, Prem Shankar : India and China : The Battle Between Soft and Hard Power, Penguin Books India, Delhi, 2010.

Keane J.: *Democracy and Civil Liberty in Afghanistan,* London, Verso, 1988.

Kilcullen, David: *Counterinsurgency,* Oxford University Press, 2010.

Nayyar, K K : *National Security : Military Aspects,* Rupa, Delhi, 2003.

Nevile, P.: *Lahore: A Sentimental Journey.* New Delhi: Penguin, 1993.

Oudha, Abdul Qadir : *Criminal Law of Islam,* Kitab Bhavan, New Delhi, 1999.

Prabla, Dixit: *Communalism: A Struggle for Power,* New Delhi, Orient Longman, 1981.

Rhodes, Richard, *The Making of the Atomic Bomb,* New York: Simon and Schuster, 1988.

Rosen, P.: *Societies and Military Power: India and its Armies,* Ithaca, Cornell University Press, 1996.

Simon, D. : *Public Administration and Policy of Indian Military,* New York, Knopf, 1950.

Singh, Amarinder : *A Ridge Too Far: War in the Kargil Heights 1999.* Motibagh Palace, Patiala. 2001.

Sumantra Bose, The Challenge in Kashmir : democracy, self- determination and a just peace, New Delhi: Sage, 1997.

Sutton, J., *Technology and Defence Market Structure,* MIT Press, Delhi, 1998.

Weber, Katja: Hierarchy amidst Anarchy: Transaction Costs and Institutional Choice. Albany, NY: State University of New York Press, 2000.

Wilborn, Thomas L.: International Politics In Northeast Asia : The China-Japan-United States Strategic Triangle. Carlisle Barracks, PA: Strategic Studies Institute, 1996.

Wishnick, Elizabeth: Mending Fences: The Evolution of Moscow's China Policy from Brezhnev to Yeltsin. Seattle: University of Washington Press, 2001.

Index

R

S

❑❑❑